Israel's Global Reach

Pergamon Titles of Related Interest

Israel's Global Reach

Arms Sales as Diplomacy

Aaron S. Klieman
Tel Aviv University

PERGAMON·BRASSEY'S
International Defense Publishers

Washington London New York Oxford Toronto Sydney Frankfurt

Pergamon Press Offices:

U.S.A.   Pergamon-Brassey's International Defense Publishers,
                   1340 Old Chain Bridge Road, McLean, Virginia 22101, U.S.A.

                   Pergamon Press Inc., Maxwell House, Fairview Park,
                   Elmsford, New York 10523, U.S.A.

U.K.   Pergamon Press Ltd., Headington Hill Hall,
                   Oxford OX3 0BW, England

CANADA   Pergamon Press Canada Ltd., Suite 104, 150 Consumers Road,
                   Willowdale, Ontario M2J 1P9, Canada

AUSTRALIA   Pergamon Press (Aust.) Pty. Ltd., P.O. Box 544,
                   Potts Point, NSW 2011, Australia

FEDERAL REPUBLIC   Pergamon Press GmbH, Hammerweg 6,
OF GERMANY   D-6242 Kronberg-Taunus, Federal Republic of Germany

Copyright © 1985 Pergamon-Brassey's International Defense Publishers

Library of Congress Cataloging in Publication Data

Klieman, Aaron S.

  Israel's global reach.

    1. Munitions--Israel. 2. Arms race--History--
20th century. 3. Israel--Military relations--Foreign
countries. 4. World politics--1975-1985. I. title.
UF535.I7K55   1985   355'.032'095694   85-3449
ISBN 0-08-031924-6

Printed in the United States of America

To Aliza Miriam and her generation

May they yet live in an Israel at peace with itself and
with its environment — free at last to confirm the prophetic motive
behind Israeli exports:

"from Zion shall go forth the Torah and its teachings"

(Isaiah 2:3)

CONTENTS

PREFACE

At the end of May, 1983, arms experts and procurement agents attending the Paris International Air Show made a special point of visiting the Israeli pavilion. Attracting their attention were the products of over twenty industrial firms from Israel specializing in aircraft construction and defense equipment and ranging from missiles and sophisticated electronics to the designs for the Lavi, a fighter plane scheduled for production at the close of the present decade. A similar scene took place at the other end of the globe during the Asia Aerospace '84 exhibition held in Singapore in January, 1984. Military hardware put on display by Israeli manufacturers again aroused a good deal of professional interest at Asia's biggest civilian and military air show.

Why this almost inordinate worldwide interest in the military offerings of so small and economically troubled a Third World country? The question is especially relevant when one considers that Israel and its policies have been so roundly condemned by large segments of the international community since 1967 and that conventional arms are so readily available in such abundance and variety from any number of alternative sources.

Surely part of the answer owes to the cynical nature of contemporary world politics and of weapons traffic in particular. The mere absence of normalized diplomatic ties with Israel is not allowed to stand in the way of a useful arms supply relationship. The rest of the answer lies in Israel's reputation of late as a serious competitor in the exceptionally competitive area of international weapons transfers. Both at Paris and in Singapore visitors to the Israeli booths sought to learn firsthand about the latest technological innovations and refinements developed for the Israel Defense Force (IDF) or being made available, perhaps for the first time, on the open international market.

Despite Israel's reputation and significance as one of the growing number of non-Western, industrializing nations now active in arms export programs of their own, its weapons trade diplomacy has yet to be analyzed either in Israel or abroad. Only sketchy treatments have been done, for example, of the local defense industry. Even worse, media coverage tends to speculate on single arms transactions at the expense of the more basic patterns and enduring relationships fostered by Israel. Much of what reaches print is exaggerated and out of proportion, oftentimes intentionally so, to make Israeli arms sales appear far greater than they are in reality. Conversely, the figures may be adjusted downward in order to draw away attention by presenting arms shipments as marginal in global terms to the point of being inconsequential.

The present study, in striving for balance, begins by offering three primary explanations for the Israeli emphasis on defense sales: (a) political incentives, (b) security motives, and (c) economic, commercial, and trade benefits. Their interlocking perspectives constitute a powerful argument for utilizing military exports on behalf of what Israelis and their leaders see and define as the vital national interest. The implications for Israel of achieving world stature as a supplier of quality military products are then analyzed at two levels: internal and external. The first employs a policymaking perspective in addressing the following four sets of questions: What specific motives compel Israel to maintain an arms transfer program at once so ambitious, so potentially controversial, and at times risky? How is arms policy formulated, and how are specific sales decisions made? What provisions and procedures are there for debating, approving, and then implementing such decisions? In particular, how influential are the defense establishment and the local arms industry in the policymaking process?

At the external level, who are Israel's clients—by region and country—and what items in Israel's armory have raised it in the last decade to the status of a prominent arms supplier, rivaling Brazil as a Third World producer and ranked among the leading world exporters? Arms transfers are generally regarded as one point where trade, security, and foreign policy converge. What types of problems might arise, however, should any of these several considerations threaten either to contradict each other or to come at each other's expense? Since bureaucratic and public enthusiasm for existing policy is sustained by the positive incentives as well as successes already achieved in the field of competitive arms sales, a balanced perspective requires asking what the limits might be on further growth.

In introducing this study of Israel's arms export diplomacy, two research problems are worth mentioning at the outset. One is methodological, the other attitudinal. The first is that of accessibility, and it concerns (a) available public sources on weapons transfers and (b) their reliability. Most governments are reluctant to divulge statistics on weapons flow, costs, utility, and exports; as a result, arms trade statistics as a rule are notorious for being imprecise and open to interpretation. Aggregate data compiled by such reputable agencies engaged in monitoring the international flow of weapons as the U.S. Arms Control and Disarmament Agency (ACDA), the Stockholm International Peace Research Institute (SIPRI), or the London-based International Institute for Strategic Studies (IISS) often reveal fairly wide discrepancies and therefore must be used with caution.

If anything the problem of obtaining accurate data is compounded in the case of Israel. Many aspects of Israeli foreign policy have always tended to be kept highly classified because of their sensitive nature and importance for national security. Nowhere is this more obvious than in the military assistance program as a whole, and in weapons transfers specifically. Hence important documentation simply is not available for publication, including material which might make the argument for Israeli arms sales more convincing. Although freely speculated upon in the daily press, arms transfers pledged or delivered by Israel invariably remain unconfirmed by government spokesmen. Silence is maintained in part owing to possible implications for Israel's own interests, but also in deference to the sensitivities of purchasing countries. Hence, as a rule this entire category of weapons transactions is purposely hidden in annual economic reports and intentionally subsumed in trade statistics as general commercial sales. Yet a great deal of information which can be corroborated is published in such detail that little doubt remains as to its accuracy. Our sources, which we cite, are all public and unclassified. Similarly, an effort has been made to use reports published abroad with considerable care and discrimination.

The scarcity of official data also means that unofficial estimates of Israeli sales volume reflect wide disparities. An accurate accounting as to the precise magnitude of Israel's weapons sales is therefore impossible. Exact figures, however, are not critical for purposes of this study nor central to our argument. The focus here is weighted toward the political and diplomatic dimension of supplying arms. Our interest lies in the outlines of the policy and in the larger issues posed by the heavy investment, monetary and otherwise, in marketing defense items abroad. This is as much a study of Israeli foreign relations as it is of Israeli arms trading. The arms may be conventional, whereas oftentimes the diplomacy involved in making their sale and transfer possible is highly unconventional.

A second, not unrelated problem is the subject's extreme sensitivity. Any reference, scholarly or otherwise, to Israel as arms merchant is certain to touch a raw nerve in Israeli society due to its implications for the moral standards of Judaism, for Zionist ideology, and for the national self-image. Similarly, one encounters the reticence of government officials to discuss so politically sensitive an area of national policy admittedly best conducted under conditions of utmost discretion.

Nevertheless, two overriding considerations prompt this enquiry. In the first instance, Israeli reticence in discussing at least the broader outlines of the country's military assistance and foreign defense sales program seems misplaced. In expanding its diversified military export campaign Israel does not so much violate or deviate from contemporary international norms as reaffirm them. Our attention has been drawn to one of the present realities of world politics—that "never before has the supply of arms been as important an instrument of diplomacy as it is today." (Stephanie G. Neuman and Robert

E. Harkavy, eds., *Arms Transfers in the Modern World*, New York: Praeger, 1979, p. v). The major difference between Israel and other suppliers lies perhaps in the heavy constraints experienced by a small state which, in addition, is engaged in a protracted struggle for survival and still finds itself threatened with international ostracism. On the other hand, Israel has found — at least until now — that smallness also affords a somewhat greater degree of maneuverability within the world market for conventional arms. In either event it has been observed that "far more than an economic occurrence, a military relationship, or an arms control challenge — arms sales are foreign policy writ large." (Andrew J. Pierre, "Arms Sales: The New Diplomacy," *Foreign Affairs*, **60**, Winter 1981/1982, pp. 266–267.) This rings especially true for Israel.

Secondly, precisely because it is "foreign policy writ large," weapons sales activity belongs in the public domain — not necessarily the specific modalities and details of each transaction, but most definitely the general principles and basic premises underlying such a diplomacy. In Israel's open and democratic society such a discussion, nearing the end of a decade of intensive arms promotion abroad, is both healthy and timely.

ACKNOWLEDGMENTS

The author gratefully acknowledges the tremendous support system which is Tel-Aviv University. This book originated with a preliminary paper undertaken at the Jaffee Center for Strategic Studies; and the comments of its highly professional research team were invaluable at the initial stage. As the project expanded into a full-length study colleagues in the Department of Political Science contributed further encouragement and insight. This later, expanded version was made possible through a timely Social Sciences Faculty grant. It owes as well to three graduate assistants — Gil Samsonov, Shmuel Tsabag, and Batya Shinhar — whose help was counted upon at each successive stage.

Towards the very end, Dr. Frank Margiotta and his production editor at Pergamon, Angela Piliouras, have been most understanding in accepting necessary last-minute revisions. All scholarly writing has its distinctive problems. This particular one seems to have had more than the usual share, making it not so much a labor of love as of commitment — to academic standards and to Israel. Only my wife and our children can appreciate what this has meant for us. Yet I wish to make it clear that by dealing with so sensitive, encompassing, and current an issue as foreign security assistance by Israel any errors of commission or omission are mine, and mine alone.

1

SWORDS BEFORE PLOWSHARES

Force majeure — circumstance far more than choice — casts Israel in the perennial role of weapons consumer. Ever since attaining sovereign independence in 1948, arms procurement at constantly higher levels of sophistication has remained a principal theme of both Israeli military preparedness and international statecraft. It is therefore fairly well documented. In the last decade military assistance from the United States has become the subject of considerable commentary, particularly the possible implications of a disproportionate reliance upon a single source of supply.[1] Little is known by comparison about the reverse side of the arms transfer relationship: Israel as merchant of arms.[2]

That annual sales at the beginning of this decade were acknowledged to have approached the one billion dollar mark is in itself sufficient testimony as to the formidable nature of the Israeli trade in weapons and military equipment. The importance of such figures is far greater still in Israeli terms, for defense sales could account for something like one-fourth of the country's industrial exports as of 1984–1985.

When pieced together, the available evidence strongly suggests that such sales, which are themselves part of a broader military assistance program, today represent a central component of Israel's external relations, defense posture, and foreign trade. This prominence, in turn, reflects: (a) approval in principle for arms transactions upheld by successive leaders of the country from Prime Minister David Ben-Gurion to the incumbent prime minister and cabinet, (b) a tremendous infusion of national resources into the indigenous military industries, (c) an energetic quest for new and additional outlets for Israeli defense products. Barring any unforeseen sharp reversal of policy, the manufacture and transfer of Israeli arms can be expected to figure prominently in the search for security, economic viability, and also as an independent course of diplomacy for the remainder of this decade and, indeed, well into the 1990s. By the same token were Israeli defense marketing strategies to fail, the impact of so sharp and sudden a reversal would be felt profoundly in each of these three vital areas. In short, the export of defense-related products has become far more than simply the tactical expedient of any single government or coalition; arms transfers in the 1980s are a strategic national commitment for Israel.

This statement, although shocking to some who would demand that Israel transcend, if not sacrifice, the "national interest" in serving as a "light unto the nations," nevertheless offers us deep insight into Israel's status and perceptions vis-à-vis the world community after thirty-seven years of sovereign existence. In the mix of motives underscoring its arms promotion activities, the argument of necessity is a most powerful one.

Arab enmity and numerical superiority still persist as the central facts of Israel's national existence and defense posture. Most recently the economic consequences of arms trading likewise have come to be expressed in terms of necessity. The logic of opportunity also enters the picture, combining with the argument based on national security imperatives to form the overarching justification for a forward weapons transfer policy. Opportunity here derives from recent global trends as well as from qualitative advantages enjoyed by Israel in both military technologies and military experience.

The point, therefore, is that Israeli arms sales diplomacy is influenced strongly by situational determinants—international, regional, and domestic. One is struck by the close interaction between military posture, economic development, internal factors, and prevailing global conditions. It is to a discussion of the latter that we now turn since as a comparatively small state actor Israel cannot help but be affected in all of its policies by the larger systemic or global crosscurrents, particularly those of militarization and rearmament.

THE INTERNATIONAL CONTEXT

Trading in weapons has been termed "the most crucial postwar political fact of life" as well as "mankind's most continuing good business."[3] Preoccupation with arms proliferation and control at the nuclear level, while understandable because of the gravity of the problem, generally results in oversight or neglect in strategic studies of the conventional level. And yet conventional arms races, including the transfer of weapons, are an issue of separate importance. They constitute a major form of international interaction; they are an undeniable source of tension, fueling local disputes and discouraging the peaceful settlement of conflict; economically, they are a drain on national resources even as they represent a leading growth industry.[4]

Limited wars still tend to dominate the world scene. The basic war/peace correlate consequently remains, as it always has, a function of ends (rival national interests resulting in interstate quarrels), means (the accessibility of instruments of force), and will (the likelihood of their being resorted to eventually). This is reconfirmed by the latest series of armed conflicts whether over the Falkland islands and Grenada, throughout Lebanon, within Chad or near the Shatt al-Arab. In each, an assured supply of arms and superior firepower became an important variable. The existence of these and many other potential trouble spots within and across state borders suggests a diverse market for conventional armaments while assuring a large demand for them. Indeed, one can argue that pressures for nuclear nonproliferation merely work to heighten demand for arms at the subnuclear or conventional level for most, if not all countries, illustrating how linkage functions in world politics while offering certainly one explanation for the unparalleled acceleration in weapons acquisition registered during the 1970s.

The statistics speak for themselves. World military expenditures (in 1979 U.S. dollars) approximated $600 billion in 1980 and about $970 billion in 1984; they are projected to pass the trillion-dollar mark in 1985.[5] Annual worldwide conventional transfers alone stood at $3.8 billion in 1965 and at $9.4 billion by 1969.[6] Thereafter even according to conservative estimates the yearly aggregate increase has been striking (Figure 1.1).

According to U.S. Arms Control and Disarmament Agency (ACDA) statistics, the value of world arms imports in constant 1979 U.S. dollars rose during the 1971–1980 period at an annual average rate of 7.4 percent.[7] Recent figures suggest the arms trade to be worth anywhere from $24 billion to $35 billion a year, or about 2 percent of the total world trade.[8] This 1982 figure is 70 percent higher than the 1972 one. The total number of arms exporters increased from thirty-two countries in 1972 to forty-four in 1982; the number with deliveries exceeding $100 million annually grew from ten in 1972 to twenty-nine in 1982.

This trend toward military expansion is at once sustained and awesome whatever the standard or measure for comparison employed. Several indicators suffice: $600 billion in military expenditures; $50 billion spent on

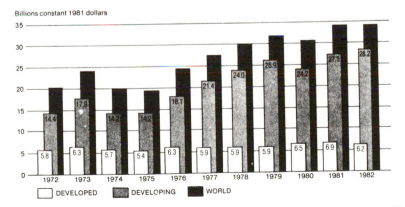

FIGURE 1.1. World Arms Imports From U.S. Arms Control and Disarmament Agency. *World Military Expenditures and Arms Transfers, 1972–1982*. Washington, D.C., April 1984, p. 6.

weapons research; $35 billion, as noted, worth of arms trade. The result is a record weapons inventory, including 150,000 tanks and some 40,000 combat aircraft,[9] underlying the fact that more armaments are being made and sold than ever before.

From such data it becomes further apparent that the volume of major weapons exports to the Third World more than doubles that of nonmilitary world trade.[10] The Brandt Commission's 1980 report makes this point in calling attention to the inverted priorities in the relationship between development and armament. For example, as many as 40,000 village pharmacies could be set up for the price of one jet fighter; or one-half of one percent of a single year's world military expenditure might pay for all the farm equipment needed by low-income, food-deficient countries to increase food production and approach self-sufficiency by 1990.[11] In light of these findings the commission strongly recommended that the international community become more seriously concerned about the consequences of arms transfers and reach agreement to restrain deliveries to areas of conflict or tension. Such appeals tend to fall upon deaf ears, whether those of the exporters or of the recipients. Prospects for the future must therefore be considered equally as promising — or ominous.

Permissiveness on the supply side of the arms transfers relationship is traceable, in the first instance, to the accelerated superpower contest. One of its features is the liberal supply of weapons to allied or potentially friendly countries. In 1980 the Soviet Union exported arms worth $8.8 billion and the United States $6.6 billion on the basis of ACDA statistics. The Soviet share of the world's arms exports was 33.7 percent, the American share 25.2 percent.[12] In fiscal year 1982 alone the United States is claimed to have signed sales agreements valued at $21.5 billion for future delivery.[13]

Soviet-American arms activity, however, is part of a larger global pattern involving other developed countries as well. The 1982 shares of arms exports to the various regions show NATO members dominating 47.9 percent of the market, those within the Warsaw Pact a further 38.3 percent (Figure 1.2). Sales of conventional weapons by the North to the South are increasing; so much so that they represent perhaps 70 percent of all arms exports.[14]

Recession and the threat of a worsening economic crisis in the Western European arms manufacturing countries underlies this accelerated flow of military products to every other part of the globe. Because of high unemployment, foreign trade imbalances, and budget deficits in the industrialized states, they attach far greater weight to the economic argument for pushing military sales than in previous years of relative prosperity. An additional source of supply are developing countries within the Third World, such as Brazil, South Korea, and India, which have achieved an export capability of their own, joining the competition for sales contracts.

Still, only a few Third World countries really have the indigenous capaci-

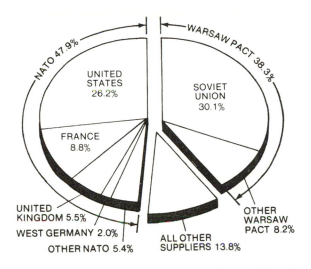

FIGURE 1.2. Shares of World Arms Exports, 1982. From ACDA, 1984, p. 8.

ty or the scientific capability to produce their own armaments, let alone to engage in the overseas marketing of weapons. As a result much of the upward demand curve at the beginning of this decade owed to the unique purchasing power of some less developed countries (LDCs), particularly those affiliated with the Organization of Petroleum Exporting Countries (OPEC), and to the often inflated military needs of all LDCs. Together they accounted for 78 percent of the value of world arms imports in 1980.[15] Confronted by multiple threats which extend from domestic challenges to the regime through border claims, insurgency, and irredentism to intraregional rivalries, these small, weak, and developing states increasingly have sought to counter their own particular security dilemma by means of the two classic increments of power—allies and arms.

The recent pattern of rearmament is distinctive, however, in at least three respects from other periods in modern history. Before the 1970s most transfers consisted of obsolete weapons or surplus stock. The demand today is for sophisticated military technologies and for ever more destructive "state of the art" systems. Of approximately 1,100 separate arms transfer agreements identified in 1981, second-hand weapons accounted for a mere 2 percent, and only 4 percent of the contracts were for refurbished weapons; whereas a full 94 percent were for new systems.[16] Reports in 1984 of the ease with which Iraq was able to secure the components necessary for waging chemical warfare from European suppliers call attention to the further erosion in international standards, but also to the lethal contents of national arms arsenals. Secondly, terms of trade in the 1970s shifted noticeably from outright arms grants to cash sales. This is due largely to those leading weapons customers enriched by the post-1973 energy revolution. Another contributing factor surely has to be the importance for the supplier countries of revenues derived from arms sales in generating foreign exchange.

The third hallmark of the international trade in conventional arms — or "the world arms bazaar," as it is often termed — is how fiercely competitive it has become. At mid-decade there are more players playing for much higher stakes. A majority of industrialized and industrializing societies are geared at present to military production and foreign sales. Yet analysts, influenced by the boom years of the last decade, for the most part have been slow to appreciate (a) how tied economic prosperity and political stability are to such sales, and (b) that the conventional arms market is at a transitional stage. Early signs have pointed to a drop in demand. Third World customers face an untenable debt load. In addition, some armed forces confront a saturation point and are unable to absorb further imports of excessively refined weapons systems for the present, further slowing their rush to rearm. Whether temporary or not, there does appear to be something of a respite in the conventional arms race.

On the supplier side, however, is a growing list of arms merchants possessing the requisite inventories of weaponry available for transfer and, more importantly, having a real perceived need to sell. Despite cautionary signs, neither the major Western arms manufacturing and exporting countries nor their less prominent non-Western competitors are likely to easily change course for fear of losing their share of the market and profits to rival suppliers. Equally great is the fear of economic dislocation at home resulting from a drying up of outlets for defense products. In short, it is the economic factor which has come to predominate, adding an element of desperation to what has always been in the best of circumstances a highly competitive and unprincipled profession.

The traffic in arms takes place essentially under what approximates free market conditions. The international management of weapons is at best only at a preliminary stage. No machinery exists by which to cope effectively with this mounting problem or to regulate arms flows. Attempts at negotiating norms or at reaching multilateral restraints all have failed.[17] Perhaps the key rule at work is that of seeking unilateral advantage. Because it is impractical to expect suppliers — newcomers as well as traditional ones — to adopt self-restraint through a voluntary code of conduct, in effect this means that supply and demand is the second and only other rule of conventional arms proliferation.

Israel, as a member of the existing international system, cannot be otherwise than deeply affected by this climate and by the existing economic and political realities. Against a backdrop of abiding insecurity shared by all countries irrespective of size, strength, or location, Israel pursues its own distinctive arms export diplomacy in a unrestrained worldwide conventional arms race at once lucrative but increasingly competitive. Global arms flow patterns and practices, by way of summary, reflect the initial blend of compulsion with expediency which lies at the heart of this diplomacy. Wider international considerations, however, are further reinforced at the regional level. It is the Middle East arms race which really best portrays the mix of necessity and opportunity behind Israel's recycling of defense skills through export.

MIDDLE EASTERN REALITIES

Israel's approach to arms transfers is necessitated more than anything else by direct participation in the escalating Palestine problem. No other significant supplier of conventional weapons can cite its ongoing involvement in a major armed conflict of such long duration or intensity by way of justification. Viewed in historic terms this dispute, raging throughout most of the twentieth century, derives from a basic Arab rejection of the right of a Jewish state to exist peacefully within secure and recognized borders in any part of what was once British-mandated Palestine.

In evolutionary terms, the Arab-Israeli conflict increasingly has assumed the nature of "one long war."[18] Beginning in the 1920s, it is characterized by four principal developments: (a) a widening of the original dispute's geographic scope, spilling over beyond the confines of Palestine proper to engulf the Middle East region and to threaten world order by posing international crises in 1956, 1967, 1973, and, again in 1982; (b) a concomitant increase in the sheer number of concerned parties perceiving their interests to be affected by the dispute; (c) the failure of most peacemaking efforts, resulting in a steady spiral of physical fighting; and (d) a progressive escalation in the means of warfare.

This progressive escalation addresses the impact of Middle East arms races upon both Israel and the Arab-Israeli conflict.[19] It bears emphasizing that Israel is hardly alone in the rush to procure arms; it finds itself in a region several of whose Arab members consistently lead the list of world weapons importers (Figure 1.3).

Over the last decade Middle Eastern countries accounted for approximately 42 percent of the international arms trade, and in 1982 they were recipients of 51 percent of all arms transferred to the developing countries (see Figure 1.4). Estimates are that the Arab members of the Middle East regional subsystem alone have spent over $100 billion on arms over the past decade.[20]

As a region the Middle East is estimated to have received over the past decade about 85 percent of all surface-to-air missiles exported to the Third World, about 70 percent of all heavy and light armor and supersonic jet fighters, 50 percent of all artillery, missile-equipped patrol boats and military helicopters, 40 percent of the subsonic combat aircraft, 30 percent of the surface warships, and 25 percent of the submarines.[21] Taking merely one of these cate-

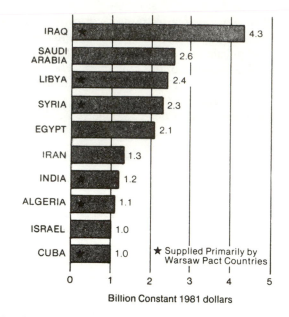

FIGURE 1.3. Leading Arms Importing Countries, 1982. From ACDA, 1984, p. 7. Note that aside from Israel, six of the top nine recipients are Arab countries, five of which (excluding Egypt) still remain in a state of war with Israel.

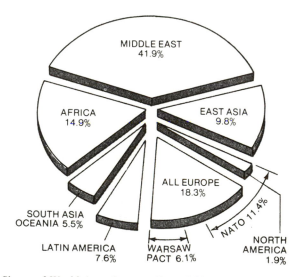

FIGURE 1.4. Shares of World Arms Imports. From ACDA, 1984, p. 6.

gories and translating percentages into volume in order to convey the true proportions of this weapons flow, the number of tanks and self-propelled guns delivered from 1977–1981 alone totaled 10,790.[22] The Arab states in particular demonstrate a collective as well as individual ability to secure arms deliveries from diverse sources.[23]

Four separate sources of supply can be enumerated: First, there is the Soviet Union, which has treaties of friendship with Iraq (1972, 1978), Syria (1980), and South Yemen (1980) and acts as their principal supplier. The Soviet Union or other Warsaw Pact nations in addition have varying types of security assistance programs with Algeria and Libya; even Jordan in 1982 accepted delivery for the first time of Russian missiles and guns.[24] China plays a complementary role through its arms relationships with North Yemen, Sudan, Egypt, Iraq, and apparently Iran.[25]

The United States is the second major supplier to Middle Eastern countries as a function of its global strategy and adversarial relationship with the Soviet Union.[26] American military assistance other than to Israel encompasses Egypt and Sudan, Jordan, Morocco, Oman, Saudi Arabia, and Tunisia. Since 1982 the Reagan administration has also poured military equipment into Lebanon as part of a desperate attempt to prop up the government and army there. These arms supplies are supplemented in a meaningful way by Western European countries acting independently of the United States as a third category of supplier, and quite often in a competitive manner. In fact, this may be one of the salient qualities of the Middle East regional arms race. Virtually every country other than Israel enjoys the leverage deriving from the ability, whenever it is rebuffed in its acquisition demands, to play off one supplier against the others.

Britain has sent arms to Bahrain, Egypt, Jordan, Kuwait, Oman, Qatar, Saudi Arabia, Sudan, and the United Arab Emirates. France has continuing arms supply arrangements with Egypt, Iraq, Lebanon, Libya, Morocco, Sudan, and Tunisia.[27] West Germany, as part of its own efforts to expand arms sales, has entered the Arab market, with particular emphasis on Saudi Arabia as a potential client. The dynamics of Middle Eastern supplier-recipient relationships are best reflected in the Iran-Iraq war. It is reliably estimated that in the first three years of the war, eighteen countries supplied Iraq and seventeen supplied Iran, while ten, including the Soviet Union, sold weapons to both sides.[28] Despite apprehension in Washington, France in October, 1983, went through with its delivery of five Super Etendard jets equipped with highly accurate Exocet missiles to Iraq.[29] This expanding Gulf War, in turn, provided Saudi Arabia and France with the justification in January, 1984, for concluding a major bilateral arms deal worth as much as $4.1 billion;[30] the Saudis cited their fear of a possible escalation of the Iran-Iraq fighting in announcing the transaction.

Each of the Arab countries thus employs the argument that it should get whatever arms it needs to defend itself against different dangers: Jordan, from Syria; Saudi Arabia, against Khomeini extremism; Egypt and the Sudan, the threat of Libyan imperialism. With the exception of countries like Syria and Southern Yemen which depend almost exclusively on Communist-supplied assistance, each state can profess to be pro-Western in orientation and hence deserving of weapons as protection against the Communist threat. Common to all, of course, is the Zionist enemy and the alleged danger of Israel military expansionism. This leads to the fourth supply pattern: arms movements within the region itself.

Weapons flows among the twenty members of the Arab League rather than from extraregional sources must be taken into account as well in discussing the Middle East arms race. The shared concern of Egypt and Sudan at the ambitions of Libya's Colonel Qaddafi at the western flank of the Middle East has strengthened military ties between them. Similarly, at the eastern extremity Iranian incitement of Islamic fundamentalists and anti-Sunni sentiment prompted Jordan and Iraq in March, 1981, to ratify a defense agreement also supported by Saudi Arabia. The Saudis also were instrumental in developing a mutual defense structure covering Bahrain, Kuwait, Oman, and the United Arab Emirates; requests by the Pentagon for congressional authorization of arms assistance and training to Jordan in 1984 were based upon the view that King Hussein's monarchy would use such equipment in the local context of the Persian Gulf. Yet ultimately there are no really effective controls preventing the reciprocal exchange or supply of arms, spare parts, and even volunteer expeditionary forces from one Arab or possibly Islamic country such as Pakistan to another.

A word needs to be said in this context of inter-Arab military cooperation about the potential importance of indigenous Arab arms production. In 1975 an Arab Military Industry Organization (AMIO) was set up in Egypt to encourage such a venture. Contracts worth over $1 billion were signed with Western companies for the local assembly and coproduction of antitank missiles, jeeps, helicopters, and jets and jet engines, in five major factories based near Helwan.[31] In the wake of the 1977 Sadat initiative and the 1979 Israel-Egypt treaty, this program aiming at further diversifying arms supply through Arab military manufacture has encountered serious problems. Egypt is pursuing a separate course through local-assembly agreements with foreign companies,[32] while Saudi Arabia appears bent upon negotiating coproduction concessions with European suppliers for the future manufacture of electronics equipment in addition to airplane assembly.[33]

For the present, however, no Arab country except Egypt has a substantial arms industry. From Israel's perspective this represents a comparative advantage, given its own advanced arms production capacity. Israel, ranked seventh in size (3 percent of the area's population) and seventh in military manpower (3 percent), makes 79 percent of the region's weapons systems.[34] Nevertheless, the ease by which the Arabs can secure their weapons needs from outside sources more than makes up for this deficiency. Arab imports of foreign arms not only fuel the regional arms race but pose additional challenges for Israel. Leave aside the fact that this entire Arab market is sealed off to Israel and left exclusively to rival suppliers. Far more serious is the need for Israeli planners to contend with the cumulative effect of this endless flow of arms to the Arab states on the regional military balance and on prospects for advancing to nuclear scenarios.[35]

Strategic assessment of the Arab-Israeli power balance is both critical for Israeli security and fraught with imponderables. What constitutes the array of forces aligned against Israel? Precisely which Arab countries comprise the "rejectionist front"? Does Egypt's adherence to its 1979 peace agreement with Israel represent an iron-clad assurance its large armed forces will not be committed again to the anti-Israel struggle? How close are the Arabs to achieving a minimal nuclear capability? What distinguishes offensive weapons from those of a defensive nature? These and many other related questions affecting Israel's military posture leave ample room for legitimate differences of interpretation, definition, and computation, as has often been the case between Israeli and American or European experts when surveying Israel's military needs.

Yet it is clear that in preparing against any eventuality, Israel's military and political leaders are duty-bound to stress "worse case" situations and the danger, ever-present in fluid Middle Eastern affairs, of the Arabs consolidating forces. Such assessments underscore Israel's quantitative disadvantage not only in manpower terms but in armaments (Table 1.1).

Since the goal of Israel is to assure a qualitative edge vis-à-vis any poten-

Table 1.1. The Israel-Arab Military Balance.

	TOTAL ARMED FORCES (IN THOUSANDS)	DIVISIONS	TANKS	ARTILLERY
Arab coalition*	1653	27	9860	7115
Israel	440	11	3600	1000

Source: Mark A. Heller, ed., *The Middle East Military Balance—1983* (Tel-Aviv: The Jaffee Center for Strategic Studies, 1983), p. 318.
*The data do not represent maximum figures based on total commitment of all armed forces on the part of all Arab countries, only those of Syria, Jordan, the P.L.O., and Egypt. Thus, only 50 percent of Saudi air and land forces are included. The figures also do not reflect quantities of Soviet and eastern bloc arms reaching Syria since the initial stages of the 1982 Lebanese conflict.

tial Arab coalition, older weapons systems must constantly be phased out at increasingly prohibitive cost in favor of newer generations of armor, naval vessels, and aircraft. Seen in this competitive context, the export of obsolete equipment, of surplus stockpiles and, increasingly, of more sophisticated items manufactured in Israel, is a logical function of the continuous rearmament process. It is another way of underlining how for Israel as well as for other struggling and security-conscious Third World countries international, but especially regional, politics stimulate defense production and recycling far beyond what would be expected from countries of comparable size and wealth.

Defense sales thus alleviate to some extent the burden of the defense budget, thereby helping to ensure the country's military competitiveness. In the absence of a comprehensive peace in the Arab-Israel zone of conflict, and given the uncertainties of a shifting Middle East balance of power, weapons transfers must remain both a major component of Israeli security and a political-military imperative.

But then the security imperative has been with Israel ever since its inception. This historical dimension is vital for the insight it offers: first, in tracing the growth of Israeli weapons manufacture leading to the export of arms to other countries; second, in underscoring how Israel — its leaders, its industrial and military sectors, its foreign relations — has responded over time to the logic of necessity posed by regional threats and systemic challenges.

NOTES

1. Unclassified data from American sources can be found in U.S. Department of Defense, Security Assistance Agency, *Foreign Military Construction Sales and Military Assistance Facts* (Washington, D.C.: U.S. Government Printing Office, September 1982). The part played by military assistance in the U.S.-Israeli relationship is discussed in Bernard Reich, *Quest for Peace* (New Brunswick: Transaction Books, 1977); see also David Pollock, *The Politics of Pressure* (Westport, CT: Greenwood Press, 1982).
2. Initial political surveys of Israeli international arms transfer activities are: Bernard Reich's chapter on Israel in Edward A. Kolodziej and Robert E. Harkavy, eds., *Security Policies of Developing Countries* (Lexington, MA: Lexington Books, 1982), pp. 203–227; and the author's *Israeli Arms Sales: Perspectives and Prospects* (Tel-Aviv: Jaffee Center for Strategic Studies), paper no. 24 (February 1984).
3. George Thayer, *The War Business. The International Trade in Armaments* (New York: Simon & Schuster, 1969), pp. 18–19.
4. United Nations Secretary-General, *Economic and Social Consequences of the Arms Race and of Military Expenditures* (New York 1983), report E. 83. IX. 2.
5. U.S. Arms Control and Disarmament Agency, *World Military Expenditures and Arms Transfers, 1971–1980* (Washington, D.C., March, 1983), p. ii; *World Military Expenditures and Arms Transfers, 1972–1982.* (Washington, D.C., April, 1984), p. 1.

6. Stockholm International Peace Research Institute (SIPRI), *World Armaments and Disarmament* (London: Taylor and Francis, 1982), SIPRI Yearbook, 1982, pp. 175–88; see also Andrew J. Pierre, *The Global Politics of Arms Sales* (Princeton: Princeton University Press, 1982), p. 9, SIPRI, 1981, p. 188.
7. ACDA, 1983, p. 29.
8. *International Herald Tribune*, 6 May 1983. The growth is somewhat less in constant dollars, although still impressive. ACDA claims total arms transfers in 1982 rose to $36.5 billion, ACDA, 1984, p. 6.
9. Ruth Leger Sivard, *World Military and Social Expenditures 1982* (Leesburg, VA: World Priorities, 1982), p. 6.
10. SIPRI, 1982, p. xxvii.
11. *North-South. A Program for Survival*. The Report of the Independent Commission on International Development Issues under the chairmanship of Willy Brandt (Cambridge, MA: MIT Press, 1980), p. 14.
12. ACDA, 1983, pp. 31, 108, 113.
13. Francis J. West, Jr., "The U.S. Security Assistance Program: Giveaway or Bargain?", *Strategic Review* (Winter 1983), p. 52.
14. Brandt Report, p. 120.
15. ACDA, 1983, p. 29.
16. SIPRI, 1982, p. 177.
17. On the dismal record of attempts at regulating the international arms trade, see Graham Kearns, "CAT and Dogma: The Future of Multilateral Arms Transfer Restraint," *Arms Control*, 2: 1 (May 1981): 3–24; and Richard K. Betts, "The Tragicomedy of Arms Trade Control," *International Security*, 5: 1 (Summer 1980): 80–110. Also useful as background on contemporary international arms trade practices are: Robert E. Harkavy, *The Arms Trade and International Systems* (Cambridge, MA: Ballinger, 1975), and Barry M. Blechman, Janne E. Nolan, and Alan Platt, "Pushing Arms," *Foreign Policy* 46: (Spring 1982): 138–154.
18. The military history of the Middle East dispute is traced in: Netanel Lorch, *The Edge of the Sword* (New York: G. P. Putnam's Sons, 1961); Martin Gilbert, *The Arab-Israeli Conflict. Its History in Maps* (London: Weidenfeld & Nicolson, 1974); Nadav Safran, *From War to War* (New York: Pegasus, 1969); Chaim Herzog, *The Arab-Israeli Wars* (New York: Random House, 1982).
19. Two worthwhile discussions are those of Lincoln P. Bloomfield and Amelia C. Leiss, "Arms Transfers and Arms Control," in J. C. Hurewitz, ed., *Soviet-American Rivalry in the Middle East* (New York: Columbia University Press, 1969), pp. 37–54, which looks at the Middle East arms race in the 1950s and 1960s; and Hurewitz's own somewhat outdated but analytical country-by-country study, *Middle East Politics: The Military Dimension* (New York: Praeger, 1969).
20. *Haaretz*, the Israeli independent daily, quoting Arab studies, 4 April 1984.
21. U.S. Department of State, "Conventional Arms Transfers to the Third World, 1972–1981" (Washington, D.C.: U.S. Government Printing Office, 1982).
22. *The Middle East*, September 1982, p. 20.
23. Regional arms flow patterns can be garnered from diverse sources. The U.S. is reported to have sent perhaps $24 billion in arms to the Middle East in the years 1955–1981, the Russians about $26 billion, *International Herald Tribune*, 4 October 1982. On the Middle East arms race and its strategic significance, see Howard H. Frederick, *The Arms Trade and the Middle East. A Primer*. (Philadelphia: American Friends Service Committee, 1977); Yitzhak Oren, "Mechirat Neshek Maaravi l'Medinot Arav" ("Western Arms Sales to the Arab Countries"), *Maara-*

chot 267 (January 1979):41–47; Geoffrey Kemp, "The Military Build-Up: Arms Control or Arms Trade," in Gregory Treverton, ed., *Crisis Management and the Super-Powers in the Middle East*, Adelphi Library (London: The International Institute for Strategic Studies, 1981), pp. 34–40.

24. On the Soviet role, see Y. Yarom, *Arms Transactions with Middle Eastern and North African Countries in 1982* (Tel-Aviv: Jaffee Center for Strategic Studies), Documentation Service, Digest no. 2 (December 1983); and David A. Andelman, "Andropov's Middle East," *The Washington Quarterly* (Spring 1983), pp. 110–114.

25. Focus upon Chinese arms activities is provided in The International Institute for Strategic Studies' *The Military Balance, 1982–1983* (London, 1982), p. 51, and in *The Economist's* "Foreign Report," no. 1979 (15 September 1983).

26. The U.S. views the Middle East, bounded by Turkey, Pakistan, and the Horn of Africa, as a strategic entity which is part of a larger "politico-strategic theater." Richard Burt, Director of the Bureau of Politico-Military Affairs at the U.S. State Department, in congressional testimony delivered 23 March 1981, official text courtesy of the U.S. Information Agency, Tel-Aviv. In encouraging local states to resist Soviet intimidation American administrations are committed to providing them with security assistance.

27. IISS, *The Military Balance*, p. 51 ff.

28. *IHT*, 14–15 July 1984, reporting SIPRI estimates.

29. *IHT*, 25 August 1983; *Haaretz*, 10 October 1983; On the Persian Gulf struggle and its introduction of newer weaponry, see Mark A. Heller, *The Iran-Iraq War: Implications for Third Parties* (Tel-Aviv: JCSS), paper no. 23 (January 1984).

30. *The New York Times*, 17 January 1984.

31. *The Middle East*, February 1984, p. 16.

32. According to Egyptian Defense Minister Abdul Halim Abu-Ghazala, local production of a version of the Soviet SAM-7 anti-aircraft missile was to begin early in 1985, *IHT*, 6 October 1983. Egypt's military industry is alleged to have received contracts for more than $1 billion worth of arms and munitions for the Iraqi army in 1982–1983, Mordechai Abir, "Whither Egypt?", *Jerusalem Post*, 8 May 1984. Details on Egyptian efforts at acquiring an infrastructure of its own appear in an article in *Maariv*, 6 May 1984, and in *IHT*, 14 June 1984.

33. "Saudis Said to Envision Own Weapons Industry," *IHT*, 17–18 December 1983. The Saudi government agreed in 1979 to help set up an $8.6 billion arms industry in the United Arab Emirates under the Gulf Cooperative Council as part of Arab sanctions against Egypt, thereby nullifying the 1975 decision in favor of an Arab Military Industry Organization based primarily on Egypt. Towards the end of 1984 Saudi Arabia reportedly signed a five-year military cooperation agreement with Brazil which will enable Riyadh to expand its own small weapons industry and transfer of arms to third parties. *Washington Post*, 12 October 1984.

34. Figures appearing in Stephani G. Neuman, "International Stratification and Third World Military Industries," *International Organization*, 38 (Winter 1984): 186. The figures include non-Arab Iran.

35. Shai Feldman, *Israeli Nuclear Deterrence. A Strategy for the 1980s* (New York: Columbia University Press, 1982). Implications for Israel of the incessant weapons competition are the items of Arye Shalev's "The Arms Race in the Middle East in the 1980s" in Zvi Lanir (ed.). *Israeli Security Planning in the 1980s* (New York: Praeger, 1984), pp. 75–90; another useful analysis is the contribution in that same work by Aharon Yariv, "The Middle East Arms Race Intensification Trap: Is There a Way Out?" pp. 91–103.

2

ARMS SUPPLIER STATUS

A review of the emergence of Israel as a serious international arms supplier serves several purposes. First, it offers preliminary insight into contemporary sales and distribution practices. The interplay between the logic of necessity and the call of opportunity may be at its strongest today; yet these same forces are found to have been at work in earlier periods, too. Second, the time perspective highlights how far Israel has come in three decades and by what effort. Third, a review can help to determine whether Israel and its arms export program are in fact a model for Third World munitions development. Fourth, the historical evidence will be of use later in answering questions about the nature and process of Israeli arms policymaking.

Defense-related industrial development leading to the export of arms is described in the literature as a step-by-step process. Moodie,[1] for example, suggests seven such "discrete stages":

1. establishment of maintenance and overhaul facilities for service and repair of imported arms;
2. local assembly of imported kits or parts under license;
3. local manufacture of simple components;
4. local production of entire systems under license;
5. introduction of locally designed modifications into such systems;
6. production of domestically designed and tested systems using imported components of more sophisticated technologies;
7. domestically designed systems using no imported components.

Such a pattern calls for a country to gradually develop the relevant expertise and industrial facilities for arms manufacture and trade by initially overhauling and maintaining imported weapons and proceeding from there to the licensed production of a selected weapon or system. The penultimate goal, therefore, is an indigenous design, development, and production capability leading to arms exporter status.[2]

Israel's experience emphasizes how difficult it is to determine where one stage ends and the next begins. As the higher stages of development and production are achieved they often overlap and can occur simultaneously. Noteworthy in the case of Israel is that it began to export arms, albeit only marginally, at a very early stage. Although the standard patterns offer independence from external suppliers as the dominant motivation for indigenous development,[3] the evidence shows conclusively that the effort at arms autarky never quite succeeds in completely alleviating dependence on external sources.[4]

DEFENSE SALES IN HISTORICAL PERSPECTIVE

In the case of Israel, direct military necessity in the form of Arab enmity and the Middle East arms race has, from the very beginning, spurred indigenous arms development. Historically, Israel's progression to the status of arms exporter can be traced through three phases:

        (1) 1948–1960
        (2) 1960–1973
        (3) 1973–present

The First Phase (1948–1960)

The roots of arms diplomacy, like so much of Israeli social and foreign policies, are to be found in the immediate prestate period.[5] Modern Jewish history emphasizes one overriding political theme — Jewish powerlessness. This sense of impotence, reflected in the wave of anti-Semitic pogroms followed later by the Holocaust, served as a potent factor in the ideas of Jewish nationalism and self-emancipation which Zionist thinkers began to spread at the turn of the century.[6] It was in large part out of a desire to end this helplessness that the early pioneers came to Palestine only to encounter, by the twenties and certainly as late as the thirties, opposition from the British mandate authorities and the resident Palestinian Arab community, which was increasingly supported by the neighboring Arab states, each possessing a standing army. While only a small fraction of the early settlers advocated armed activism as the way to compel Great Britain to evacuate Palestine, the leaders of the Jewish community, or *yishuv*, did set out to build up a local self-defense capacity against periodic Arab riots and the harrassment of Jewish farm settlements, buses, etc.[7]

In the final stage of the struggle for Palestine and for Jewish independence in the years 1946–1948, the military strategy continued to be premised upon self-reliance. It was in this context that early efforts were made at improvising a munitions base able to provide the *Haganah* (defense) fighters[8] with desperately needed small arms and explosives. Parallel attempts at breaking the British arms embargo of the *yishuv* by taking advantage of the opportunities for securing surplus weapons in postwar Europe also led to a number of clandestine activities abroad.[9] In the War of Independence these acquisitions — ranging from rifles to airplanes for a primitive air force — proved of critical importance. But they also exposed Israel's vulnerability and dependence on diverse foreign sources for the most rudimentary means of defense.

During the first decade of independence the security threat not only persisted but increased in intensity. Arab hostility to the Jewish state hardened as neighboring countries prepared for the so-called "second round." What made Israel's position acute, however, was the pledge by the Western Great Powers to restrict military assistance to the region as enunciated in the Tripartite Declaration of May, 1950, issued by Britain, France, and the United States.[10] This policy worked decidedly against Israel in light of Britain's special military relationship with the frontline Arab states, Egypt, Iraq, and Jordan, reinforced by the dangling of arms by the United States seeking to draw Baghdad into the anti-Soviet "northern tier" security system. This Tripartite Declaration, given its monopolistic nature and implicit discrimination against Israel, was bad enough; what compounded the situation even further was its abject failure in point of practice. The Soviet Union, in sponsoring the 1955 Czech arms deal to Egypt, in effect served notice that hereafter it would be a major competitor against the West in supplying weapons to the Arabs.[11]

Such developments compelled the government of Israel after 1948 to redouble its efforts in the field of arms and security. Excluded from preferred supply sources, Israel was forced to seek austere alternatives in the fifties. As early as 1949 Prime Minister David Ben-Gurion determined to convert the several scattered and primitive factories left over from the Haganah period into a military industry.[12] In 1951 his orders to form an aircraft company began to be carried out, with the formation of Bedek in 1953 representing a modest start.

The 1950s therefore witnessed the expansion of several military-related industries under prodding from the Ministry of Defense (also headed, except for a brief period of retirement, by Ben-Gurion) and from the army command. In the years after 1948 Israel slowly acquired greater degrees of self-sufficiency in small arms and mortars and showed an ability to modify and overhaul tanks, aircraft, and even electronic systems. Faced with permanent scarcity, the Israeli military turned arms-grafting into something of a fine art.[13] The desperate effort in 1946–1948 to secure munitions from every available source led to the problem of standardization. Old tanks had to be fitted with freshly bought cannon; planes were given a new look in keeping with the specific requirements of local warfare; trucks regarded as unusable were fitted with new spare parts, making them roadworthy and even adaptable to desert fighting. Improvization, in short, became a way of thinking in the war against scarcity as local producers learned by trial and error to manufacture spare parts of different makes and calibers. Indeed, national planners throughout have stressed the need for an indigenous military production capability despite the country's limited resource base, or rather, because of it.

By the late 1950s what have since become the three pillars of the military industry were already in place: Israel Military Industries (IMI); Israel Aircraft Industries Ltd. (IAI), an outgrowth of Bedek; and the National Weapons Development Authority (Rafael). All three operated under the aegis of the Defense Ministry, and a good deal of the credit for their spurt in development owed to the initiative and imagination of Shimon Peres who, as director-general and deputy defense minister from 1953 until 1965, took direct responsibility for programs of applied military science and technology.[14]

Ben-Gurion provided the catalyst and inspiration, whereas Peres saw to the mundane matters and myriad details necessarily involved in so ambitious an undertaking. Under his influence the Ministry took over the prestate "home cottage" factories and set them up on a corporate footing. Modern capital equipment and machinery necessary for independent production were purchased abroad. The government expanded into aviation, established an electronics division, and pushed ahead with nuclear research and development.[15] Milestones included:

- design of the Uzi submachine gun (1952)
- Bedek workshop for handling jets (1956)
- expansion into electronic equipment (1959)
- work begun on what was to be known as the Gabriel sea-to-sea missile (1959)
- first Fouga plane assembled in Israel delivered to air force (1960)

These efforts presented the state not only with the capacity to strengthen its own armed forces but by the 1960s to explore seriously the prospects for supplying low level, conventional military aid to friendly countries.

Parallel with this domestic program of arms manufacture Ben-Gurion continued to seek other, more immediate and political ways of meeting Israeli military needs in countering what was regarded as a discriminatory policy on the part of the Western Powers in refusing Israel's applications for arms while continuing to furnish military aid to Arab countries like Iraq and Jordan. The regional arms race, for example, and Israel's procurement concern help to explain two critical decisions reached in the 1950s: the acceptance of German reparations and an agreement to coordinate military plans with France and Britain against Egypt in the 1956 Sinai campaign in return for their supplying Israel with advanced armor and planes.[16]

A less known chapter of Israeli external relations in the 1950s was the initial arms sales completed with foreign governments. 1944 serves as the date for charting Israel's gradual emergence as arms supplier. That year found Israel involved in negotiating five arms deals. One of the earliest recorded sales came in August, 1954, when Burma bought Spitfires worth $1 million from stocks no longer needed by Israel as well as 50,000 rifles for $700,000.[17] Also in 1954, an agreement was concluded with the Dutch, whereby an Israeli order for artillery shells was partially covered by payment in cash with the balance in the form of Israeli-manufactured military products.[18] Belgium and Turkey appear to have purchased some form of military goods from Israel and were followed soon after by Italy.[19] At about the same time two reconverted frigates were sold to Ceylon.[20] And in the mid-1950s arms deals were also consummated with two Latin American countries, Nicaragua and the Dominican Republic; these orders were worth $1.2 and $15 million respectively.[21]

The most significant transaction during this initial period, however, was the secret decision by Ben-Gurion in 1959 to sell the Federal German Republic mortar bombs produced by the Israeli firm, Soltam. During the crisis which broke out subsequently in the Knesset, the Prime Minister revealed something of government thinking at that stage and of procedures on arms transactions. In defending his decision before the Cabinet, Ben-Gurion read the protocol of an earlier meeting in December, 1958, when a resolution had been passed which, although not mentioning Germany explicitly, nevertheless gave him and the Ministry of Defense general approval "to sell arms to foreign countries in all cases in which the Ministry of Foreign Affairs has no objection."[22]

We can already see certain outlines emerging: decisions reached at the sub-Cabinet level rather than by the full Cabinet; Defense Ministry dominance; a case-by-case approach in place of a comprehensive policy; in effect, a carte blanche authorization based upon a predisposition to sell rather than the reverse, requiring that each such arms deal first be justified. Whatever objections there were took issue with the particular purchaser, West Germany, under the shadow of the Holocaust, and not with the principle itself of Israel's involvment in arms traffic. And as former Chief of Staff Moshe Dayan argued publicly in 1959 in defending the sale: "Germany would become strong with or without Israeli weapons—but would Israel?"[23] Although this argument would come to the fore again in the late 1970s and early 1980s it figured less prominently during the second phase which lasted throughout the decade of the 1960s.

The Second Phase (1960–1973)

This period was marked by several key developments. First, further technological strides by the defense industries brought Israel closer to self-sufficiency in an increasing number of armaments categories. Thus, by 1965 the country had reached defense production capability not only in small arms but in aircraft and electronics as well.[24] Full production also put Israel in a better position to export certain types of weapons. Equally important, this export capacity coincided with a willingness on the part of Israeli leaders to use it as an element of foreign relations. The effectiveness and speed with which the Israel Defense Force (IDF) acquitted itself in 1956 and, again, in 1967, established Israel as having a military force of recognized competence. Weapons either adapted or made by Israel also earned a favorable reputation.

As a result, arms diplomacy came to be employed more directly in attempts at breeching the wall of Arab hostility politically. This can be derived from the relationship Israel opened up with Ethiopia during the reign of Emperor Haile Selassie. Located on the periphery of the Middle East, Ethiopia nevertheless was regarded by Israeli strategists as a friendly regional actor of particular importance. Pro-Western, non-Arab, and a Christian enclave menaced by surrounding Muslim countries, Ethiopia also dominated the Red Sea route to Africa and Asia seen by Israel's planners as vital for future trade growth. Like Israel, it had a strong interest in preventing the Sudan's full participation in the expansionist designs of Egyptian President Gamal Abdul Nasser. For a number of reasons combining diplomatic, strategic, and commercial considerations Ethiopia for a while became the largest recipient of Israeli economic aid in Africa and the object of close cooperation in military affairs. In return, as many as forty Israeli advisers reportedly helped train an elite counterinsurgency force maintained by Ethiopia in the province of Eritrea.[25]

As seen in the example of Ethiopia, there appears to have been a marked preference for indirect rather than direct arms relationships. In all likelihood, this was due to a combination of Israel's timidity about earning a reputation as an arms merchant, and possible conditions imposed by recipients of Israeli assistance because few customers were so eager to purchase from Israel as to risk Arab censure. Still, the emphasis was more on military assistance and training than on the actual supply of weapons. As a result, the arrows pointed more in the direction of an inflow of promising young officers and maintenance personnel from the newly emergent countries into Israel, where they participated in special courses such as paratroop training school, rather than to the outflow of arms per se.[26]

The 1960s saw Israel establishing cooperative relations with more than sixty countries in Africa, Asia, and Latin America. While a special division of the Foreign Ministry administered these far-flung agricultural and technical assistance projects, the defense establishment was no less active in promoting bilateral military programs with many of these same countries. In fact, a unit operated separately by the Ministry of Defense was responsible for any aid of a military nature to developing countries. Transfers of conventional arms on the whole, however, still tended to be rather limited and to play a relatively small role in this diplomatic initiative.

The main emphasis of the special assistance at that time was never truly military in nature. Rather, it consisted of civic action programs relating primarily to Nahal-type rural cooperative projects based within a quasimilitary framework such as were adopted in a number of Latin American countries.[27] Not infrequently these projects took the form of paramilitary kibbutz-like farming outposts in isolated or border regions of a Third World country. The primary emphasis, to be sure, was on agricultural guidance, technical aid, and public service assistance rendered by civilian experts.

This fairly low profile of export diplomacy throughout the sixties is reflected statistically. At the beginning of the decade arms sales were estimated at only $6.5 million, and between $12 and $15 million by 1966. Official Israeli sources predicted that total arms sales, including engine overhauls, would approach only $30 million in 1967; one-third actually being weapons, the remainder, ammunition.[28]

Yet there are grounds for viewing the decade of the sixties as a transitional and preparatory stage. Israeli ambassadors and agents were active in opening and then deepening basic military relationships of a bilateral nature with Third World countries. Moreover, the arms industry at home used this interval to make additional product breakthroughs and refinements with future implications for the arms export program. Work was begun by IMI, IAI, and Rafael on projects which would later catapult Israel onto the world market. To cite but one example, the first production models of the Israeli-manufactured Kfir combat aircraft came off the assembly line in 1973. And as the arms industry grew it deliberately cultivated an export market; in several instances 30 to 40 percent of the output of some companies went abroad.[29] The benefits of export were quite apparent even then: hard currency earned from such sales could be used to purchase strategic raw materials and capital equipment, thereby making further expansion of facilities and production possible.

In recalling this second phase (1960–1973), special mention must be made of the role played, unwittingly, by France. In the overlapping decade 1956–1967, France ranked as the main external source for Israel's heavy weapons. French military assistance went far beyond the supply of Mirage, Mystère, and Super Mystère planes and other major systems. The French arms industry served as a model for national, industrial, and economic growth generated by weapons production. The local arms industry manufactured jet trainers under French license, and Franco-Israeli scientific cooperation extended into a number of military areas.[30] French policy toward Israel, however, changed abruptly in 1967 following the Six Day War. To express his displeasure at Israel's rejection of advice against opening the fighting, President Charles de Gaulle unilaterally imposed an immediate embargo on the further shipment of weapons to Israel. Undelivered orders, even those for which Israel had already paid, including gunboats at Cherbourg and fifty Mirage V aircraft, were withheld; nor were further orders of weapons accepted.

The initial impact of the French arms boycott was traumatic for Israeli leaders. But rather than forcing a halt to their aspirations for local military production, de Gaulle's action had the opposite effect; it merely forced the pace of sophisticated manufacture. Money previously invested in France and other foreign countries now was diverted to local munitions firms. In keeping with the decision immediately after the war to proceed with an intensified effort to develop and enlarge Israel's own weapons industry, cost-benefit calculations were set aside in favor of producing essential items in Israel. Still, at every phase there have been civilian as well as military skeptics who take issue with both the feasibility and cost-effectiveness of Israeli home production and prefer instead to order arms abroad.

In the first three years after 1967 the military industry quadrupled its output.[31] Research and development intensified and the independent design and manufacture of major subsystems came to be favored over licensing or coproduction arrangements involving foreign companies. Israel's entry into the age of building and producing sophisticated aircraft later would be attributable to French cancellation of the Mirage V deal[32]; it was not long before an Israeli version of the plane, known as the Nesher, was produced, which led in turn to the higher performance Kfir fighter aircraft.[33]

The period of major investment in the defense industrial sector also took place between 1968 and 1972. The number of persons employed by it rose by about 20,000 during that time. In those years the purchase of weapons systems from local industry underwent a real growth of approximately 86 percent. Metals and electronics were the chief beneficiaries: these branches of industry growth were accelerated by increasing demand for defense products; and they absorbed about one-third of industrial investments. Their relative share in the nation's industrial export, exclusive of diamonds, rose from about 14 percent in 1967 to approximately 21 percent in 1968; by 1975 the figure was in the neighborhood of 31 percent.[34]

Clearly, the military industries, their infrastructure and production techniques in place by the end of the decade, more than rose to the challenge. Once again, necessity and adversity had been turned to Israel's advantage through a combination of ingenuity and forced improvization.

As part of this redoubled effort to produce most, if not all of its own armament needs before 1973 (this, after all, being a time of mounting U.S. military aid to Israel), Israeli arms enthusiasts hoped in the long run to reduce the heavy manufacturing costs by means of mass production. Such logic could only imply one possible outlet other than to the Israeli army: the export of remodelled or originally developed weapons to foreign countries. As though to give this awareness institutional expression, it was in 1972 that the Deputy-Director General's Export Department came into being within the Ministry of Defense, warranted by new trade prospects.

Nevertheless, Israel in this period had yet to reach the takeoff stage in capitalizing fully upon the emergence of so many new states with a need for conventional armaments occasioned by the rising incidence of international tension and conflict. This would be reached, however, in the following phase of Israel's drive to arms maturity.

The Third Phase (1973–present)

The 1973 Yom Kippur War represents something of a turning point in the transformation of arms sales diplomacy from a peripheral or secondary position to one of greater centrality. Until then Israeli sales, with only several exceptions, were based primarily upon servicing and repairs, upon reconverting older generations of foreign-made products, and upon the export of small arms, such as the popular Uzi submachinegun. Statistics then show a sharp rise after 1973 in both the allocation of resources to the Defense Ministry and in the transfer of more sophisticated arms. In 1975, exports amounted to $50 million; according to the United States Arms Control and Disarmament Agency (ACDA) figures they nearly trebled in 1976 to $140 million and by 1979 had reached, at a conservative estimate, $250 to $300 million.[35]

Just how conservative ACDA figures consistently tend to be (in 1971, for example, it reported Israeli sales as zero), can be inferred from an exceptional statement from a Defense Ministry spokesman in January, 1977. Departing from the practice maintained throughout of avoiding official references to the arms trade, the spokesman gave the total export of military equipment at the time as slightly in excess of $300 million – an amount not claimed by the ACDA for Israel until 1979.[36] Using the 1977 Israeli government report as a basis, Stockholm International Peace Research Institute (SIPRI) analysts by 1979 showed Israeli exports as having doubled within three years to $600 million and, extraordinarily, having multiplied again in a single year to $1.2 billion by 1980.[37] The hypothesis reinforced by these albeit unsubstantiated and divergent figures, nevertheless, is of policy following segmented decisions or, put differently, that an arms sales "policy" only emerged as the opportunities presented themselves.

The explanations for such a dramatic increase in the flow of arms from Israel are of importance for illustrating the powerful mix of motives in force at present. First, necessity took several forms: the erosion of Israel's international standing; the need to counteract Arab pressure and the oil factor; but, above all, renewed urgency in achieving a higher degree of selective self-sufficiency in weapons systems stocks and manufacturing capabilities. During the war, and especially those events surrounding the delayed United States airlift of desperately needed replacements, Israelis appreciated anew the bitter lesson about dependency first learned in 1948, repeated in the mid-fifties and again with President de Gaulle's arms embargo.

Second, during the 1970s the IDF underwent an amazing degree of sophistication in its weapons modernization programs. Once the flow of weapons from the United States accelerated following the war this had the effect of releasing older weapons systems. By 1975 Israel had rounded out its defense manufacturing capability by adding aircraft engines, warships, armored fighting vehicles, and missiles to its list of electronics, small arms, and aircraft.[38] Of the four categories of major weapons reportedly sold by Israel in the years 1977–1980, 18 percent were covered by missiles and 37 percent by aircraft, while 45 percent consisted of naval ships.[39] It is in this same period that production of the Kfir intensified, that the decision was made to undertake manufacture of an Israeli tank, the Merkava, and that the Lavi fighter plane project received the preliminary go-ahead. In effect, the seeds of earlier planning, investment, experimentation, and design were now bearing fruit as all three preconditions for military export — necessity, capacity, occasion — came to prevail.

International opportunities provide the third explanation. The chance to merchandise arms, whether to established clients like the Shah of Iran or to new purchasers like South Africa canvassing the world market in quest of their own defense needs, enters the equation in the seventies as a function of worldwide rearmament. The shipment of arms came to exceed in importance the dispatch of advisers and technicians or the range of paramilitary and training courses offered in Israel itself. Despite the public antagonism encountered in such international forums as the United Nations, Israeli emissaries had little difficulty in opening new doors to prospective clients in every region.

A combination of factors thus facilitated and help to explain the takeoff in Israeli arms sales in the late 1970s: the upgrading of the Israeli army which released large surplus stocks; the ability to produce sophisticated weapons systems at competitive prices; the seemingly limitless demand for weapons and for alternative suppliers.

Supportive Israeli governments are yet a fourth, and final, factor. Personalities figure prominently after 1973 just as they had done from Ben-Gurion onward throughout the evolution of the arms sale diplomacy. The period immediately following the Yom Kippur War found the defense industries at the peak of technological and scientific excellence. It also found leaders sympathetic to the entire thrust of military production and export in key positions of power and influence. People like Premier Yitzhak Rabin, the former chief of staff, come to mind and perhaps even more Shimon Peres who as defense minister in the Labour Government from 1974 to 1977 had the opportunity to stimulate or complete programs he had personally initiated as director-general of the Ministry some twenty years earlier. The third member of the Labour triumvirate in those years was Foreign Minister Yigal Allon, a former top commander in the War of Independence, and hence less likely than his predecessors to raise diplomatic niceties as an argument against weapons exports claimed to be serving national security and military preparedness.

The timing for the post-1973 takeoff in weapons transfers is politically significant in yet another respect. It argues that the changing of the guard in the 1977 Israeli elections, replacing Labour governments for the first time in the country's history with the Likud, represents more of a reinforcement and acceleration of the previously existing pro-arms orientation than a fresh policy initiative identified with any leader, political ideology, or government. Israel in the role of arms supplier predates the Begin era. Foreign military assistance, of which the sale of weapons is a major component, is a deeply entrenched national practice. It is not therefore, in any way a new brand of Israeli diplomacy or a departure from pre-1977 practices.

Two final observations deserve mention in concluding this survey of the history and evolution of Israel as arms exporter. The first is that judging from its historical experience, the Israeli model may be atypical in terms of the development of other nations into major suppliers, certainly unlike the Soviet Union or the large Western producers. Brazil's emphasis on indigenous production leading to, or coinciding with, an export campaign has owed little to an inability to obtain arms from foreign suppliers, whereas Israel found itself repeatedly subjected to arms embargos, even including multilateral agreement in 1950 to restrain arms transfers. Its response to the constriction of supply at each critical juncture may have been characterized by short-term access to alternative sources of acquisition—first the Eastern bloc, then the smaller European manufacturers like Belgium, followed by West Germany and the United States acting indirectly through the Germans, then Britain and France before turning openly, and increasingly, to the United States. But the really important and lasting response to interrupted supply has been to build the most impressive conventional arms industry in the Middle East, and possibly anywhere outside of the United States and Europe. Scarcity of suppliers, in sum, has had a positive effect, with self-sufficiency in a wide range of less sophisticated hardware being achieved over a relatively short span of time along with a growing ability to produce and also market more advanced equipment. Given the unrestrained nature of the recent conventional arms trade, few other countries are likely to experience such acute problems of denial; perhaps only South Africa and Taiwan come closest to emulating the Israeli route to weapons export through adversity.

The last point to be made on the basis of the three phases of Israeli growth from exclusive import to a mixture of import and export is that there are prospects for Israel's possibly being on the threshold of a new and fourth phase. Having moved from the marketing of second-hand equipment and small arms through the provision of military training and advice to the higher level of increasingly conspicuous boats, armor, missiles, or planes and of complete systems, Israel could encounter—indeed, has already encountered—certain obstacles to continued expansion in these areas. On the other hand, in the early part of the 1980s its exports of technological know-how, data packages, and the most sophisticated electronics, computer programs, and optical components of direct or indirect military application have met with singular suc-

cess in finding a ready market. Less conspicuous and therefore less politically sensitive, such scientific items are highly promising, especially if Israel
continues to enjoy a comparative advantage and headstart in their refinement.
Technology transfers consequently offer at least the prospect that Israeli
defense manufacture and foreign sales promotion may be entering what may
well come to be seen as a distinctive fourth phase, in which case it would assure
that military-related industrial exports remain a major Israeli foreign policy
instrument.

NOTES

1. Michael Moodie, *Sovereignty, Security, and Arms* (Beverly Hills: Sage Publications, 1979). Georgetown University's Center for Strategic and International Studies, Washington Papers no. 67, pp. 45–48.
2. Ilan Peleg, "Military Production in Third World Countries: A Political Study,"
   in Pat McGowan and Charles W. Kegley, Jr., eds., *Threats, Weapons and Foreign
   Policy* (Beverly Hills: Sage Publications, 1980), pp. 209–230.
3. Frank Barnaby and Ronald Huisken, *Arms Uncontrolled* (Cambridge: Harvard
   University Press, 1975), p. 34.
4. Neuman makes the case persuasively in her article in *International Organization*.
5. Dan Horowitz and Moshe Lissak, *Origins of the Israeli Polity* (Chicago: University of Chicago Press, 1978), especially Ch. 8, "The State of Israel and the Political
   Heritage of the Yishuv."
6. On Zionism, see Arthur Hertzberg, *The Zionist Idea* (New York: Meridian Books,
   1960); Ben Halpern, *The Jewish State* (Cambridge: Harvard University Press,
   1961); Walter Laqueur, *A History of Zionism* (New York: Holt, Rinehart, &
   Winston, 1972).
7. The origins of the arms industry are traced as far back as 1929 and the Arab anti-
   Jewish riots that year in Palestine. Gerald Steinberg, "Israel," in Nicole Ball and
   Milton Leitenberg, eds., *The Structure of the Defense Industry* (New York: St.
   Martin's Press, 1983), pp. 278–309. In fact, Ta'as, forerunner of today's Israel
   Military Industries (IMI), was born in the years immediately following the 1921
   riots and concentrated on turning out hand grenades and low-grade explosives,
   Zev Schiff and Eitan Haber, eds., *Lexicon L'bitachon Yisrael* (Tel-Aviv: Zmora,
   Bitan, Modan, 1976), p. 547.
8. On the *Haganah* and its evolution in the 1948 War of Independence into the
   modern Israel Defense Force, see Samuel Rolbant, *The Israeli Soldier. Profile of
   an Army* (New York: Thomas Yoseloff, 1970); Edward Luttwak and Dan Horowitz, *The Israeli Army* (London: Allen Lane, 1975). On the contribution of such
   improvized arms as the Davidka mortar used in liberating Safed, see Yehuda Slut-
   sky, *Toldot Hahaganah* (Tel Aviv: Ministry of Defense, 1978), pp. 496–501. Lorch,
   op. cit., describes how the real groundwork for a domestic war industry was laid
   during the two years prior to the 1948 war, as Sten guns, hand grenades, two-
   inch mortars, and their shells were produced clandestinely despite British efforts
   at locating the small factories, p. 42.
9. These arms exploits are vividly portrayed in Col. Benjamin Kagan, *The Secret
   Battle for Israel* (Cleveland: World Publishing Company, 1966); also Lorch, pp.
   329–332. Some of the arms secured from European dumps, scrap, and stores of
   surplus equipment or from Czechoslovakia arrived at critical junctures in the

fighting. Dominique Lapierre and Larry Collins offer a colorful description of the emergency supply effort in their *O Jerusalem!* (London: Weidenfeld & Nicolson, 1972).

10. Text in J.C. Hurewitz, ed., *Diplomacy in the Near and Middle East: A Documentary Record, 1914–1956* (Princeton: Van Nostrand, 1956), vol. 2, pp. 308–309; On American arms policy at that time, see John C. Campbell, *Defense of the Middle East* (New York: Praeger, 1960).

11. The exact details and timing of the transaction remain unclear. An interesting interpretation of the genesis of the Czech arms deal is Uri Ra'anan's *The USSR Arms the Third World* (Cambridge: MIT Press, 1969).

12. Yoav Lavi, "B.G. as Decision-Maker," *Skira Khodshit* **30** (October 1983):11.

13. Steinberg, pp. 280–281; Rolbant, p. 300.

14. Peres, who was subsequently to serve as Deputy Defense Minister and, from 1974–1977, as Minister of Defense, continued to promote arms manufacture of increasingly sophisticated systems. On his personal role, see Matti Golan, *Shimon Peres. A Biography* (London: Weidenfeld & Nicolson, 1982); also, Shimon Peres, *David's Sling* (London: Weidenfeld & Nicolson, 1970).

15. A history of the Israeli arms industry and its eventual incorporation into the overseas diplomatic effort is documented in a number of sources. Anthony Sampson, *The Arms Bazaar* (London: Hodder & Stoughton, 1977) recalls Israel's experience in the 1950s with unreliable Western suppliers which provided the catalyst to local manufacture. A personalized account if offered by Shimon Peres, *David's Sling*, especially chapters 3,4,5; and Shimon Peres, *Lech im Ha'anashim* (Jerusalem: Eydanim, 1978), pp. 46–47. Yosef Evron's *Ha-taasiya Habitchonit B'Yisrael* is the best treatment of the arms industry's development from the prestate period to the present (Tel-Aviv: Ministry of Defense, 1980). A fascinating behind-the-scenes glimpse of military technology in Israel after statehood is Munya M. Mardor's *Rafael* (Hebrew) (Tel-Aviv: Ministry of Defense, 1981).

16. On the reparations agreement signed with the government of West Germany on 10 September 1952, see Michael Brecher, *Decisions in Israel's Foreign Policy* (London: Oxford University Press, 1974), pp. 56–110.

17. Golan, p. 46, claims thirty Spitfires were involved; Schiff and Haber, p. 543, refer to eighteen planes.

18. Golan, p. 46; Schiff and Haber, p. 548, mention that Holland in 1954 purchased explosives from Israel worth $140,000.

19. Schiff and Haber, p. 548. Israel's chief military censor during the 1950s later makes reference to a sale negotiated in January, 1957, by which Israel was to supply 80,000 Uzis to the Dutch Army. Avner (Walter) Bar-On, *Stories Never Published* (Tel Aviv: Yediot Achronot, 1981), pp. 90–91.

20. Cited in Michael Brecher, *The Foreign Policy System of Israel* (New Haven: Yale University Press, 1972), p. 412.

21. Golan, pp. 81–82.

22. Details of the Cabinet crisis related in Brecher, pp. 418–426; Bar-On, p. 126, refers to the order from Bonn of 250,000 mortar shells worth 12 million marks.

23. Quoted in Brecher, p. 419.

24. Kolodziej and Harkavy, p. 11. By 1959–1960 Israel, with its own trainer plane, was one of fourteen Third World producers of at least one major weapons system; but by 1969–1970, save for the People's Republic of China, it was the only developing country to be included in all categories of major systems, including missiles, Neuman, pp. 172–173.

25. Several details of Israel's assorted military and economic links with Ethiopia are found in Fred Halliday and Maxime Molyneux, *The Ethiopian Revolution* (Lon-

don: Verso, 1981), pp. 232–233; also in Haggai Erlich. *The Struggle Over Eritrea, 1962–1978*. Hoover Institute Studies (Stanford: Hoover Institute Press, 1983).

26. Edy Kaufman, "Israel's Foreign Policy Implementation in Latin America," in Michael Curtis and Susan Aurelia Gitelson, eds., *Israel in the Third World* (New Brunswick: Transaction Books, 1976), p. 130.

27. Samuel Decalo, "Israel and Africa," *The Politics of Cooperation* (Ann Arbor: University Microfilms, 1970), Ph.D. dissertation, pp. 151, 290. See, also: Abel Jacob, "Israel's Military Aid to Africa, 1960–1966," *The Journal of Modern African Studies*:9:2(1971):165–187.

28. Lewis A. Frank, *The Arms Trade in International Relations* (New York: Praeger, 1969), p. 126.

29. Hurewitz, *Middle East Politics*, p. 368.

30. On the impact of French aid prior to 1967, see Steinberg, pp. 280–281; also Sylvia K. Crosbie, *A Tacit Alliance. France and Israel From Suez to the Six Day War* (Princeton: Princeton University Press, 1974).

31. Michael Handel, *Israel's Political-Military Doctrine* (Cambridge: Harvard University School of International Affairs, 1973), p. 63.

32. Dov Goldstein, interview with Gavriel Gidor, Director-General of the Israel Aircraft Industries, "Israeli Aeronautics: Thanks to De Gaulle," *The Israel Yearbook* (Tel Aviv: Israel Yearbook Publications, 1982) pp. 258–263.

33. Steinberg, p. 282.

34. Data provided in Naftali Blumenthal. "The Influence of Defense Industry Investment on Israel's Economy," in Lanir, especially pp. 169–173.

35. U.S. Arms Control and Disarmament Agency, *World Military Expenditures and Arms Transfers, 1970–1979* (Washington, D.C.: U.S.Government Printing Office, March, 1982), p. 105. SIPRI gives the figure of $300 million in arms exports already in 1976, SIPRI, 1980, p. 85.

36. Israel, Prime Minister's Office, The Government Press Office, Press Bulletin, 25 January 1977, p. 1.

37. SIPRI, 1982, p. 188.

38. Kolodziej and Harkavy, p. 11.

39. SIPRI, 1981, p. 188.

3

ARMS AND THE NATIONAL INTEREST

The national consensus in Israel in support of foreign military assistance and defense sales is, as we have seen, firmly rooted in, and takes its cue from, the past. Yet it is also built on the realization that for the present and the foreseeable future the export of weapons is likely to continue to be a unique, multipurpose instrument in pursuit of fundamental national interests. Until quite recently such security assistance was conceptualized, and justified, by most knowledgeable Israelis as a crucial policy tool for achieving foreign and defense objectives. As of late, however, the economic argument and the interests of the private or semiprivate industrial concerns appear to be in the ascendant. To the extent that this trend toward viewing armaments as a key currency in its international trade and politics comes to dominate policymaking in Jerusalem, Israel's motives for selling arms will emulate those of the principal arms merchants, Communist and non-Communist alike.[1]

Nevertheless, while the economic interest looms large, the enduring foundations for Israeli weapons transfers still lie in security and diplomatic considerations given the highest national priority. Indeed, the arms sales program is perceived of as promoting, as well as deriving from, three sets of essential, overlapping determinants: military, political, and economic.

MILITARY INCENTIVES

It was the late Moshe Dayan who once argued that "Small nations do not have a foreign policy. They have defense policy." For a country and leadership elite long dominated by what can best be termed a national security mentality, any distinction between diplomacy and defense is blurred under the larger rubric of national security. This is especially true of arms sales policy. In some ways the military-security argument is the very centerpiece of Israeli arms diplomacy. Certainly military considerations are pivotal in policy discussions of whether or not to expand the assistance program just as they are in

29

decisions to authorize a particular sale. The military rationale for transferring Israeli weapons in effect serves as the intermediate link between political and foreign policy incentives, on the one hand, and economic motives, on the other. Like them, the security argument reflects the close interplay between the logic of necessity and of opportunity.

Provision for an indigenous military industry has been an element of security planning virtually since independence. The justification on military grounds for trading in arms originates in the sustained Arab threat to the country's existence and security predating statehood and provides the earliest case for a defense industry and, at a later stage, for an arms export effort. Such exports therefore need to be viewed as a function of the larger defense effort and of the drive to achieve selective even if not absolute self-sufficiency. This merits being repeated because the material imbalance of power has been etched now in the minds of Israeli leaders for more than three decades.

Arab superiority in the tangible indices of military power is a primary factor behind Israel's emphasis upon arms exports in taking full advantage of Israeli assets and their maximum exploitation. To begin with, Israel's Arab opponents enjoy at least two advantages in securing arms: sources and resources. They possess both the financial means and ease of access to a number of willing suppliers in both the East and West blocs. The resultant inpouring of arms buttresses longstanding Arab hostility, thereby posing a two-fold threat: to (a) Israel's qualitative advantage and deterrent capability, and consequently to (b) a stable regional balance of power. In countering these threats Israel remains, for the present, the most advanced Middle Eastern country in terms of its defense industry. The "rejectionist front" Arab states (those states rejecting peace), and most notably Syria, continue to be heavily reliant on outside suppliers, and hence susceptible, in theory at least, to political pressure at critical moments as well as to irregular arms flows, particularly of more advanced systems.

Solely from an Israeli standpoint, therefore, these conditions alone warrant utilizing its singular advantage in pursuing arms aid and trade as an adjunct of its broader military posture and state of preparedness.

In the brief presented by advocates of military sales, however, weapons transfers outside of Israel are presented as serving, directly or indirectly, at least four additional military and defense functions. These are: (a) strengthening the Israeli army's immediate, intermediate, and longer-range preparedness goals; (b) enhancing Israeli deterrence capability by projecting a positive image of strength; (c) fitting into a wider strategic perspective; and (d) doubling as a tool of diplomacy through supporting countries friendly to Israel.

In the first instance, military exports enable close to full production to meet the immediate and ongoing needs of the IDF. Until now few items have been produced exclusively for export; rather the emphasis has been primarily on servicing the Israeli army. Its needs center upon assuring adequate supplies of conventional equipment under routine and sudden crisis situations, together with a need to introduce increasingly more sophisticated systems. Foreign commercial transfers of particular weapons originally designed for the IDF in this sense must be viewed as essentially a derivative benefit: the byproduct of Israel's own accelerated pace of armed forces modernization.

Still, pressure by the military in support of the munitions industry and the development of certain newer systems necessitating a huge public investment of capital, becomes harder to resist and more convincing once overseas sales show a respectable monetary return. The likelihood of foreign orders has served in the past as a rather persuasive factor in the government's determination of whether or not to authorize projects backed by IDF planners.

The expansion of the market for local arms manufactures to include overseas purchasers arguably sustains production at full capacity, and thus also figures in strategic planning by going beyond immediate IDF orders. Military preparedness for conventional war situations includes the notion of a surge capability, i.e., the maintenance of a sufficient peacetime capacity to ensure a rapid increase in military output when necessary. The role of arms sales in preserving this capacity in terms of replenishment, lead time, reserves, and safety supplies has received increasing emphasis in other countries as well, although Israeli leaders had arrived at a heightened awareness of the problem during the 1973 war. Excess output should enable Israel to withstand an arms embargo, for example, or to endure a prolonged war of attrition. As happened during the 1982 fighting in Lebanon, in an emergency stockpiles consigned for foreign delivery might have to be rerouted to units of the IDF in the field. While government economists have a strong commercial interest in arms exports and Israeli ambassadors respect defense sales as a powerful diplomatic wedge, the value of such transfers from the standpoint of the country's military planners would seem to lie in their sustaining production lines, keeping the defense industries viable, and assuring supplies when needed for the armed forces. Each of these is in itself a strategic interest.

On an even longer-term basis arms exports are a factor in weapons systems development and recycling. Science and technology, research and development — these are critical elements in Israel's overall strength and security. From the military standpoint, a successful R & D process contributes to the continuum of military objectives: deterrence of war, control of conflict, and, where possible, success on the battlefield. Investment is one problem; perceptions of lead time and effective management of system development or replacement are other serious issues.[2] In response Israel shows a heightened sensitivity to the need for guaranteeing that additional aircraft and other weapons components are always "in the pipeline," making for a fairly regular and predictable pattern of acquisition and supply. Access to sufficiently large foreign markets figures in these calculations by supporting the cost of developing newer weapons, either by initial coproduction and licensing agreements aimed at sharing costs or by sales revenues at a later stage of production.

The short shelf-life of weapons and the pace of turnover between generations of sophisticated systems act as a constraint on Israel in the Middle East arms race. Simply to be able to preserve the option of manufacturing an advanced system for the IDF at a future date may make it necessary to produce an unprofitable short-term, intermediate generation. Foreign orders, particularly in the West, and purchases in advance of production, all other political and diplomatic considerations being equal, would at least then reduce the initial costs while ensuring that the IDF and its industrial support system remain in the forefront of weapons technology, avoiding dependence on external suppliers in the midst of spiraling military competition.

Defense sales also help to alleviate the problem of weapons obsolescence by permitting Israel to dispense with older items at a profit, politically as well as financially. Accordingly, attempts in the 1980s at preserving the qualitative edge include not only the export of military know-how acquired in the series of wars, but also the sale of older generations of armor and aircraft replaced by more advanced models. It is at this point that the market among Third World countries enters the picture.

Because of such domestic considerations it is important that weapons transfers be analyzed not only at the level of Israel-Arab rivalries but also within the context of the tremendous burden upon Israel's national economy and defense budget. Maintaining large peacetime forces and a constant state of military alert along Israel's several fronts imposes a prohibitive cost on an economy already severely constrained by manpower and financial limitations. Armed forces proponents of foreign military assistance obviously are sensitive to the persistence of the high defense expenditure over a very long period, nor are they insensitive to the charge that such expenditures are mortgaging Israel diplomatically while draining it economically. Perhaps as much as half of all government funding for research and development, for instance, is reported as going to the defense sector. Such a situation tends to underscore the positive and beneficial side of rising arms sales abroad.

Not surprisingly, one finds professional military officers in Israel, whether on active duty or retired, in the forefront of those alert to the full implications, military as well as political, of dependence on external suppliers, primarily the United States. Former Chief of Staff Raphael Eitan in 1982 listed among the four goals before Israel that of reducing all such subordination; he urged ending requests for aid so that "those conferring the assistance will be unable to determine our limits for us."[3] The IDF's head of planning disclosed that priority would continue to be given to making Israel self-sufficient in air, land, and sea armaments "not only to achieve technological freedom of action" but in particular because of the "urgent and critical need" to progressively narrow "our reliance upon American money," with the very grave consequences it has "for our political independence, but also for the national pride and values of the Israeli society as a whole."[4] Arms sales, in this military conception, are prized as manifestations of how Israel might restore its lost sense of independence through self-reliance and initiative.

Arms sales, from a military viewpoint, satisfy a second function not unrelated to the symbolic or psychological component of Israeli security policy. They contribute to Israel's deterrence capacity and military reputation. Military proponents highlight the fact that, whether Israel wants it or not, foreign buyers are attracted to Israeli weapons because of their proven worthiness under actual combat conditions, as reconfirmed in the 1982 Lebanon war. In contrast the aim of rival suppliers is often to have others do the testing, or they sell products which fail to meet today's high standards of performance. Again, solely from a military perspective arms exports are proving to be "a quick and profitable way to translate the nation's war experience into economic advantage."[5]

Each successive war seems to have added to the reputation of Israeli arms and of Israel as a military power in the Middle East. In the 1973 Yom Kippur War, for example, the Israeli navy, relying largely on its own resources, outperformed Arab navies equipped with the most up-to-date Soviet technology. Electronic support measures devised by Israeli engineers surprised Western defense experts in their proven ability to detect enemy radar and missile activity beyond the horizon.[6] Israel's military performance resulted in orders over the next decade for its Gabriel missiles and induced many navies around the world to adopt the fast missile boat pioneered by Israel. Once again, in Lebanon in 1982 Israel's reputation was reconfirmed by the successful use of pilotless aerial reconnaissance equipment, stimulating international sales. One perception shared by all three categories of observer countries—sympathetic, hostile, and interested but neutral—was an image of Israel as a nation with limited resources but capable of defending itself. Witness the justification offered by Sri Lanka's national security minister for turning to Israel for counter-insurgency advice: " . . . why can't Sri Lanka get the world's best consultants to help eliminate terrorism in this country?"[7] In terms of the "rules of the game" in the Middle East and of regional deterrence, such intangibles of national power as Israeli credibility, global respect for its military prowess and defense capability—when given tangible expression by the successful sale of weapons made or refined in Israel—should not be minimized in any estimate of its total strength.

Just as the reputation of Israeli arms has spread, so has there been a concurrent extension of Israel's security interests. A primarily regional focus has given way to a more global geopolitical perspective. One manifestation in the 1980s is intermittent attempts by Washington and Jerusalem to give meaning on a broader scale to what is referred to as their "strategic understanding", in which Israel is seen—and sees itself—as part of the global effort at containing Soviet advances. Implicit in such a world view is the assumption that:

(a) Israel has something of importance to contribute, such as military aid, for example; (b) its own particular interests dovetail with those of the United States and the West.

A leading proponent of this view was former Minister of Defense Ariel Sharon. In articulating an Israeli defense policy for the 1980s, Sharon postulated that Israel's sphere of strategic and security interests extends beyond the traditional belt of Arab confrontation countries to include countries such as Turkey, Iran, and Pakistan, and regions such as the Persian Gulf and Africa. These interests are to be met, he maintained, "by an active effort to increase our exports to countries who share our strategic concerns and with whom we maintain security relationships."[8] This is as clear a statement of direction on arms policy as one finds from an authoritative Israeli source. And in highlighting the value placed on arms transfers as contributing directly to the national security, rather than being merely a derivative of diplomatic or economic strategies, it may also serve as an accurate mirror of the thinking current among the nation's policymakers.

Less exceptional is the fourth and final military consideration behind heightened arms activity: arms in the service of foreign policy in general. Israel, despite Entebbe and the Osirak air strike against the Iraqi nuclear reactor, does not have the capability of long-range military action, shows of force or other symbolic uses of power beyond its immediate area. Nor is it able to finance the military acquisitions of other countries. Hence its ability to influence worldwide military or security developments is circumscribed. One instance where Israel is able to exercise some influence lies in the transfer of military-related equipment. Once Israel's own needs have been met, arms become an impressive security asset at the disposal of the government to invest in other developing countries or revolutionary movements satisfying its immediate or long-range interests.[9] Put differently, weapons transactions may become, for a small power such as Israel, an important substitute for the overt political presence generally sought by the more prominent international actors.

From the outset military spokesmen and civilian members of the defense establishment were quick to point out diplomatic as well as economic and military advantages. Thus it was Shimon Peres who, in 1961, made the argument for a military aid policy to the new countries of Africa and Asia in order "to surround the belt of enmity with a belt of friendship in the new independent countries."[10] This argument has been made by Ariel Sharon who also sees military assistance and arms as supporting Israeli foreign policy, with aid to Zaire as the model for reopening relations with additional African countries.[11] Nevertheless, there is a difference, primarily of emphasis. Israel's political-military doctrine as presently revised commands far greater respect for its utilization of weapons transfer relationships as part of a more aggressive strategy.

Support for friends and allies thus becomes a further selling point, simultaneously improving Israel's own geopolitical position, opening markets to Israel as a supplier country affiliated with the West and resulting in the increased military strength of friendly countries in an otherwise menacing international environment. For a people that previously had been an object of ridicule and a symbol for powerlessness, the accomplishments of the Jewish state in the realm of international defense and security affairs is of no trivial or passing importance in the total picture of Israel among the nations.

DIPLOMATIC INCENTIVES

The ability to sell its arms abroad leads to the interesting proposition that Israel's military influence goes well beyond its diplomatic influence. No such distinction seems to exist, however, in Israeli eyes. Arms transfers are employed as a dual political-security instrument, essential to Israel's defense posture but also an indispensable component of foreign policy. Consequently, current Israeli arms export diplomacy serves as an extension of the country's overall approach to external affairs. In fact, defenders of this present course maintain that given forced diplomatic isolation the sale of arms and technology is one of the few effective techniques remaining to further Israeli goals overseas.

All Israeli governments, Labour or Likud and irrespective of ideological orientation, have shared a set of basic objectives in confronting the real world. Priorities, emphases, and styles may differ, but the goals of foreign policy remain constant: (a) to repel hostile attacks and guarantee defense of the state; (b) to gather in as many of the dispersed Jewish people as possible in their ancient homeland; (c) to secure Israel's place in an inhospitable environment and, to whatever extent possible, to alter that environment from a condition of enmity to one of amity; (d) to offset the country's immediate Middle Eastern isolation by setting up a worldwide network of mutually beneficial cultural, commercial, and diplomatic ties.[12]

Historically, as discussed in the previous chapter, the export of small arms and ammunition on a modest scale had its beginnings in the late 1950s and early 1960s as part of precisely this broader diplomatic offensive which aimed at leaping beyond the wall of Arab hostility. Early supply relationships were developed with France, Great Britain, and West Germany. Even though the relationships were markedly one-sided, Israel had some success in penetrating these European markets with its military products, most notably the Uzi. Military assistance also proved surprisingly effective as an opening wedge for cultivating friendly ties with ethnic minorities in the Middle East and with the newly emergent Afro-Asian countries. Notwithstanding the subsequent diplomatic setback in the years between the 1967 victory and the 1973 trau-

matic Yom Kippur War, when many of these formerly friendly Third World
governments defected to the Arab side and cast their votes with the anti-Israel
bloc in the United Nations, selling weapons has been valued as primarily an
instrument for implementing foreign policy objectives. If anything, because
of the contacts it has provided with countries less disposed toward Israel on
the surface than in point of fact, an aggressive arms sales campaign is regarded
as one of the few successes in Israel's foreign relations over the last two
decades.

Influence and leverage, friendship and symbolism are the more obvious and
most explicitly political ends toward which arms transfers contribute. While
these four objectives are applicable to Israel or to any other supplier of
weapons, there do seem to be as many as eight separate diplomatic factors
at work in Israel's present pursuit of international defense relationships.

Arms as Influence. One of the more overworked and unscientific concepts
in world politics is the notion of political influence among nations. Still enjoying wide currency is the obvious truism that there is a high correspondence
between Great Power arms transfer patterns and, for example, the granting
of strategic access or major bases.[13] Perhaps the closest that Israel came to
employing defense assistance as a quid pro quo for access rights was with
Ethiopia during Emperor Haile Selassie's reign, stemming from a mutual
security concern over revolutionary political trends in the Red Sea area. Otherwise, Israeli arms diplomacy is not guided by any such quest for direct political
presence or leverage.

Surely the American experience in Iran teaches that arms transfers of
themselves do not ensure stability in a country or region, nor do they guarantee the continued goodwill and cooperation of the recipient. Recent cases,
like those of Egypt and Somalia in which arms clients successfully turned their
backs on the Soviet Union after years of alliance and are now obtaining
weapons from Western suppliers, provide other illustrations, were they even
needed by Israeli diplomats and strategists, of the dubious thesis that arms
shipments in and of themselves assure a direct policy input upon the arms
recipient. Israel's own experience, both as recipient and supplier, offers ample
proof of the need to avoid exaggerating the amount of political leverage deriving from defense relationships.

Nevertheless, Israel does subscribe to the commonly accepted thesis that
friends can be won and nations influenced to some degree and by indirect,
day-to-day access by providing some of their security needs. A question yet
to be clarified however is the extent to which the leverage of a small supplier
differs from, or remains more limited than, a Great Power supplier. In Israel's
case the correlation between weapons and influence is unclear as yet. However, it is clear that military assistance enhances bilateral political relationships which already exist. It facilitates collaborative efforts of a functional

nature in such areas as information-gathering and antiterrorism. Also, an arms relationship may offer the opportunity to present Israel's position on political issues, particularly those relating to the Middle East conflict, although it must be noted that dependence upon Israeli military advisers and equipment did not inhibit Afro-Asian countries from severing ties after 1967 or from supporting resolutions condemning Israel at the United Nations. Equally questionable is whether the threat of withholding further arms from uncooperative recipients is an effective sanction and mechanism of control, or even a possibility for Israel.[14] Initiating negative sanctions as a form of political pressure is of dubious value and can serve little purpose under present marketing conditions in which diverse alternate suppliers provide an option to Israel's clients. It could lead to unforeseen and undesired consequences for Israel as a peripheral supplier to any single target customer.

Despite such reservations, Israel's leaders early on were prepared to accept the risks inherent in contending for international influence. In part this reflected the realization that states often differentiate among various types of relations. Second, arms transfers by Israel as a rule have tended to be a more effective short-term instrument for maintaining and expanding its influence, especially in the Third World, than have economic aid or trade.

Third, the lesson is that influence may be transient and yet still worthwhile. It was Shimon Peres, one of the early proponents of utilizing military assistance in the service of foreign policy objectives, who expressed this pragmatic viewpoint. "Relations do not arise on their own", he said,

> but are made up of similarity of outlook and experience, political connections, and even personal connections. They do not develop by themselves and they do not remain forever. In some countries security relations do not necessarily run parallel to ordinary foreign relations and . . . we must take cognizance of the fact.[15]

Perhaps for this reason, and despite the experience in Iran, and in East and West Africa, a conception of arms transfers as bestowing political benefits and influence, however defined, continues to dominate thinking in Jerusalem. Indeed, the argument will be made shortly that the inability to assert direct influence, to either dictate or punish, actually becomes advantageous, making Israel attractive to prospective buyers suspicious of the interference or dominance of outsiders.

Whether because of ingrained realism owing to its status as a small state or chastened in those instances where it perhaps exaggerated the direct political impact of defense relationships, Israel re-entered the global arms competition during the 1970s far more mature in its international outlook and arms sales expectations. Eschewing direct presence or influence, arms diplomacy enthusiasts instead are quite content to settle for the prestige value and tangible contacts accruing from these defense relationships along with trade opportunities.

Arms as Prestige. Being associated with the international traffic in weapons is admittedly a double-edged sword. It draws exaggerated prominence to Israel and subjects it to criticism. But at the same time it does confer certain positive symbolic benefits, especially upon a small state like Israel for whom power is a function of reputation, of how it is perceived by others.

In this sense, arms are a signal to friends and enemies alike of Israel's strength and determination to act in defense of its vital interests. Arms from Israel serve as a gesture of symbolic political support. They suggest that it pays to be on good terms with Israel; that Israel has something more tangible than moral support to offer governments prepared to deal with it; that it has a global reach.

At the level of the small state or middle-range power in today's world, the marketability of one's armaments also represents its visibility — the equivalent of showing the flag. This is amply demonstrated by the interest shown each time Israeli defense products are put on open display. Certainly in the case of Israel a good deal of its credibility has come to depend upon its export profile and has been further enhanced by the caliber and proven effectiveness of its weapons. Should the Conventional Arms Transfer (CAT) negotiations aimed at regulating conventional arms transfers, which broke down in 1978, be resumed, Israel's status as an arms supplier would ensure it of an invitation to attend as a direct participant alongside the major exporters.

Even without this acknowledgement, current defense sales have helped to revive Israel's image, particularly in the Third World and with the less developed countries (LDCs), which had declined after the sixties. The interest of these nations is aroused in no small part by the diversity, quality, and reputation of Israeli arms for sale on the open market. Success in this arms market, in short, confirms not only that Israel is a reality of international life but that it is also a factor to be reckoned with in world as well as in regional politics. Here again, the symbolic importance is inestimable given Israel's continuing diplomatic struggle for legitimacy and international recognition. Such recent triumphs of Israeli statecraft as the resumption of diplomatic relations with Zaire, Liberia, and Sri Lanka, together with the decision by the governments of El Salvador and Costa Rica to return their embassies to Jerusalem, thereby recognizing it as Israel's capital, are attributable in large part to the interest these countries have in gaining military support from Israel.

In keeping with the realization that transfers alone have little long-lasting positive impact, Israeli diplomacy stresses the importance of different forms of contact. The following three diplomatic incentives thus have in common the opportunities arising from weapons supply relationships to reach certain distinctive domestic groups: the local military, business circles, and Jewish communities.

Arms as Military Contacts. Rather than striving for dominance over any customer state or its government in the sense of pervasive influence and control, Israel's preference appears to be for the concentration of attention upon narrower, quite specific target groups within many of the recipient countries.

Weapons can be a singularly serviceable tool of diplomacy in Third World countries under direct or indirect military government. Whether such regimes are desirable is a moot question given Israel's inability to determine the nature of a recipient's political system, especially where the armed forces are already in power. Ongoing military training and assistance programs, rather than pre-science, established personal contacts between Israeli personnel and junior officers like Idi Amin or Col. Joseph Mobutu with ambitions but also prospects of eventually coming to power in their countries. Even in those countries where civilian government still prevails, the military chiefs are a powerful interest group with a strong behind-the-scenes influence upon their country's budget as well as foreign policy orientation.

One consideration in furnishing Iran with arms has always been to preserve good working relations with that country's armed forces. Similarly, arms supplies provided an opening for a low-level relationship after 1976 with one Lebanese political faction, the Maronite Phalange forces of Bashir Gemayel, first under the Rabin government and then by the Begin government. Again, it was more than mere coincidence that found Liberia's defense minister visiting Israel in August, 1983, even before the announcement in Monrovia that ties were to be renewed. So, too, the following year with Sri Lanka, whose defense officials apparently took the lead in pressing government officials in Colombo to make the diplomatically significant gesture of upgrading relations with Israel as the price for securing a defense relationship.

Moving to a different part of the world, the central position of the military in the Latin American political process is an acknowledged fact. Israeli military transactions have established liaison with this most significant political elite in the majority of Central and South American countries. Military establishments in these countries are impressed with any of several Israeli attributes. If modernizing elites, they may choose to use Israel's socioeconomic progress as a source of inspiration and a guide for action. As professionals, the Latin American military are swayed in their recommendation for or final selection of weapons purchases by Israel's demonstrated military capability. Finally, as national patriots and anti-Communists, representatives of the armed forces consider aid from Israel no less effective than Big Power assistance, while at the same time not jeopardizing their national sovereignty.

Arms as Commerce. Military sales and assistance often provide the opening wedge for a variety of other commercial contacts which would otherwise have been difficult. Where Israelis have shown resourcefulness is in their use of this economic resource in advancing political as well as security interests in a manner comparable to the sale of oil by other developing states.

Military assistance has proven its usefulness in the larger diplomatic sense of achieving a degree of influence with the recipient through economic and cultural activities. Israel's thrust today in many parts of the world is toward improving its economic position and creating avenues for trade. Military sales frequently do provide such entry into civilian and commercial sectors. Trade has followed not the flag but, symbolically, the Uzi submachine gun, with contacts extending in the course of time to nonmilitary commerce. The maintenance of weapons, especially of the more sophisticated types, training in their use, and orders for spare parts suggest the dynamic for an ongoing relationship and the possibility of exerting influence, particularly where Israel has to offer tangible benefits as an inducement to countries willing to consider commercial if not diplomatic links.

An outstanding example is the role of Israeli firms in areas such as housing, construction, and irrigation during the period of modernization in Iran. Israeli-Iranian relations during the 1970s also point to another logical if as yet potential commercial use of weapons. Were arms deals to be contracted on favorable terms of trade or, more important, on a barter arrangement of military hardware in exchange for vital resources such as oil, this, too, might indirectly enhance Israel's diplomatic position. In light of the arms relationship developing between Israel and Zaire, another expression of the commercial implications is the air traffic agreement signed in April, 1983, between the two countries, allowing El Al, Israel's national airline, to extend its services to central Africa and to open new routes to Latin America via Africa. To cite these few examples is merely to hint at the enormous economic possibilities for commercial relationships of both a nonmilitary and military nature throughout Africa, the Americas, and parts of the Far East. Arms transfer successes further suggest that at least until such time as normal diplomatic relations are reestablished with a whole range of developing countries, formal ties are not even needed in order to maintain trade links with many of them.

Arms and the Jewish Factor. A central tenet of Israeli foreign policy has always been a sense of commitment toward world Jewry and the use of diplomatic contacts with host governments in over eighty countries where the more than ten million Jews residing outside of Israel live. This extraordinary sensitivity for the safety, welfare, and rights of Jewish communities in distress and, in addition, for ensuring the right of Jews to emigrate, preferably to Israel in keeping with the essence of Zionist teaching, is indeed the true hallmark of Israeli statecraft. This concern for maintaining links to fellow Jews and for fostering bonds with them is often overlooked in the rush, even by Israelis themselves, to identify hard-bitten political or monetary motives for pushing arms. Yet this Jewish connection provides a significant moral balance to these more commonly cited pressures in the total arms sales calculus.

A survey of Israeli arms sales patterns and preferences discloses in a number of instances a rather strong correlation between the presence of Jews in a given country and its being the recipient of Israeli defense aid or equipment. This suggests the application wherever possible of military assistance relationships on their behalf. While not necessarily the principal consideration in whether to authorize an arms transaction, the Jewish factor nevertheless was a component of Israeli thinking vis-à-vis Iran; it remains so in terms of Argentina, with its 300,000 Jews, and South Africa which has 120,000 Jews.[16]

If the objective is to maintain free and continuous contact with every one of these Jewish communities, with their ingathering to Israel ultimately in mind, then military relationships and the supply of equipment represent one such vital opening. This "primordial and pre-eminent aspect of the political culture" has been commented upon;[17] it found an articulate exponent in David Ben-Gurion and found later expression in the thinking and policies of Menachem Begin, which may also help to account in part for the upsurge in arms sales following his electoral victories in 1977 and 1981.

This Jewish connection also works of late in a different and interesting way. In the eyes of many Third World leaders Israel is seen as the key to improving their image in the United States. It is assumed therefore they will have better prospects of gaining an appreciative ear among U.S. congressmen for their own requests for economic and security assistance by cultivating ties with Israel, including at the military level. In exploiting such perceptions Israeli diplomats are not above suggesting the purchase of its military goods as an acceptable and fair quid pro quo for using the near-legendary strength of the pro-Israel lobby in the Congress and its influence with the American Jewish community on behalf of the arms client; rumors of such an understanding circulated in the instance of Zaire for example.

Arms as Preemption. A sixth political function asked of arms diplomacy lies in the area of Israeli security and competitiveness. Military aid and equipment are meant at a minimum to deny advantages to Arab adversaries.

Israeli statesmen have never forgotten the constant attempt by Arab opponents ever since 1948 to further weaken and isolate the Jewish state. In fighting back against measures such as the Arab boycott, blacklist, and funds dangled before countries willing to honor Arab and Muslim demands to avoid all contact with the Zionist entity, they are duty-bound to exploit even momentary opportunities to frustrate Arab designs which amount to a policy of denial—denying Israel allies, markets, access, and influence. Military assistance and arms sales are therefore an important part of this Arab-Israeli rivalry and of Israel's resourceful counteroffensive.

In instances where a commonality of interest arises between a prospective client and Israel, such as the shared desire to resist Arab or Muslim ascendancy on the African continent, weapons transfers have been singularly effective in cementing relationships. Moreover, in the past at least, arms, as op-

posed to oil or money, were a commodity which Israel could offer a potential
anti-Arab or anti-Muslim country like Ethiopia. Cases arose where either the
Arab states were unable to satisfy another country's even modest military
needs or refused to do so for political reasons; similarly, the recipient might
find the acceptance of such Arab aid either inopportune or anathema. Arms
transfers to Ethiopia, Kenya, and Uganda at one time or another have fit neat-
ly into this strategy of aligning Israel with countries opposed to the spread
of Arab radicalism or of Islam beyond the Middle East. Transactions with
Morocco, Kurdish separatists, Lebanese Phalange and the Iranians only suggest the subtle uses of arms within the region itself and Israel's ability to exploit inter-Arab and intraregional rivalries in order to blunt the Arab political
and military threat.

Increasingly this diplomatic offensive by Jerusalem has assumed global proportions as part of efforts at combatting the Palestine Liberation Organization and international terrorist groups linked to it. Reported supplies of arms
to different African and especially Central American countries in recent years
can be viewed as a function of this campaign to support governments that
oppose radical forces closely allied with Arab extremists like Colonel Qaddafi of Libya aided by the P.L.O. This is apparently the case with assistance
to Guatemala, Honduras, and to a lesser extent Costa Rica, confronted by
Cuba and Nicaragua, neighboring countries that strongly support the P.L.O.[18]
This is apparently also the case in the instance of Sri Lanka where the Palestin-
ians are said to be among those foreign guerrilla groups training and arming
Tamil terrorists.[19]

Preemption has a dual meaning for Israeli arms sales practices. In the first
sense it refers to this broad diplomatic strategy of countering Arab and P.L.O.
influence or pressure upon third party countries whenever, wherever, and
however possible, including through the use of arms leverage. The second
meaning, however, is narrower and applies exclusively to the international
arms trade. Israeli leaders, having committed themselves and the indigenous
arms industry to a competitive export drive, and perfectly aware that other
sellers show few inhibitions in closing contracts, must confront the choice of
either gaining influence by making sales or of losing it by refusing to compete because of unilateral restraint. Israeli arms diplomacy aims, therefore,
at precluding others from achieving those very same goals of influence and
income which it seeks for itself.

Arms, Western Security and the United States. Fortunately for Israel and its
goal of promoting conventional weapons transfers, there is a great deal of
overlap between its anti-Arab, anti-P.L.O. policies and the two separate yet
related goals of closer alignment with the West in general and with the United
States in particular.

Israeli diplomacy dating back to the early 1950s has sought to identify the country with the West and with the democratic Free World. In stressing Israel's great value to the West in the event of a direct confrontation with the Soviet Union, Ben-Gurion maintained: "We have to explain . . . that the whole of Israel—strengthened, in military and industrial terms—is a base . . . available to the free world on a day of need."[20] Israel's self-image is that of a significant Middle Eastern component in the system of anti-Communist containment and collective security. But because the other members of the Western alliance also perceive of Israel as problematic if not a liability in the narrower regional and Arab-Israeli contexts, there is always a need for Israel to demonstrate its usefulness short of the event of war and to reconfirm the positive contribution which it makes to the security of the West.

In making this argument, spokesmen in Jerusalem would surely cite Israeli arms as performing an important service in defense of Western interests. Since those interests lie in preventing small and vulnerable countries favorably disposed to the West from falling prey to destabilization efforts by the Soviets or their Arab clients, any Israeli success in enhancing the ability of such governments to cope with internal or external threats must be regarded as serving this larger community of interest. Earlier timely assistance to Emperor Haile Selassie of Ethiopia and to the monarchy in Morocco helped them to withstand the wave of Nasserist revolution which threatened their pro-Western regimes. Supplies to Honduras or Costa Rica in the face of Caribbean subversion are a more recent example.

When placed in this broader geopolitical context, the Israeli role in building up the armed forces of Zaire, units of which were rushed in to Chad in 1983 to prevent a takeover by Libyan-backed insurgents equipped with Soviet weapons, becomes more meaningful; so, too, rumored Israeli contacts with the government of Mengistu Haile Mariam still waging its war against Arab-backed Eritrean separatists and perhaps less inclined than before to advance Soviet influence in Ethiopia and in the Horn of Africa.[21]

In contemplating the emerging strategic map at the end of this decade, the Israeli arms relationship with southern hemisphere countries similarly assumes greater clarity (Figure 3.1).

From this maritime perspective the South Atlantic emerges as the focus for global attention.[22] It calls attention to vital Western strategic interests: considerable oil deposits on the coast of West Africa, oil supply routes and sea lines of communication from the Persian Gulf, fish resources, and some of the world's largest deposits of scarce minerals. It also underlines the Soviet Union's vulnerabilities, given the absence of adequate major overseas bases in the vicinity, but especially the pivotal defense role of states like South Africa, with its major naval base at Simonstown, Argentina, and Brazil.[23]

The political significance of Israeli arms for its relations with the United States is directly related to this larger community of Western strategic interests. First, as part of the strategic decision to align Israel with the West,

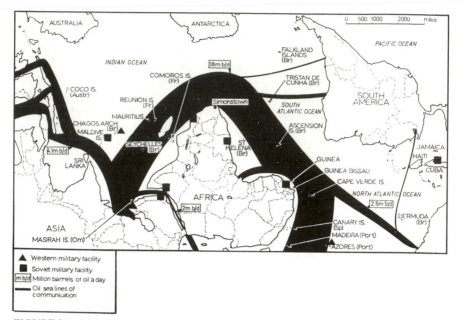

FIGURE 3.1. A Maritime Map of the Southern Seas. From: Geoffrey Kemp, "The New Strategic Map," *Survival* **19** (March–April 1977):51. Reprinted with permission.

principal stress was placed on convincing the United States to make Israel, in Ben-Gurion's words, "the base, the workshop and the granary" of the Middle East.[24] How Israel is perceived by the U.S. is therefore crucial for the way it is accepted or kept at arm's length by the other Western allies. Second, arms support for various pro-Western regimes is part of what Israeli representatives allude to when describing Israel as a proven strategic asset—a fact better known to Pentagon and State Department officials from classified documents than to the American public at large.

Looked at more closely this Israeli support significantly augments United States policy. As a result of its mounting defense burden, the United States is no longer able to meet the proliferating calls for more help from nations whose security and stability are vital to Western interests, particularly in the Third World. Israel's program thus falls within the larger context of an effective security framework for the Free World, led by the United States, and answers the call of the American administration for greater contributions from allied and friendly countries able to render different forms of such assurance.[25]

In cases where it is important to the United States that a given country adopt its military doctrine and equipment, but where political considerations preclude supplying arms directly, Israel might be asked to act as an alternative supplier, assuming the interests and political assessments of the two governments run parallel. Arms to the Lebanese Christians, Argentina, and

Central American republics illustrate this approach. Out of fear of angering Beijing, and not wanting to abandon Taiwan or its supporters in the United States, the Reagan administration might choose to have a request for such items as additional American-made M-48 tanks met by Israel. Each instance of close military cooperation strengthens Israel's claim that it has a right to be regarded as an ally and strategic asset, while at the same time justifying American support for Israel as payment for services rendered.

When questioned about American reactions to reported Israeli military assistance to various countries, American officials may resort to bureaucratic terminology in stating that the United States "is not displeased" but they cannot, or do not choose to, hide a basic American satisfaction with Israel's positive role. On the other hand, Israeli arms sales diplomacy may sometimes have to be conducted without consultation with Washington; the sale of spare parts to Iran for a while after 1979 comes to mind. Moreover, Israel's push might succeed to the point of rivaling or even preempting American defense contractors in the competition for some markets. Consequently, whereas until the 1980s the modest export program worked positively as a lubricant facilitating the principal goal of Israeli foreign policy—strengthening the U.S.-Israeli relationship—it demonstrates a potential for becoming a source of friction in the near future. This leads us to the eighth and final diplomatic goal for which foreign military assistance has been justified in Israeli terms.

Arms as Independence. The unwritten rules of the arms trade cannot prevent most suppliers from anticipating increased leverage over those to whom it provides military aid, but by the same token they counsel the beneficiary to avoid the danger of becoming too dependent upon any single supplier. Some clients have opted, or been forced, to rely solely upon either the Russians or the Americans. Most countries, however, are anxious to establish alternative sources for armaments as a hedge against resupply problems, extreme dependence, or undue interference. The possibility of meeting some of its security requirements through the auspices of Israel presents a viable third option to a proud yet dependent country, more so because the former is perceived of as posing no real threat. Israeli aims, by comparison with those of the major suppliers, are less complex. Israel is interested neither in a direct military presence nor in a high profile arms relationship. Moreover, it simply has less capacity than do the other leading suppliers to extract political concessions. Sensitive issues of domestic jurisdiction like human rights policy or state sovereignty, such as the actual stationing of forces, which dominate arms negotiations with the superpowers, therefore are unlikely to enter diplomatic negotiations over the terms of sale.

Evidence suggests that Israeli salesmen and diplomats are quite successful in presenting Israel as a buyer's attractive second or third option as well as a dependable source for arms acquisition. As a result, weapons transfers account for a substantial part of the total volume of bilateral trade relations between Israel and those non-Arab and non-Muslim countries still determined to pursue a narrow course of nonalignment in a balancing act between formal neutrality and too close or open an association with the United States. Regarded in this light, close ties with Washington are a definite advantage to Israel, positioning it intermediately between the Western superpower and skittish developing countries. In short, it permits their utilizing the leverage deriving from the availability of competing sources.

Ironically, however, such an intermediate position, forcing Israel into a delicate balancing act of its own, poses a critical challenge for Israeli statecraft and independence in seeking to avoid too close an association with the United States. This applies to relations in general and to defense sales in particular.

Israel's position as arms recipient is the reverse of that enjoyed by some of its own clients. In terms of supplier preference it has no comparable third or even second option, being reliant upon the United States in certain critical categories of sophisticated equipment. In attempting, nonetheless, to diversify its sources, besides investigating alternative European suppliers, Israel has been able to meet a sizeable portion of its needs through a local arms industry. In the process national leaders have discovered that while far from removing this basic condition of dependency, military exports do help to relieve it somewhat. Thus, for example, it can be argued that the export of arms enables Israel to produce greater quantities at less cost for itself, to stockpile emergency reserves, and to produce its own substitute version of a previously imported item such as the Merkava tank in place of U.S. tanks, all of which translates into decreased dependence.

Israel is susceptible to overreliance. It is also open to criticism for supporting Washington's arms assistance policies to Central America almost to the extent of becoming to the United States what Cuba is to the Soviet Union: an arms surrogate and indirect supplier. Staking out a course of its own within certain limits serves to counter the negative side of the close association with the United States. If pursued carefully, a distinctive Israeli policy represents a small safety net and, in the symbolic context, a declaration of sovereign independence.

If the notion of sovereignty for all modern states is meaningless in absolute terms, then in this sense arms should be seen and esteemed as permitting a greater *degree* of latitude politically. In offering an essential margin for diplomatic maneuvering, the sale of weapons contributes to the national interest and provides the foundation for a more independent foreign policy. For Israel, its options so limited to begin with, pragmatism argues for exploiting every reasonable opening or advantage. This view is consistent with the pursuit of other diplomatic goals, such as ongoing political contacts, even if the latter should happen to derive from a coincidence of interests — perhaps only momentary — rather than being anchored in ideological affinity.

If Israel clings to its tenuous independent role, political and military, in world politics, at least some of this success can be traced to military sales.

SUCCESSES AND FAILURES

In concluding this discussion of the possible range of diplomatic interests generally thought to be served by the sale of Israeli arms, it is important for the sake of balance to consider some of the dilemmas as well.[26] First, in various times and places one of the eight diplomatic rationales may have come at the expense of any one of the others because of competing foreign policy aims. Second, as we shall see, the potential exists for a clash between diplomatic objectivities and economic motives. A third possibility is that taken on their own merits each of the eight political goals threatens to be offset by disadvantages and heavy costs diplomatically.

Let us take the first, the quest for influence. It is precisely because Israel possesses so little capacity for exerting leverage that it appeals to many customers as a suitable supplier with few demands. This in itself makes Israel susceptible to betrayal by Third World clients, as indeed happened between the years 1967 and 1973. The offer of arms does not guarantee political success —even when accepted—in and of itself. One illustration is the supply of Israeli-manufactured mortars to Nehru's India at the time of its wars with China and Pakistan, which, nevertheless, did not provide the breakthrough in diplomatic ties hoped for by Ben-Gurion.[27]

Prestige, too, is a double-edged sword. Whatever the gains for Israel's positive image to be derived from its reputation as a military power and supplier threatens to be cancelled, particularly in Western liberal circles, by the notoriety of gun sales as a general practice and by the identity of some of its internationally less respectable customers. Furthermore, the prestige value of being known as a formidable supplier is vitiated because Israeli policymakers and arms merchants prefer not to attract undue attention, stressing the sale rather than the effect of the attendant publicity.

Third, as previously alluded to, the emphasis upon establishing contacts with Third World leaders and military elites renders Israel open to guilt by association. Many of its best military clients also happen to be countries or leaders with serious image problems. It must honestly be noted that regardless of other possible political considerations and without denigrating them, having been identified with the Somoza regime in Nicaragua raises unavoidable questions as to the possible value of such contacts. Moreover, given the often repressive and precarious rule of some of these leaders and governments they often prove to be transient. Their removal or departure from office would deprive Israel of the access it had patiently sought to acquire. Also, there is the danger that as the contacts deepen and expand, Israel may inadvertently become entangled in local or regional squabbles to which its clients are a direct or indirect party; Central America, of course, is presently the best case in point.

International trade was the fourth rationale. And while defense relationships have made a contribution, it should be noted that: (a) aside from agriculture, arms, and technological know-how, Israel enjoys little comparative economic advantage and certainly cannot compete with the larger suppliers in terms of resources, trade, or markets; (b) the very fact of its diplomatic isolation precludes ease of access to otherwise lucrative markets.

Concerning the fifth, or Jewish, interest, one encounters the problematic nature of arms diplomacy in its fullest intensity. In one recent case, the insistence upon fulfilling arms commitments to Argentina at the height of the Falklands fighting found Israel in the political crossfire as Argentinian Jewry encouraged Israeli actions as cementing their own position in the country whereas Anglo-Jewish leaders argued that for their sake Israel had best terminate all such arms activities. The case of Argentina is instructive in a second sense. Israeli foreign ministry officials insisted that the sale of weapons to the military junta had been morally sound and that consequently many Argentinian Jews were spared the fate of the *desaparacedos*. It was argued, for example, that at the height of the arms flow in December, 1982, Foreign Minister Yitzhak Shamir had made an official *démarche* (protest) on their behalf, but that any more dramatic action by Israel would have made no practical contribution.[28] This followed accusations by some Argentinian Jews that the Israeli government and Foreign Ministry had not intervened, possibly out of concern lest defense contracts be cancelled by offended authorities in Buenos Aires.[29] Be that as it may, some of the potential advantage in using arms sales as diplomatic and Jewish leverage would seem to be diminished because of the less than wholehearted or enthusiastic view held in certain Jewish circles, primarily outside Israel, of the general practice of representatives of the Jewish state marketing lethal weapons.

Arms, when employed for purposes of preventing Arab political inroads or as preemption of other arms supply contenders, do not necessarily suffice. The danger exists that in retaliating, the Arab camp, reinforced by friendly Muslim countries, might be capable of mobilizing sufficient pressure to frustrate Israel's efforts at cultivating a prospective arms client and hence potential diplomatic supporter. Not to be forgotten is the traumatic diplomatic setback suffered in 1973 when eighteen African states previously on friendly terms in one month ordered the closing of Israel's embassies. Their actions are interpreted as having been governed in large part by Arab pressure mixed with promises of massive alternative aid and supplies of oil.[30] Israel has no assurance that in the future as well smaller countries pursuing military ties with it will be able to withstand Arab pressures; Costa Rica and El Salvador, in persisting with their ties despite a decision by Egypt early in 1984 to sever diplomatic relations with them, may only be the exception proving the rule.[31] While impossible to verify, it is safe to assume that any number of prospective clients have entered arms negotiations only to be dissuaded at the last moment by political considerations.

Likewise, in instances where the arms competition is intense, Israeli defense proposals, however generous or attractive, may not suffice against stronger competitors precisely because Israel has so little political clout, in which case it runs the danger of being squeezed out of prospective markets and deprived of important contracts. Certain countries might prefer Israeli defense exports for political reasons—no threat of Israel's interference or direct influence, a "window" to the United States— but too often the opposite is true. In the case of the Kfir interceptor, for example, political factors prevented the export of an otherwise attractive plane. This, too, would have an adverse impact upon the overall diplomatic position of the country.

Even the close identification with the United States and the West has a less desirable side to it from the standpoint of Israeli foreign relations. As part of the U.S.-Israeli dialogue American military and intelligence officials may be prepared to cooperate bilaterally with Israel on an entire range of security, economic, and diplomatic issues, but may be anxious to see, in return, a higher Israeli profile in support of administration policy. One recent illustration was reported efforts by the Reagan administration, and especially the Central Intelligence Agency, to get Israel to become more active in overtly and covertly helping to weaken the Sandinistas in Nicaragua and in backing the Contras.[32]

On the one hand, Israel is so beholden to the United States that it becomes not only difficult but unpleasant to turn down such requests. Yet, on the other hand, to acquiesce in such adventures exposes Israel to the charge of being used in a proxy, interventionist role similar to that played by Cuba for the Soviet bloc. Just how sensitive Israelis are to this image can be seen from the denial of a senior but unnamed official: "We are not a surrogate for the United States."[33]

This leads to the eighth argument on behalf of defense exports: that they provide an added degree of political independence. Yet here, too, weapons transfer diplomacy can, and has, boomeranged. First, in some ways it serves only to make Israel even more dependent. Second, by seeking to distance itself from the United States and other friendly Western countries, Israel risks increasing friction: commercially, in competing for arms clients; politically, by happening to be on the opposite side, as was the case in the early stages of the Iran-Iraq conflict. Third, arms as pragmatism and political expedience, even as they make a significant contribution to the country's national security and international status, nevertheless impose a serious tradeoff. They raise questions, oftentimes from sympathetic parties, about Israel as a principled state representing a clear set of moral values covering both human rights and relaxation of global tensions. Rumors of arms activities, even if baseless, are a convenient means for critics and detractors to cast a slur upon Israel's integrity and its international standing. In addition, Israel finds its own aggressive promotion of weapons sales thrown back at it, as happened when the Israeli government protested West German plans to sell sophisticated arms, including the Leopard II tank, to the Saudis only to have Chancellor Helmut Kohl and the German press counter by citing many of those very same arguments used by Jerusalem in justifying Israeli arms diplomacy.[34]

There is no reason to assume that Israeli policymakers are unaware of the risks and drawbacks of arms assistance from the standpoint of foreign relations. Statesmen are neither naive nor blind to realities. The negative side of the balance sheet is fairly obvious. The sale of weapons offers no lasting influence; at times it may appear to be unselective, mercenary, and immoral, encourage the wrong kinds of contact, and go unappreciated in the Jewish world. Those same policymakers may find Israel outmaneuvered by Arab enemies, foreclosed in a long list of countries and markets, and dismissed as a tool of the West even as its narrow pragmatism leads those in charge of national policy to lose sight of genuine and larger foreign policy goals.

But Israel persists. For while the record is mixed, on balance the concrete, short-term accomplishments outweigh the drawbacks. This is especially so once the economic rationale, as we shall see in the following chapter, is added to the security and diplomatic determinants analyzed here. If Israel has prevailed in clinging to the tenuous role of an independent small, security-conscious state in world politics, at least some of this success is traceable to military assistance and weapons transfers.

Israel's diplomatic isolation within the international community is well known and taken for granted by outside observers. One is accustomed to the one-sided votes against Zionism and the Jewish state, such as the resolution passed in 1982 by the U.N. General Assembly calling upon members to end aid, trade, and diplomatic ties with Israel "in order to totally isolate it in all fields."[35] An overwhelming majority (86 to 21, with thirty-four abstentions) voted in favor, and Israel's representative promptly denounced the action as "unjust, illogical and unbalanced." On the practical plane, however, in contrast to bold gestures, Israeli arms salesmen have mounted the more effective response.

Such assistance has given Israel some small yet crucial influence over events in many areas where other instruments of foreign policy do not work. Considering the evidence of arms sales relationships with well over thirty countries, the linking of arms transfers to foreign policy has proven a success in promoting each of the twelve political-military incentives discussed here. Defense exports in the instance of Israel are anything but an imprudent escapade or caprice.

NOTES

1. Individual country studies include: Andrew J. Pierre, ed., *Arms Transfers and American Foreign Policy* (New York: New York University Press, 1979); Lawrence Freedman, "Britain and the Arms Trade," *International Affairs* **54** (July 1978): 377–392; Edward A. Kolodziej's essay on "French Arms Trade: the Economic Determinants," contributed to the 1983 SIPRI Yearbook, pp. 371–390, as well as his chapter, "Determinants of French Arms Sales: Security Implications," in McGowan and Kegley, pp. 137–175. Soviet and Eastern European assistance patterns are dealt with in J. F. Copper and D. S. Papp, eds., *Communist Nations' Military Assistance* (Boulder: Westview Press, 1983). Activities of the Soviet Union and of the United States are compared by Andrew K. Semmel, "Security Assistance: U.S. and Soviet Patterns," in McGowan and Kegley, pp. 267–288.

2. See CSIS Panel on Science and Technology, "R & D for National Strength," *Washington Quarterly* **6** (Spring 1983): 149–160; also relevant is Lewis W. Snider, *Arabesque: Untangling the Patterns of Supply of Conventional Arms to Israel and the Arab States and the Implications for United States Policy on Supply of "Lethal" Weapons to Egypt.* University of Denver, Graduate School of International Studies, Monograph Series in World Affairs, **15**, Book One (1977), pp. 78–79.

3. *Haaretz*, 29 December 1982.

4. Interview with General Ehud Barak, Chief of Planning, IDF General Staff, *Bamahaneh*, 29 December 1982, pp. 14–15.

5. H. Bonner Day, "Israel's Quest for Military Independence," *Nato's Fifteen Nations* (December, 1978–January, 1979), p. 53.

6. Respect for Israel's position in the forefront of modern weapons testing and development is expressed, for example, in an interview with U.S. Rear Adm. Julian Lake in the *Jerusalem Post*, 11 May 1984.

7. Quoted in *JP*, 27 May 1984.

8. Remarks prepared for delivery to an international conference on "Defense and National Economy in the 1980s" at Tel-Aviv University, 14 December 1981. Official text reprinted as an appendix in Efraim Inbar, *Israeli Strategic Thought in the Post 1973 Period* (Jerusalem: Israel Research Institute of Contemporary Society, 1982), pp. 24–29.

9. This point is made by Bernard Reich in his contribution on "Israel" in Kolodziej and Harkavy, p. 211.

10. Brecher, p. 343.

11. Goldstein interview with Sharon, *Maariv*, 17 December 1982.

12. On the constants of Israel's international behavior, see the author's chapter, "Israeli Diplomacy in the Thirtieth Year of Statehood: Some Constants and Discontinuities," in Asher Arian, ed., *Israel. A Developing Society* (The Netherlands: Van Gorcum, 1980), pp. 33–58.

13. The practice of using arms sales by Great Powers to gain access rights and permanent basing facilities is explored in Robert E. Harkavy, *Great Power Competition for Overseas Bases* (Elmsford, N.Y.: Pergamon Press, 1982).

14. Arms as an instrument of political leverage on Third World recipients is discussed in Snider, especially pp. 11–22.

15. Brecher, p. 342.

16. World Jewish Congress, *The Implications of Israel-Arab Peace for World Jewry*, A Report of the International Economic and Social Commission (New York: Walden Press, 1981), p. 29.

17. Jewishness and its impact upon Israeli foreign policy is analyzed in Brecher, pp. 229–233; highly instructive is a more recent article on the subject, in Hebrew, by Israeli journalist, Moshe Zak, "The Jewish Consideration in Israel's Foreign Policy," *Gesher* 1/110 (Spring 1984): 32–43.
18. *Haaretz*, 29 April 1983; *Time*, 28 March 1983; *International Herald Tribune*, 28 April 1983.
19. *The New York Times*, 29 April 1983.
20. Quoted in Michael Bar-Zohar, *Ben-Gurion. A Biography* (New York: Delacorte Press, 1977), p. 194.
21. Such reports increased following disclosure of Israeli rescue efforts on behalf of Ethiopian Jewry at the beginning of 1985. See, for example, *The Washington Post*, 4 January 1985.
22. Geoffrey Kemp, "The New Strategic Map," *Survival* **XIX** (March–April 1977): 50–59, also Andrew Burrell, "The Politics of South Atlantic Security," *International Affairs* **59** (Spring 1983): 179–193.
23. In countering this strategic weakness and as a hedge against the possible loss of influence in Angola, Moscow is reported as attempting to convert the Western African island nation of Sao Tome and Principe off the coast of Gabon into a South Atlantic military stronghold on the oil tanker route around the Cape of Good Hope, *IHT*, 23 March 1984.
24. Bar-Zohar, p. 194.
25. One such appeal by an American Assistant Secretary of State for International Security is, West, p. 55.
26. Our attention to the costs and political risks of arms sales is drawn by Andrew Pierre in his 1979 work which offers a good general discussion using references to the American experience.
27. Reference to Nehru's urgent requests for mortars in Moshe Zak, *Maariv*, 2 November 1984.
28. *JP*, 28 March 1984.
29. *JP*, 30 December 1983.
30. *Newsview*, 31 January 1984. A detailed postmortem is Susan Aurelia Gitelson, "Israel's African Setback in Perspective," in Curtis and Gitelson, pp. 182–199.
31. *JP*, 22 April 1984.
32. *IHT*, 21 May 1984.
33. *IHT*, 21 May 1984.
34. Aspects of the Leopard negotiations in the weekend magazine of the *Jerusalem Post*, 30 March 1984, remarks by Kohl on Israel's own arms deals covered in *IHT*, 28–29 January 1984 and by *Maariv*, 18 May 1984.
35. *NYT*, 7 February 1983.

4

THE ECONOMIC IMPERATIVE

Meriting separate discussion is the third pillar of the pro-arms sales strategy: the economic rationale. True, there is always some linkage and overlap between a country's status in world affairs, its defense posture and role as munitions supplier, on the one hand, and its national economy. But in the case of Israel this economic variable is noteworthy for going beyond merely supplementing or further reinforcing those diplomatic and security arguments analyzed in the previous chapter. For one thing the relationship between weapons transfers and economic strength appears to be inverse: foreign sales are increasing even as the nation's economy has stagnated in the first four years of the present decade. And as a result considerations of an economic nature have become extremely important of late in arms decision making, causing, for example, a lessening of restraints on the export of military products.

ISRAEL'S ECONOMY

A brief picture of the economy in the 1980s suggests a number of indicators and trends relevant to the larger context of arms transfer policies. To begin with, the impression of a major economic crisis is inescapable and overwhelming. The most immediate symptom is rampant inflation, approaching 1,000 percent in 1985. A second alarm signal is a halt in economic growth. In 1982 the Central Bureau of Statistics had released figures which showed that for the first time since the early 1950s the Gross National Product had not increased at all; whereas during 1981 the total output of goods and services had risen by some 5 percent.[1] Third, Israel's balance of payments and balance of trade position worsened. Imports of goods and services by a consumer-oriented society exceeded exports by some $4.9 billion in 1982. The external deficit on goods and services projected for Israel by the International Monetary Fund (IMF) was $5.3 billion in 1983 and over $6 billion by 1985.[2] In 1984 foreign reserves fell to $2 billion — well beneath the $3 billion mark Israeli economists and the government regard as the safe minimum.

Traditional earners of foreign currency, such as agricultural exports, diamonds, and even tourism, have experienced periods of decline in recent years.[3]

Owing in part to this, Israel's foreign debt has assumed alarming proportions. By the end of 1984 Israel was shouldering a foreign debt estimated at $24.2 billion, requiring that it pay out about $3.5 billion in capital and interest on long-term and medium-term loans. In 1982 Israel had to repay over $800 million to the U.S. alone, a sum exceeding the $785 million received in American economic aid.[4] These payments of principal and interest on domestic and foreign debts are believed to have soaked up a full 32 percent of export earnings in 1982.[5]

The implications of this crisis are best reflected in Israel's abnormal budget. Debt servicing alone consumes about one-third of all government expenditure. Another third, or about $7 billion, goes for defense — as opposed to 7 percent in the United States and compared to 2.5 to 4 percent for most other countries.[6] This staggering military outlay leaves only the last third to be spent on social services.

In contrast to these and other indicators of a troubled and declining national economy — what has been referred to as a "siege economy" — is the image of Israel as a booming, vibrant center of manufacturing and technological research. Since the 1967 Six Day War the country's industrial base has expanded enormously and Israel itself has been transformed from a rural economy dependent upon citrus exports to a sophisticated producer of computers, electronics, medical and biotechnological products, and aircraft. While in 1972 only $103 million, or 7.5 percent of all exports, were in the category of high technology, a decade later, in 1983, the figure had jumped to $1.5 billion, or 30 percent of all industrial goods.[7] Rapid industrial expansion and continued industrial development geared to foreign trade, moreover, are acknowledged by economic experts as one of the keys, along with cutting government expenditures and reducing the defense budget, to stemming Israel's economic decline and resuming economic growth.

It is here that military production and foreign sales enter the discussion. Admittedly the defense budget and defense needs are a drain on the nation's resources. A heavy armament program, imposed upon a narrow and shrinking economic base, generally tends to divert funds to socially unproductive investment. Yet, for Israel, the arms industry and export program are presently one of the few bright spots in this otherwise rather dismal economic picture as well as a central component of the strategy for moving the Israeli economy into the twenty-first century.

DEFENSE AND THE ECONOMY: THE ISRAELI EXPERIENCE

The discussion about the domestic economic effects of military expenditure on arms transfers is one familiar to economists. It is widely accepted, for example, that in the long run economies are ill-served by massive investment in the defense sector; Benoit, Kaldor, and others have shown how military

expenditure, and the pursuit of ever more modern and sophisticated technology, are detrimental to development, compete directly with civil projects,
entail "opportunity costs" by diverting funds from social and other economic
goals, and even then do not necessarily increase military effectiveness.[8]

In terms of Israel, the discussion at the level of macroeconomic theory is
somewhat academic. There was little if any element of choice involved historically in the determination of military as opposed to other economic priorities. These were imposed upon the country, dictated by threats from the
external environment. Or as expressed in the advertisements of one military
exporter: "unfortunately we have the experience." The only matter open to
question was whether to seek the country's security needs solely by importing arms from foreign sources or to give attention to indigenous manufacture as well. And for so long as the security problem continues to demand
maximum attention, the production and marketing of defense equipment will
remain characteristic of the Israeli economic system.

Beyond that, however, lies a second observation. Contrary to the notion
that military industrialization is dysfunctional, Israel stands as a model,
possibly unique, for the opposite view.[9] The manufacture and export of
defense-related products have served as a stimulant to growth, or what Kolodziej prefers to describe as "a mechanism of modernization."[10] The defense
effort and the local armament process, while costly, provide the main impetus
behind industrialization. Military industries have pioneered in a number of
nonmilitary sectors, offering spinoff, or side benefits, and creating a standard
for high-quality products which, in turn, has had a marked effect on civilian
production. Moreover, they have given Israel an operational base for modern
weapons systems design, development, and production without condemning
the country to "an industrial structure that is perpetually backward by the
standards of the most advanced industrial nations";[11] and all this while challenging the contention that militarization "can be carried out only through
authoritarianism and repression."[12] As judged by a foremost student of the
impact of defense upon economic growth in developing societies, "the economic payoffs to Israel of its large defense program appear . . . to have been
substantial."[13]

This judgment goes beyond the past tense. The defense industry and its export drive are of vital importance to Israel's present economy and future performance through a logic which is straightforward and rests upon economic
and commerical pragmatism. It goes as follows: to remain viable the economy
must be oriented toward industrialization and foreign trade. Total exports
are spearheaded by industrial products. Industrial exports, in turn, are dominated by three sectors—metals, electronics, and aerospace equipment. Each
of these includes defense-related items, meaning that while Israeli leaders
studiously avoid making the point quite so unequivocally, the fact remains
that in recent years defense output has become a critical factor in the growth

of industrial as well as total exports, hence of the economy as a whole. As for the defense industry itself, Israel, emulating the leading arms merchants, depends upon the weapons trade to achieve an array of economic interests, including domestic employment, lengthening production runs, achieving lower per unit costs of research and actual manufacture while also protecting the local industry from fluctuations in domestic demand.

We find that while not an unmitigated success and although achieved at great cost, on balance the defense sector, of which arms transfers are an integral part, has had a net positive effect on civilian growth capacity. In Israel's case the economic benefits, domestic and external, tend significantly to outweigh the burdens. In fact, three factors have been providential in keeping Israel's economy from declining even more sharply than it has. Two of these are external: American assistance and the fall in the price paid for oil. The third factor, however, owes more to Israel's own initiative and determination, namely, the successful defense sales program. Yet, in our opinion the economic imperative for pushing arms and what has been termed the "arms transfer-economic development nexus"[14] are not sufficiently appreciated.

CONTRIBUTION OF ARMS SALES

Five principal arguments, dividing into domestic and external, are most often heard in the case made for Israeli defense sales on economic grounds. The first set of three are: employment, economies of scale, and spinoffs. In the second category are foreign exchange and the balance of trade.

The Labor Market

Military production provides a major source for employment in all industrializing and arms exporting countries. In Britain military exports are estimated to contribute to the direct employment of 70,000 to 80,000 people and indirectly to perhaps another 100,000 people.[15] The French arms industry employs approximately 300,000 military and civilian personnel — or about 1.3 percent of the active population and 5.5 percent of the industrial labor force.[16] U.S. Bureau of Labor Statistics reveal that every $1 billion in arms sales is equivalent to 50,000 more jobs for Americans.[17] In Singapore the national arms corporation has only 4,500 salaried people and yet is regarded as an important employer in a country of some 2.5 million people.[18]

Compared to the larger Western arms manufacturers the figures for Israel will perhaps appear numerically less significant at first glance. But because of the country's origins in socialism, its struggle for economic viability, and its extreme sensitivity to societal unrest, claims that the armament effort contributes to near full employment are not to be dismissed as a myth.[19]

It appears that anywhere from 58,000 to as many as 120,000 Israelis are employed currently in the defense industry. These are merely estimates since detailed information is not published on employment in the defense sector. Also, it is hard to know precisely where the military industry ends, given the profusion of subsidiaries. Nor do such figures fully reflect the magnitude of such employment, given the fact that beyond the wage earners are their immediate families; the director of the Israel Aircraft Industry admits to feeding "more than 80,000 mouths."[20]

Even accepting the lower figure of 58,000 people employed in arms manufacture as a base point, the implications are clear. The Bank of Israel reported a labor force of 1.3 million Israelis in 1982. Of these, fully one quarter, or 309,000 people, worked in the industrial sector.[21] In which case, no less than 20 percent of the entire industrial work force and 5 percent of the country's employed are connected, directly or indirectly, to an expanding military industry with markets both at home and abroad.[22]

Furthermore, in qualitative terms the defense industry eases the manpower situation by absorbing technically-skilled immigrants and in mitigating the "brain drain." A high percentage of scientists and engineers are concentrated in this one sector. Until recently at least Israel enjoyed a comparative advantage over other Western arms exporters because of its human resources, featuring a skilled, motivated work force and low labor costs.[23] The large military firms have a reputation for excellent labor relations and high worker motivation, with wage strikes and lost work days kept to a minimum. Because the arms industries have been a source of growth and jobs, the employment benefit of defense sales is quite high. In the context of Israel's present economy it is a dubious proposition that this industry is replaceable by other substitute employers.

In a recessionary period the spectre of labor cutbacks in any sector is a source of concern to the Western democracies. In Israel every government since 1948 has pledged, as a matter of social and economic policy, not to consciously wield unemployment, which has been kept as low as 3.5 to 5 percent, and never topped 6 percent, in the fight against inflation. Quite the opposite. As the jobless rate increases, the government comes under mounting pressure to act; one way would be to create additional jobs in the defense industries if foreign orders can be obtained. On the other hand, the weapons trade is notorious for being singularly unpredictable as markets dry up. In Israel, where it is calculated that some 700 job slots are closed for every 1 percent drop in industrial exports,[24] the success or failure of arms sales diplomacy directly affects employment. In 1983 it was rumored that 100 employees (over 10 percent of the 900 employed) might have to be released by the Israel Shipyards due to a drop in foreign orders; the 1985 budget suggested 1,500–2,000 workers might be laid off at IMI, and 500–700 at Rafael.[25]

Economies of Scale

Economists generally are agreed that by extending production runs and spreading development outlays, arms exports serve to reduce unit costs of defense items locally manufactured. Economies of scale mean that each additional tank or plane built and sold lowers the cost per unit of all the rest, with the result that adding foreign sales to contracts with the IDF makes it possible for Israel to produce for its own use weapons it otherwise could not afford. Cost-cutting considerations and the export argument are especially weighty in the development and production of the more sophisticated weapons systems because of their enormous start-up costs.

At several stages in Israel's history the internal debate has focused on the principle of local military production as opposed to the advantages of overseas procurement.[26] Export potential as an argument figures in decisions taken on at least three ambitious — and costly — projects: the Kfir fighter, the Merkava tank, and, most recently, the Lavi jet plane. Because of their high cost the manufacture of sophisticated armaments such as these deemed essential for Israel's defense would be all but impossible to justify on economic grounds were it not for the existence of a potential foreign market. Foreign orders can thus be the necessary element in a favorable decision to undertake a production run intended, in the first instance, to equip Israel's own forces. Whether these favorable prognoses actually have materialized or not is another matter to be dealt with later.

In terms of existing production military experts are agreed upon the desirability of maintaining the constant capacity to produce beyond levels suggested by peacetime defense needs as a precaution against sudden military emergencies. Ongoing weapons exports are a good way of preserving such an ability since they permanently mobilize factors of production like labor, plants, and machines at a level ensuring that when necessary expanded military production can be realized smoothly and rapidly. Israel has had more than its share of acute, unanticipated military crises in the last three decades — in 1956, in 1967, in 1973, and again in 1982 — which called for a major domestic military supply effort both during and subsequent to the fighting, in addition to large defense imports. Sales abroad thereby provide such a reserve capability. On a less ambitious scale foreign sales have allowed Israel periodically to reduce large stocks of surplus and outdated military equipment and to make a profit at the same time.

Of mounting importance in unit-cost considerations at present are the direct, long-term implications of cuts imposed upon the defense budget since 1982 because of the rampant inflation. The immediate effect is reduced local procurement by the Ministry of Defense for the IDF. The Ministry is taking whatever measures it can, such as continuing production of the Merkava tank rather than purchasing American tanks, specifically in an attempt to soften the blow of limited procurement orders for Israeli arms manufacturers.[27]

Rather than protesting to little avail, the larger arms industrialists have been quick to appreciate that the national budget and the domestic demand for weapons are no longer able to assure the expansion of the military sector. Their only alternative is to fill the gaps arising from the contraction of the home market through production for export, thereby lengthening production runs.

The government and the defense establishment have their own reasons for reinforcing this logic. State-directed arms industries are being encouraged as well to intensify their overseas marketing. The hope is that exports will allow the production of advanced weapons systems without excessive cost or confining defense manufacture to a narrow range of weapons, and that the real cost to the economy can still be absorbed abroad as foreign purchasers take up much of the slack. The effects of this joint governmental-managerial strategy are already apparent. Formerly, the military industry in Israel existed primarily to service the IDF, and exports represented only a small part of total production. Today the emphasis has shifted markedly. Export sales of military products account for upwards of 50 percent and may perhaps exceed 60 percent of the total volume of defense production.[28] Comparable figures for both the United States and Great Britain are in the neighborhood of 25 percent. And should reduced local purchasing continue, the proportion seems bound to rise further, implying an even greater dependence upon the arms trade.

This trend suggests that Israel has fallen into the plight common to other arms exporting countries which have invested heavily in the strategic decision to gear much of the industrial sector to military manufacture. One of the few developing countries to support a military industry, Israel, too, is at great pains to avoid a situation prevalent in other Western advanced industrialized countries, namely, that of idle production capacity. At this point the quest for arms contracts might take on an air of desperation, given the overwhelming importance for the economic, social, and political stability of the country in finding alternative outlets for the defense industries, some of whose production lines may be kept open only by the success of these efforts.

Research and Development

The military industry and foreign military sales are economically beneficial in the third sense of spurring scientific research and high technology. Reliance on technological superiority has been a keystone of Israeli economic growth as well as its defense posture throughout. In this emphasis the military and civilian sectors converge, reinforcing each other by sharing advances in knowledge and technology.

For the defense establishment the importance of R & D in the process of competitive weapon development is clear. Modern warfare, extending to the Middle East, underscores the technology of precision and stimulates the qualitative arms race to which Israel, of necessity, is committed. Its leaders, therefore, are the first to subscribe to the definition of military research and development as

> the effort to extend knowledge and technical expertise wherever there are thought to be military applications, existing or potential, in order to create more effective weapons, more effective means of using them and more effective ways of making these same weapons (when used by the other side) ineffective.[30]

Operationally, this awareness of the strategic importance of defense technologies for the national security effort has resulted in heavy capital investment in the defense industries and defense production;[31] and preference shown in government expenditure for military research on behalf of superior military technologies.[32]

The military industry has been the principal although not the sole beneficiary of this preferential R & D treatment. Like Israel in its quest for maximum security, the industry is staking much on enhancing defense technologies and in pushing the frontiers of military technology forward. But in doing so it has helped provide a climate conducive to industrial innovation in general. This in effect is the thrust of the "spinoff" or derivative benefits argument typically heard on behalf of the huge defense industries and their arms promotions.

Proponents contend that advances in the military sector perform an important modernizing function by stimulating scientific advances in other, nonmilitary industries also having export potential and as a source of new ideas. Since critical civil and military technologies increasingly converge, research funded and conducted ostensibly for military purposes has led to impressive breakthroughs, ahead of many other countries, in the fields of optics and lasers, for example. Research in the areas of aeronautics, computer technology, and electronics, innovative in itself and conducted initially for defense reasons, has provided the necessary impetus for efforts to move industry into higher technologies and gives Israel a definite advantage in the relentless civilian technological race. A prime example is the rapid growth of the electronics industry; another is the manufacture of communications systems through the application of military know-how to civilian products. Two explanations may account for this. One is that many Israeli firms manufacture both military and nonmilitary products; Tadiran Israel Electronics Industries Ltd. is but one example. The second explanation is that scientific knowledge does not lend itself to compartmentalization but rather that lessons learned in one field, the military, are more broadly applicable, for example, in metallurgy and engineering, too.

In Israel branches of civilian industry have been made viable and new industrial sectors have evolved parallel with the military industries. This is readily acknowledged by Israeli business managers; Eli Hurvitz, chairman of the Industrialists' Association admitted as much when he cited the military firms as a role-model whose success was attributable to concentrated effort and an innovative spirit.[33] The ambitious Lavi fighter project earned approval, in part, because of confidence that its production will provide yet another fresh stimulus for the technological advancement of sophisticated industry in Israel. Yet another spinoff arises from the type of highly skilled labor required by the military industry; provided with additional training and experience, many of its technicians, researchers, and managers later transfer to other firms, making a contribution to the growth of non-military areas as well.

R & D military know-how and science-based information thus generate spinoffs. They also are exportable. According to Commerce Ministry spokesmen, at the beginning of the seventies high-technology exports amounted to less than 1 percent of total industrial exports. By 1981 they were 33 percent, or $1.2 billion. The goal is to reach $6.8 billion, or 62 percent, by 1991.[34] There is little question but that all such ambitious forecasting rests upon the implicitly assumed proposition that the military industry will figure prominently in contributing toward this end. Now at an advanced stage of indigenous manufacture it can provide a market for military hardware and know-how which can be exported.

In short, the generalization often made that the emphasis upon military R & D together with the large number of research scientists and engineers engaged in it "diverts scarce expertise and intellectual effort from the civil sector, reducing civil technological development and so depressing rates of economic growth"[35] does not easily fit Israel. Rather, its experience does nothing so much as suggest that if properly scaled and channeled, a viable, advanced defense R & D coupled with a refined industry open to adaptation can be maintained by a small country with a fairly small domestic market. How much better, though, if the market can be expanded further afield through export.[36] Equipment with a large R & D component, if exported on a substantial scale, helps appreciably to defray the original scientific investment by producing downward pressures on the price of that particular weapon.[37] It helps to cover at least some of the sunk costs by recouping the investment through an extended production run. For each of these reasons it is not surprising that Israelis to an overwhelming extent are convinced that the defense industrial base is a national resource and consequently support both military production and overseas sales.

Foreign Exchange

Arms sales, in addition to everything else, are regarded as one of the ways for a country to earn as well as to save foreign exchange. Israel's monetary system and balance of payments both contribute to and are affected by the national economic crisis gripping the country in recent years. Foreign debts at the end of 1984 stood at over $23 billion—the highest in the world on a per capita basis. In order to preserve its credit and credibility at never having defaulted on loan repayments, in 1984 it had to return the staggering sum of $2.4 billion as loans and interest to international creditors.[38] The lion's share was earmarked for the United States to whom over $800 million a year must be repaid just in servicing debts. Low foreign reserves, a drop of perhaps 11 percent in foreign grants during 1982 and the resulting necessity to fall back upon additional negotiated loans, plus arms imports still valued as high as $2.2 billion, merely compound an already serious situation. In addition, tourism, traditionally a major source of foreign capital, has also proven a disappointment at times in the past few years[39] (Table 4.1).

Seen in this context, defense exports in the neighborhood of even $1 billion assume a greater significance in the face of national indebtedness and the outflow of gold reserves to pay for fuel, arms purchases from the U.S. and, not least, the unabated inflow of consumer goods.

Such weapons sales contribute in Israel's present search for relief from its aggregate international balance of payments pressures by financing some of the import surplus.

Similarly, from a different perspective, domestic military manufacture, bolstered by production for foreign clients, alleviates some of the need for the IDF to import arms, freeing valuable funds for alternative uses, including local reinvestment. Arms transfers stabilizing annually at over $1 billion in effect ease the credit side of the ledger by roughly approximating the portion of defense assistance from the United States given as a loan: $1.1 billion out of the 1983 total of $1.7 billion, $500 million of which is in the form of an outright grant. The need to counterbalance the outflow of American dollars only increases pressures for defense sales abroad. Such sales, while obviously not able to arrest the overall economic decline, nonetheless, act as a compensatory mechanism in two ways: by creating foreign exchange savings through substitution of domestic production, premised upon economies of scale, and foreign contracts for exports; and by earning hard currency.[40] Since so much of the national deficit is attributable to high military expendi-

Table 4.1. Earnings ($ Million) by Sector, 1982.

Tourism	$875
Agricultural exports	500
Diamond exports	200

From *Newsview*, 10 May 1983, p. 32.

tures, the policy of arms deliveries by and from Israel helps indirectly to defray the cost of defense.

Then, lastly, there is the value added factor. Economists use the term to distinguish gross receipts from exports from their foreign exchange cost. Added value is thus meant to reflect net foreign exchange earnings by underscoring the difference between the value of the exports and the cost of imports, such as raw materials or parts, originally used in their manufacture.

Value added in foreign exchange varies between economic sectors: from as little as 20 percent for diamonds to as high as 75 to 80 percent for tourism and agricultural exports. Industrial exports, by comparison, are in an intermediate position, averaging some 50 to 55 percent.[41] The added value of Israeli exports in general has been in a decline curve in the past decade— from 52 percent in 1971 to 47 percent in 1981[42]—caused, ostensibly, by the rise in the price of imported fuel necessary for running export industries.[43] But because agricultural exports and the tourist sector, those with the highest added value, have been troubled of late, while industrial and defense exports are in a growth pattern, the contribution of the latter in bringing a high economic return for relatively low material cost investment becomes noteworthy in the balance of economic considerations.

The Trade Contribution

Each of the major political parties in Israel shares the view of professional economists that both for the short- and long-term the country must stimulate exports. The trend in recent years has found a natural increase in capital goods exports spearheaded by industrial and defense exports. In fact, based upon the available evidence foreign military sales at present reflect a disproportionate share of total exports.

Just how large are these military sales? An approximate figure, extrapolated from various statements and Government statistics scattered under the loose categories of metals, electrical equipment, communications, and transport, is anywhere between $1 and $1.5 billion. Thus, for example, unidentified officials admitted to having shipped $1.2 billion worth of domestically produced or refurbished defense equipment abroad in 1981.[44] By computing the 1982 export figures for each of the major industrial branches under which arms are subsumed, one arrives at a total of $2.372 billion (Table 4.2). Accepting the word of industrialists in each of these branches that their companies' production and exports are heavily weighted toward defense-related items, and allowing for other military sales unreported in these five categories, we are left with a figure somewhere in excess of $1 billion. Exactly how much *above* that figure remains a matter for conjecture.[45]

Sophisticated industrial exports in general have increased over the past decade, as represented in the area of metals, machinery, and electronics

Table 4.2. Exports by Economic Branch, 1982 ($ Million).

Metals, machinery, electronics	1,567.7
Electronic equipment for "control," science and medicine	177.9
Aircraft and parts	406.5
Communication equipment	167.8
Scientific measuring and controlling equipment	52.4
TOTAL	$2,372.3

Derived from Central Bureau of Statistics, *Israel Foreign Trade Statistics Quarterly*, **33** (October–December, 1982):10–13; *Israel Economist*, January, 1984, p. 32.

(Table 4.3). Industrial products thus have become the key to Israel's international trade position and to its export drive. This was particularly apparent in the peak years, 1980–1981, and remains so today despite a percentage decrease in 1982 which continued into 1983 as well. Of a total of $10.5 billion in capital goods exported during 1982, nearly 30 percent – $3.5 billion – were industrial, not including diamonds.[46] Total exports of electronics alone grew in 1979–1982 from $171 million to $466 million – a rise of over 170 percent in just three years.[47] Even in a year of poor economic performance, 1982, export of metals and electronics suffered only a slight (0.5 percent) drop, relative to a 3 percent decline in all industrial exports, not including diamonds.[49]

In part, the prominence of industrial exports in the overall export profile reflects the effect of the shift in the structure of industry toward the specialized output of goods for shipment overseas. A second reason, however, is the poor

Table 4.3. Exports, Metal, Machinery, and
Electronics ($ Million).

1970	70.0
1075	194.0
1976	456.2
1977	795.1
1979	968.2
1980	1,251.2
1981	1,538.5

From *Israel Foreign Trade Statistical Quarterly*, **33**
(January–June, 1982):9.

showing of other traditional export branches. The textile industry lost 20 percent of its export market in 1981; at the same time agricultural exports dropped by some 9 percent.[50] Foreign sales of diamonds likewise have been erratic in the 1980s. They fell from a peak of $1.4 billion in 1980 to only $900 million in 1982 before climbing again to over $1 billion in 1983.[51] Yet despite recent setbacks the economic strategy calls for tripling industrial exports by 1990.

To whatever extent such optimistic projects are realistic, they rest on the strong performance of foreign defense sales. For while the nonmilitary markets have been sluggish, military ones have proven active and, in the view of economic planners, promising. Until 1982 arms exports increased at an impressive rate: by 15 percent in 1974, 80 percent in 1975, and 85 percent in 1976.[52] Using the figure of $1 billion in various forms of security assistance, it represented something on the scale of one-tenth of Israeli exports in 1982, and between one-fourth and one-third of all industrial exports.[53] Should the ratio of arms exports/total exports only be in the vicinity of 5 percent rather than twice that figure, this would still be of major significance for the national economy.[54]

In sum, it has been the arms export program, riding the crest of a global boom in military expenditures and weapons transfers, which in effect salvaged Israel's trade position in the face of a chronic trade deficit.[55] They have helped the country to become one of the world's ten leading export nations on a per capita basis. Nor is it an accident that defense sales climbed at the same time as the volume of Israeli exports rose by 17 percent in the years 1978–1983.[56] As concerns the future, more military sales overseas would provide jobs and increase trade, and would therefore be welcome at a time of excess industrial production, threatened unemployment, and shrinking trade. Conversely, should defense-related exports fall drastically for any number of reasons, the serious adverse effects would be felt not only in the balance of trade but in the economy as a whole.

By way of concluding this discussion of the triad of incentives for Israeli arms sales diplomacy, two trends are apparent. The first is that Israel's weapons transfers go far beyond political, defense, strategic, and security concerns. Economic trade, industrial growth, and scientific development are vitally affected by the degree of success in finding outlets for military products to such a point that what might once have been engaged in as a matter of economic opportunity now gives the appearance of being an economic necessity. The current structural crisis in the Israeli economy all but precludes any serious deemphasis of arms diplomacy. A figure of somewhere near $1 billion in defense export earnings is not to be scoffed at in the context of Israel's economic recovery program. Industrial and commercial arguments reviewed here have become cardinal national interests to the extent that greater weight in policymaking could be attached to these economic arguments than to diplomatic sensitivities. In short, as has been detected in the instance of other arms suppliers,[57] in Israel, too, arms policy threatens to float increasingly away from its initial moorings in diplomatic and strategic considerations. Should the arms policy indeed become a commercial rather than a political or a strategic venture it would owe in large part to the powerful influence and private interests represented by the defense industries which are the subject of the next chapter.

NOTES

1. *Jerusalem Post*, 31 December, 1982, 3 and 17 January 1983; *IHT*, 13 December 1982; *Newsview*, 31 August 1982. A useful profile of the economy at mid-decade can be found in the staff report, "The Economic Crisis in Israel" (46 pp.), prepared for the Committee on Foreign Relations of the United States Senate (Washington: Government Printing Office, 1984).
2. International Monetary Report findings, *New York Times*, 10 July 1983, 16 October 1983. Israel's Central Bureau of Statistics officially reported the payments deficit in 1983 as being $5.1 billion, *J P*, 1 January 1984.
3. Bank of Israel, Research and Development, "Recent Economic Developments," no. 34, Jerusalem (April 1983), p. xi.
4. *NYT*, 26 June 1983.
5. *NYT*, 10 July 1983.
6. This budget breakdown into three basic areas is disclosed by two Cabinet members, Ministers Patt and Arens, in separate interviews, *J P*, 23 May and 31 May 1984. The defense budget is analyzed in Paul Rivlin, "The Burden of Defense: The Case of Israel" (Appendix 7D), in SIPRI, 1983, pp. 191–194.
7. Figures presented by Industry Minister Gideon Patt in addressing the Jerusalem Economic Conference and reported the following day in the *JP*, 23 May 1984.
8. An extensive literature exists on the controversy sparked by Emile Benoit in his early research and findings, *Disarmament and the Economy* (New York: Harper and Row, 1963). Negative effects of militarization are emphasized in Miroslav Nincic, *The Arms Race. The Political Economy of Military Growth* (New York: Praeger, 1982). Frustrations of a military nature are the theme of Mary Kaldor's *The Baroque Arsenal* (New York: Hill and Wang, 1981); whereas the social costs are underlined in the 1980 report of the Brandt Commission and the Boston Study Group, *The Price of Defense* (New York: Time Books, 1979) p. 262. A balanced presentation of both the pluses and minuses of arms manufacture and export is in an article by Debbie J. Gerner, "Arms Transfers to the Third World: Research on Patterns, Causes and Effects," in a special issue of *International Interactions* **10** (1983) devoted to arms transfers.
9. A dissenting view is taken by Gavin Kennedy, *The Military in the Third World* (London: Duckworth, 1974), especially pp. 283–301. He concludes that domestic military production is not necessarily a diversion from industrialization programs and finds a positive association between the expansion of both defense and the metals and engineering sectors.
10. Kolodziej, in McGowan and Kegley, p. 165.
11. Kaldor, p. 160.
12. Kaldor, p. 160.

13. In a later study Benoit finds much to praise in Israel's coping with the implications of disproportionate emphasis on the defense sector, Emile Benoit, *Defense and Economic Growth in Developing Countries* (Lexington MA: Lexington Books, 1973). He singles out Israel for closer analysis (pp. 251–257) to show that defense programs, "though not *intended* to contribute to the civilian economy, may in fact do so in indirect ways that have not hitherto been adequately recognized" (p. XX).

14. Gerner, p. 28.

15. Freedman, p. 380; also figures for the UK in Frederic C. Pearson, "The Question of Control in British Defense Sales Policy," *International Affairs* **59** (Spring 1983): 220.

16. Kolodziej, SIPRI 1983, p. 387; additional French data in Edward A. Kolodziej, "Re-evaluating Economic and Technological Variables in Explain Global Arms Production and Sales." Paris (June, 1982), p. 12.

17. Figures range between 38,000–50,000. Roger P. Labrie, John G. Hutchins, and Edwin W. A. Peura, *U.S. Arms Sales Policy. Background and Issues* (Washington, D.C.: American Enterprise Institute, 1982), p. 47; see also, Pierre, *The Global Politics of Arms Sales*, p. 26.

18. *IHT*, 30 June 1983.

19. Alfred Kastler makes this contention in his argument on behalf of disarmament in the introduction to a special issue (no. 95) of the *International Social Science Journal* devoted to "Burdens of Militarization," **35** (1983).

20. Gabriel Gidor, interviewed by Dov Goldstein, *The Israel Yearbook*, p. 259.

21. Bank of Israel, *Annual Report* (Jerusalem, May 1983), p. 68,70.

22. Using higher figures one journalist depicts overseas sales as employing a third of the country's work force. A. J. McIllroy, "Israel: Arsenal of the Third World," *Sunday Telegraph*, 28 August 1983. Closer to 20 percent is the figure offered by Steinberg, p. 290.

23. According to the IMF, low labor productivity and wage increases have sent unit labor costs up by 28 percent since 1979. This, in turn, reduces to some degree Israel's foreign competitiveness, including in arms sales terms, *NYT*, 10 July 1983.

24. Ministry of Industry and Commerce, Center for Industrial Planning, *Industry in Israel, 1982* (Jerusalem, July, 1983), p. 30.

25. *Haaretz*, 9 June 1983.

26. On the domestic debate see Paul Rivlin, "The Burden of Israel's Defense," *Survival* **20** (July/August 1978): 146–151.

27. *Haaretz*, 4 January 1983; *Maariv*, 19 April 1985.

28. "Israel's Expanding Capabilities," *Defense Attache*, no. 1/1981, p. 35. *The Sunday Telegraph* quotes a figure of only 40 percent for the home forces.

29. The Boston Group, p. 262; Freedman, p. 380.

30. This is the definition offered by SIPRI, 1983, p. 213.

31. Steinberg (p. 289) figures that one-third of total annual governmental investment reaches the defense industries.

32. This imbalance has prompted calls for boosting civilian research. One expert claims that in 1982–1983 only $132 million from all sources, government and private, was spent on civilian industrial R & D and forecast that the future would have to grow to $500 million in 1990, Professor Baruch Raz, *JP* 17 November 1983.

33. *Maariv* interview, 23 September 1983.

34. *Forbes*, 7 November 1983, p. 142.

35. SIPRI, 1983, p. 214.

36. R & D is examined in Franklin A. Long and Judith Reppy, eds., *The Genesis of New Weapons: Decision Making for Military R & D* (Elmsford, N.Y. Pergamon Press, 1980).

37. The experience in Britain suggests otherwise, that the biggest consumers of R & D funds, such as aircraft, do not generate a large share of arms exports; Trevor Taylor, "Research Note: British Arms Exports and R & D Costs," *Survival* **22** (July/August 1980): 259–262. Pearson, p. 223, citing Taylor, takes a similarly critical position, arguing that while exports lengthen production runs they may not reduce unit costs very much. He also shows that R & D costs are not necessarily recovered through exports since British weapons requiring the most research were generally the least successful exports.

38. *Haaretz*, 10 May 1984.

39. The number of foreign visitors to Israel fell significantly, 12 percent, in 1982. Receipts from tourism are believed to have dropped by 8 percent from 1981 and totalled approximately $875 million in 1982, *Newsview*, 10 May 1983.

40. Needing to be factored in are expenditures in foreign currency at the early stages of production, investment costs, and the import of raw materials necessary for military production.

41. See Nadav Halevi, *The Structure and Development of Israel's Balance of Payments*, The Maurice Falk Institute for Economic Research in Israel (Jerusalem, 1983), discussion paper no. 83.02, pp. 14–16.

42. *Haaretz*, relying upon Central Bureau of Statistics figures, 4 January 1984.

43. *Israel Economist*, March 1984, p. 31. If in 1971 Israel had to import $2.50 worth of oil for every $100 of gross exports, in 1981 it had to pay $10.

44. Quoted by *NYT*, 18 March 1984, p. 4; SIPRI, 1982, (p. 188) presented arms exports by Israel in excess of $1.2 billion as early as 1980, doubling the 1979 record. Even the $1.2 billion for 1982 is felt by European arms analysts to be understated. That Israel's arms sales are more than a billion dollars was confirmed by U.S. intelligence officials cited in the *J P*, 22 April 1984.

45. Cabinet Minister Mordechai Tsippori on one occasion was quoted as claiming that arms sales for 1981–1982 were nearer to $2 billion. Ran Goren, "Indigenous Advanced Fighter Aircraft in Israel: Considerations for Decision-Making," unpublished paper prepared for the Naval Postgraduate School (Monterey, Calif., December, 1981), p. 48. He has since denied any such statement or that sales anywhere approximated such sums, in a communication to the author, 26 July 1983.

46. Bank of Israel, 1982, p. 2; *Israel Government Yearbook 1982/3*, p. 92.

47. *Newsview*, 17 January 1984. The main increase was in electrical communications equipment, most of which was military in nature, *Israeli Industry*, 1982, p. 10.

48. *Haaretz*, 13 January 1983. Dun and Bradstreet (Israel) noted that the fall in exports would have been considerably worse had it not been for a real growth in the export of electrical items of 20 percent, *JP*, 21 July 1983. Later figures covering 1983 show the decline has continued, although not as steeply as other export branches. For example, industrial exports in 1983 dropped by 6.5 percent, those of agriculture by 9.5 percent, *Israel Economist*, January, 1984. p. 33.

49. *Israeli Industry*, p. 11.

50. *J P*, 10 November and 18 October 1982.

51. *Newsview*, 17 January 1984. p. 16; *Israel Government Yearbook, 1982/3*, p. 92.

52. Rivlin, pp. 152–153. Arms exports are estimated as increasing at an average annual rate of 20 to 30 percent. *Newsview*, 20 April 1982; see also, M. Dunn, "Israel's Arms Exports Booming," *Strategy Week*, 24–30 November 1980, pp. 8–9.

53. Some economic analysts actually place the figure even higher, and closer to one-third of industrial exports. See, for example, Gad Yaacobi, Labor Party member of the Knesset Finance Committee, *Maariv*, 17 May 1983. Government officials usually insist that defense sales not exceed one-quarter of industrial exports, *Maariv*, 6 May 1983. *The Sunday Telegraph* report claims 21 percent. Industry Minister Patt, writing in a special twenty-two page advertising supplement in the 19 September 1983 issue of *Fortune*, gave figures of $5.5 billion in exports and of $3.5 billion worth of industrial goods (excluding diamonds), hence the figure of one-third. Exports of goods in 1984 were $5.5 billion.
54. Freedman (p. 380) shows British arms exports constituting only 3.5 percent of total exports.
55. In a statement of exceptional candor the governor of the Bank of Israel, Dr. Moshe Mandelbaum, conceded that were it not for dollars earned from worldwide trade in arms the country in 1982 might have gone under economically. *Maariv*, 8 June, 18 October 1982.
56. *Israel Economist*, March, 1984. p. 7.
57. Kolodziej in McGowan and Kegley, p. 162.

5

THE DEFENSE INDUSTRIES

One group within the Israeli society which readily associates itself with the commercial and economic necessities of weapons manufacture leading to foreign sales is the defense industry. Not only do its members embrace the economic thesis behind Israel's arms transfers diplomacy, but they can usually be found at the forefront of those most actively engaged in promoting the cause. Thus located at the apex, the military-industrial sector has developed into the country's fastest-growing industry and, as seen in the previous chapter, has become a major exporter.[1]

In point of practice there is no single arms industry in Israel. The reference is to a number of local business enterprises fusing advanced technology with a broad spectrum of skills and producing an impressive inventory of systems and equipment having a direct military application. If the term "military-industrial complex" enters the discussion, it is not used in the American context, to suggest anything sinister or conspiratorial against genuine Israeli national interests, but rather in the sense of "a subtle interplay of interests and perceptions"[2] shared by those comprising the defense manufacturing sector.

The armaments industry is, by Israeli standards, of vast proportions. A recent edition of Israel's arms exports register contains advertisements by no fewer than 112 companies variously involved in the manufacture of exportable military equipment.[3] The list, while not inclusive, is fairly representative.

Achidatex Ltd.
A.E.L. Israel Ltd. (Elisra Electronic Systems)
Aerotec Consultants
Agat Ltd. — Polyurethan Products
   Design & Manufacturing
Alchut Electronic Engineering Ltd.
Alexander Schneider Ltd.
Amcor Export Ltd.
Aryt Optical Industries Ltd.
Astronautics C.A. Ltd.
Automotive Industries Ltd.

Bet-Shemesh Engines Ltd.

Chemoplast Ltd. — Plastic Factory
CLAL Group Ltd.
   Beta Engineering & Development Ltd.
   Electra Mikun Ltd.
   Electronics Corporation of Israel
   Isrex-Israel General Trading Co. Ltd.
   Microguide Ltd.
   Rubber Factory Franz Levi Ltd.
Cyclone-Aviation Products Ltd.

Datic Cable Works Ltd.
Degem Systems Ltd.

Eagle-Military Gear Overseas Ltd.
Elbit Computers Ltd.
Elbit Nes-Ziona Plant
Electra (Israel) Ltd.
Elul Technologies Ltd.
Eshed
Explosives Industry Ltd.
Eytan Building Design Ltd.

Fibrotex Ltd.

Gamid Rubber Products and Plastics
G. Shoef Laboratory

Haargaz Ltd.
Hagor Company Ltd.
Hanan Rabinovitz Ltd.
Hancal System Engineering
Haogenplast Ltd.-Plastic Industries
Hish Steel Works Ltd.

IAI — Israel Aircraft Industries Ltd.
   Aircraft Manufacturing Division
   Bedek Aviation Division
   Combined Technologies Division
   Electronics Division
   Elta Electronics Industries Ltd.
   Engineering Division

Golan Metal & Electronics Industries Ltd.
Magal-Detection & Alert Systems
Mata Helicopters, Jerusalem
Mamta-Composite Structures
MBT Weapon Systems
PML-Precision Mechanisms Ltd.
Ramta-Structures and Systems
SHL-Hydraulics Services Lod
Tamam-Precision Instruments Industries
Teud-Technical Publications
IDC-Industries Development Corporation Ltd.
IMI-Israel Military Industries
ICS-International System Consultants
Iscar Blades Ltd.
Ispra-Israel Product Research Co. Ltd.
Israel Shipyards Ltd.
Israel Winding Wires Ltd.

Jolan-Engineering & Consulting Co. Ltd.

Koor Communication & Security Systems Ltd.
Koor Electric & Electronics Ltd.
Koor Inter-Trade (ASIA) Ltd.
Koor Metals Ltd.
  Agan Engineering Works
  Ramim Engineering Works Ltd.
  Simat Works
  Vulcan Engineering Works
Koortrade Ltd. – Defense Supply Department

Limat – Metal Polishing Ltd.

Mamor Works Ltd.
Metal Works Netzer Sereni
Mifal Mivza Co. Ltd.
Ministry of Defense
Moore Architects Ltd.
Motorola Israel Ltd.
MTLM Mechanica Karmiel Ltd.
M. Urman & Co. Ltd.

Nimda Ltd.

Odmat Rotem-Export & International Trade

Orbit-Advanced Technologies Ltd.
Orlite Engineering Co. Ltd.

Polyziv-Plastics Products

Rad Computers Ltd.
Raem Gears Ltd.
Rafael-Ministry of Defense

Scientific Translations International Ltd.
Shalon-Chemical Industries Ltd.
Shtoolplan—Metal Works Ltd.
Soltam Ltd.
Spectronix Ltd.

Tadiran Israel Electronics Industries Ltd.
Tama Plastics Industries
Tamuz-Systems Ltd.
T.A.T.-Aero Equipment Industries Ltd.
Technical Writing Ltd.
Talkoor Ltd.-Electronics Industries
T.G.L. (Aviation) Rubber Co. Ltd.
The Electronic Wire & Cable Co. of Israel Ltd.
Thermofil Ltd.
Thermonir Ltd.-Thermotechnics & Mechanical Works
T.I.L.-Aviation Consultants Ltd.

Urdan Industries Ltd.

Vishay Israel Ltd.
Vulcan Foundries Ltd.
Vultex Ltd.
Ypoos Ltd.-Design & Counseling

At least 58,000 people, comprising a large part of the entire Israeli work force, are employed by the military industries. Whether as manufacturer or prime employer the fact is that managers and companies constituting this complex form a powerful interest group. Their influence upon the economy is substantial. More particularly, their support for the government and its pro-arms sales orientation is enthusiastic and unequivocal, justified in their eyes by the compelling arguments of jobs, profit, foreign trade, and national economic growth.

As a group the military enterprises are identifiable by a distinctive set of characteristics. To being with, there tends to be a high degree of concentration around a few large firms. These "prime contractors"—a handful of companies—are engaged in the design, development, and production of entire weapons systems. Most of the other companies are subcontractors engaged in the production of components or specialized parts. As a rule there exists a division of labor, since the industry is organized in such a way as to encourage company specialization and to avoid wasteful duplication.

In one of the rare instances of duplication and intercompany rivalry, both the Israel Aircraft Industry and Tadiran Israel Electronics Industries entered the market at about the same time with similar versions of a pilotless drone, the Scout and the Mastiff respectively. Once it became apparent that their stiff competition might jeopardize overseas marketing prospects, other parties intervened, and in January, 1984, IAI and Tadiran announced they would be forming a joint company to produce the drone. According to a senior defense source the agreement was made possible after the IDF submitted its own specifications for the vehicle, encouraging both sides to realize it would be more economical for them as well to join forces in exploiting the market at home and abroad.[4] In another recent instance, three companies submitted bids on a defense ministry contract worth $10 million to supply a computer system for the Lavi fighter project.[5] However both instances are the exception rather than the rule. The decision to undertake manufacture of the Lavi plane is itself symbolic, being premised upon a multicompany collaborative effort.

In one sense, geographically, the attempt is being made to achieve decentralization of the industrial complex. For a combination of reasons—demographic, strategic, and economic—the national policy is to use employment in steering Israelis away from the coastal plain and the triangle Jerusalem-Tel-Aviv-Haifa by locating branches of the larger military producers or new firms in such areas as Judea and Samaria (the West Bank), the Negev, and northern Galilee, which have been targeted for development. But this decentralization of businesses, personnel, and communities engaged in military manufacture has also created a broad base of vested interest in, and support for, the arms industry, applying pressure for a strong weapons export campaign.

As a group the defense enterprises are distinctive for their excellent management and labor relations. At the same time, because of the nature of the work in which they are engaged, motivation is exceptionally high due to the perceived sense of contributing to the nation's ultimate security. This *esprit* is reflected by such comments as "we need entrepreneurs, not military heroes," implying that bravery was no longer enough in defending Israel; or "we need $10 billion in exports, not $10 billion in aid."[6] In keeping with this extended definition of what makes for a strong Israel, one of their aims is to keep the IDF at a high level of military preparedness. Appealing to this patriotism, Defense Minister Moshe Arens told the Aircraft Industry engineers: "Should

I come to the conclusion that we can't count upon your total dedication and willingness to work day and night without interruption, I would have no choice but to cancel the entire Lavi project!"[7] IAI, for example, has suffered virtually no slowdown in production due to strikes or slowdowns for twenty-eight years.[8]

Military contractors on the whole share a third characteristic, what might be referred to as a pioneering spirit. Their entire approach is progressive. Company directors remain open to fresh ideas and innovative techniques;[9] they employ advanced technology, insist on quality and product reliability, work at constant upgrading and product improvement, have not been impeded by institutional inertia, and have had to grapple less with theoretical problems than with practical ones arising from actual rather than simulated war conditions. Such guidelines alert the defense firms to the ever-present need for additional strides if Israel is to outpace both the Arab countries and its major arms competitors. These qualities, therefore, extend to aggressive overseas marketing as well; and they have enhanced the reputation of Israeli military products abroad.[10]

Export-consciousness logically becomes the fourth characteristic shared by the firms constituting the military industries complex. This originates in the growth of the larger corporations and their transformation from modest beginnings in the fifties into highly-productive concerns; they geared themselves to continued high levels of production and sales, only to witness by the late seventies a real decline in the national budget base. Defense cuts were imposed and IDF orders no longer consume full output.

In response, some of the companies have tried to organize in fighting defense ministry cutbacks and its preference at times to purchase equipment in the United States. Otherwise, however, what has happened is that having outgrown the home market, save for wartime, yet obviously interested more than ever in doing business, the companies are drawn increasingly toward foreign markets and the opportunity to sell overseas, not infrequently with the government's full encouragement. Alarmed at the economic recession, their collective answer lies in technology, efficiency, and export. Foreign arms sales gradually have come to exceed domestic sales[11] in keeping with this so-called "substitution effect"[12] and quest for profits. Two factors have contributed to this: one, the defense industries remain the beneficiaries of between 20 to 33 percent of the national defense budget, part of which is used for further weapons research and development;[13] two, that some of these industries have demonstrated an ability to penetrate foreign markets and to compete with Western giant defense contractors.

The latter point raises another aspect common to all Israeli firms which are building their corporate futures on the growth of defense exports. There is a strong element of risk. The growing imbalance in the origin of procurement orders exposes the defense manufacturers to the danger of depending too much on external market conditions, upon the standards and policies of the pace setters in worldwide conventional arms transfers, and, lastly, upon Israel's diplomatic standing. For the present, however, corporate thinking within the military industries complex remains upbeat in meeting these challenges. Following an export slump in 1982–1983, the recession at home and the opening of new markets abroad combine with the reputation of Israeli arms in accelerating arms and military technology transfers by many of Israel's leading companies.

One final point needs to be mentioned before concluding this profile of the defense industry as a whole and turning to some of its individual components. Military procurement in Israeli terms has created an industrial giant, perhaps the single most powerful interest group in the country today. Its influence is felt, for example, in the decision to go ahead with the Lavi project, expected to cost well upwards of a billion dollars, with many local firms awarded government contracts.

Moreover, the larger defense companies and most aspects of their operations, including foreign sales, are free from public examination for reasons of national security; only rarely, such as in the annual report of the state comptroller, is behind-the-scenes insight provided into some aspects of these firms' practices and administration. And while it is true that pressures for arms exports derive from two sources—national and private—nevertheless, in some important respects the military industries complex has assumed a corporate life of its own. Private interests (jobs, production, sales, profits), therefore, can predominate, as when profit motives apparently were behind the attempt to supply spare parts and other military equipment to Iran in its conflict with Iraq.

EXPORTING FIRMS

It will help to appreciate the centrality of the Israeli defense industry by surveying the principal manufacturers, their areas of expertise, and export emphases. Various attempts have been made to identify those industrial subsectors relevant for arms production.[14] A catalog of Israeli military products and exports encompasses the following eight basic categories:

- *aviation*: aircraft, weapons and control systems, flight control systems, aircraft equipment and instruments, manufacturing and maintenance, airfield equipment.
- *ships*: ferrying and bridging facilities, naval craft and weapons, marine equipment.
- *ordnance*: small arms and ammunition, hand grenades, mines, demolition charges, weapon control systems, tear gas, maintenance.
- *armor*: tanks and ancillary equipment, military vehicles, fire control and navigation systems, parts.

- *communications*: communications systems, radar, electronics, command and control systems, training systems, antennas and accessories, wires and cables.
- *optics*: glasses, lenses and optical equipment, laser rangefinders, night vision, power supplies.
- *personal gear*: helmets, gas masks, protective clothes and covers, webbing and tents.
- *security items*: field security equipment, intruder detection systems, military support equipment.

Three central pillars of the military industry are active in nearly all of these areas of production: the Israel Aircraft Industries, the Israel Military Industries (IMI) and the Armament Development Authority. In a class by themselves, they are state-owned and under governmental control.

THE ISRAEL AIRCRAFT INDUSTRIES (IAI)

Established in 1953 and initially known as "Bedek," or the Institute for the Reconditioning of Planes, the IAI is the largest industrial enterprise in the State of Israel, the largest employer, and the largest single industrial exporter.[15] It is also the biggest and the most prestigious of the arms producers. The IAI has had corporate status since 1968; government-owned and autonomously controlled by the Ministry of Defense, today it is a sprawling network of five divisions and some fourteen subsidiary firms. On its executive board sit representatives of the ministries of defense, finance, transport, commerce, and industry.

These links to the defense establishment have served the company well. Close collaboration with the IDF enables designers to make rapid improvements in current models deriving from battlefield experience; as IAI's director boasted: "we have the wisest, most sophisticated, experienced and knowledgeable customer in the world."[16] Consequently, in the 1960s IAI — or *Hata'assiya Ha'avrit* in Hebrew — was a world pioneer in naval missilry and one of the first to station sea missiles on small patrol boats. Second, the IDF's successful employment of IAI systems provides ample advertisement to foreign purchasing missions. A third benefit of government ties is the U.S. market which has opened to IAI as a result of offset agreements between the two countries; in the last four years the company has increased its work as a subcontractor to such American military aircraft manufacturers as McDonnell-Douglas (F-15) and General Dynamics (F-16).

Some of the 400 products and services marketed by the company on five continents are explicitly nonmilitary, such as the refurbishing of Boeing aircraft. Yet even some of its civilian products, like the Arava and Westwind planes, are advertised by IAI itself as being adaptable for military use. Though designed primarily for civilian use, the former is billed as a multimission military aircraft.[17] The Arava 202 version, in addition to range performance and fuel efficiency, is designed to perform a variety of missions including: parachuting, assault transport, casualty evacuation, cargo paradrop, and motor conveyance as well as passenger transport. So, too, the Seascan maritime patrol plane derived from the Westwind executive jet. An all-weather, long-range aircraft, the modified Westwind is deployed by the IDF and the armed forces of several other countries for marine reconnaîssance, signal intelligence, antisubmarine warfare or even, depending upon its configuration, as an air-to-sea missile platform.

In 1975 the IAI delivered its first Kfir planes, designed and produced in Israel, to the Israeli Air Force. Success in undertaking local manufacture of so sophisticated a plane as the Kfir, together with its performance in actual warfare, stimulated the interest of prospective customers abroad. Under pressure from the IAI, the Rabin government gave its approval in 1976 for marketing the Kfir abroad; however, the export initiative ran into political obstacles, especially from Washington, and therefore has been a disappointment. The ambitious Kfir experiment at assembling an indigenous fighter plane with a value added of 60 to 70 percent has encouraged IAI and government agencies to undertake an even more venturesome project in the 1980s, one whose export potential is no less uncertain. IAI planners aim at full production by 1991 of the Lavi tactical fighter aircraft. In the interim, until the Lavi becomes operational, IAI is filling the gap by producing the newer version of the Kfir C-2, the Kfir C-7, praised by experts for accuracy and versatility in ground attack as well as aerial combat.

With an eye upon the international market, the IAI aerospace complex is emphasizing two forms of diversification. Acknowledging some of the problems of selling costly and sophisticated aircraft to Third World customers, it has lowered its sights somewhat. One result is its program of combat aircraft upgrading or retrofit. Spiraling fighter plane procurement costs to the point of prohibiting acquisition of modern aircraft are common to smaller countries. In order to compete in the modern combat arena the alternative lies in improving the operational capabilities of existing aircraft; and the IAI has made a name for itself by offering comprehensive upgrading packages to countries whose air forces are built around Western planes, such as the French Mirage or the U.S. A-4 Skyhawk. Similarly, directors of the firm are hopeful that in addition to Israel's own air force those of other countries will be interested in buying its improved version of the Fouga-Magister trainer plane, the Tsukit.[18]

The second area for diversification does not fall squarely under the category of aviation. Responding to IDF requirements the IAI years ago moved into other areas, predominantly naval warfare and missile development. Easily the most popular export item manufactured by IAI is the Gabriel MK III, a third generation of the combat-proven Gabriel missile family.[19] As reflected by the Israeli Navy's operational experience in 1973, the Gabriel is a radar-guided missile which can be launched from an aircraft or ship to skim at low level across bodies of water at an effective range of 36 kilometers. Another advanced sea-skimming supersonic missile system sold by the IAI is the Barak, used as a defense for ships against aircraft and missiles. Other naval needs met by IAI designers are filled by the Dvora 71 combat boat which is described as a fast missile craft capable of serving as a long-range patrol boat or for harbor police and customs duties, armed escort and in-shore assault. In this same category are earlier models, the Dabur and Shapirit fast patrol boats, also manufactured by the IAI, in active service with the Israeli Navy and reported to be operational in several foreign navies. Reported under development at present are an antimissile missile and a helicopter pad capable of being assembled on small ships of 400 tons or more.[20]

Lately, the IAI has come to international attention by pioneering in yet a different field, that of unmanned drones. Its SCOUT mini-RPV (remotely piloted vehicle) system is considered one of the most advanced on the market. Employed extensively in the 1982 Lebanese War, the SCOUT is locally designed and manufactured; it is pneumatically catapulted into the air from a truck-mounted launcher, enabling takeoff without any landing strip. Similarly, retrieval is accomplished by guiding the aircraft semi-automatically toward the center of its recovery net. While in the air the SCOUT fulfills such missions as target identification, missile site reconnaissance, and battlefield combat. Here, again, it is important to stress that like a number of other Israeli military items part of the RPV's appeal to a buyer, beyond that of cost-effectiveness, is its conversion to peacetime duty, in this instance coastal and waterway control or damage assessment. In fiscal year 1983–1984 local and foreign orders for the SCOUT totaled $36 million.[21]

Foreign sales figures provided by company officials since 1981 reflect both IAI's tremendous export potential and the difficulties it encounters when Third World clients claim an inability to pay for past deliveries and present orders.[22] In 1981–1982 the company's exports for the first time approached the half-billion dollar mark only to decline by approximately 8 percent the following year.[23] The IAI's recovery is suggested by 1983–1984 export orders worth more than $500 million and represented some 65 percent of company sales; the 1984–1985 figures for total sales were $900 million.[24]

THE ISRAEL MILITARY INDUSTRIES (IMI)

The Israel Military Industries (*Ta'as*, in Hebrew) is the pioneer in the country's defense industry, its origins being in the clandestine workshops of the prestate period. 1983 marks the fiftieth anniversary of its establishment. IMI was also the first to export arms, having contracted sales in 1953–1954 with Holland, Burma, Belgium, and Turkey, followed by Italy.[25] Also government-owned and directed, IMI is the second largest defense employer, and operates thirty-one factories in eleven regional districts throughout Israel.

IMI is the principal ordnance manufacturer, supplying virtually all the needs in small arms and ammunition of the Israeli army. Of its 500 exportable products certainly the best known is the 9 mm Uzi submachine gun, found in the hands of the armed forces, anti-terrorist units and secret service of many foreign countries, including some who have no direct ties with Israel. Battle-proven in environments ranging from snow to desert, the Uzi appeals to foreign armies because it is relatively inexpensive, lightweight, and can be fired full or semi-automatic from the hip or shoulder, and therefore is equally adaptable by security police as well. Since 1973 the Uzi has been joined by another IMI product, the Galil 5.56 mm and the Galil 7.62 mm assault rifle, in service throughout the world. Of rugged and durable construction, also automatic or semi-automatic and firing standard NATO ammunition, the Galil in its different versions (including the short-barreled SAR model) can be used by any kind of military force, infantry, airborne, amphibious or armored troops.

Rocketry is another area of specialization by IMI weapons developers. Items sold abroad include Arrowhead *Chetz* tank shells, artillery shells, bomb carriers, grenades, and rocket propellants used in the Gabriel and Shafrir.[26] On the occasion of Israeli Independence Day, in May 1984, *Ta'as* displayed two of its newest items: a multiple rocket launcher which reduces reloading time from forty-six minutes to only five minutes; and an armor-piercing warhead adaptable to the TOW antitank missile capable of penetrating the Soviet T-72.[27]

Although the manufacture and development of munitions for export are given as only secondary goals of the company, evidence strongly suggests otherwise. One indication is that the position of assistant director-general includes responsibility for export as well as local sales. However, the growing emphasis upon weapons transfers is best reflected in IMI sales figures. IMI exports for the past decade have increased dramatically as seen in Table 5.1. Foreign currency income from exports during 1980 alone increased by 40 percent.[28] In 1981 this trend intensified. Exports exceeded $300 million out of a total of $500 million in the company's turnover.[29] At the end of the year its order books listed foreign contracts worth $540 million for future delivery.[30] In 1982 this distinct orientation toward foreign markets was confirmed by company spokesmen who reported total sales of $535 million, of which $350 million were in the form of overseas sales to some forty countries.[31] Noteworthy is the fact that a large share (over 53 percent) of IMI exports are the fruit of Israeli ingenuity and design.[32] Equally indicative is the shift in outlets away from the home market, as seen in Table 5.2.

The obvious inference is that world arms market conditions permitting, IMI will continue to pursue the present strategy of channelling more than 60 percent of its output to foreign customers.

Table 5.1. IMI Exports, 1970–1980.[33]

YEAR	EXPORTS (MILLION $)	ANNUAL GROWTH RATE
1970	10.1	—
1971	17.1	+ 69%
1972	20.5	+ 20%
1973	13.7	− 33%
1974	19.2	+ 40%
1975	46.8	+144%
1976	85.5	+ 81%
1977	111.5	+ 30%
1978	186.6	+ 67%
1979	200.0	+ 7%
1980	288.7	+ 44%

THE ARMAMENT DEVELOPMENT AUTHORITY (RAFAEL)

The third of the three large firms representing the core of the Israeli defense industry sector is the Rafael Armament Development Authority. It is attached to the Ministry of Defense and, as its name implies, bears major responsibility for research, design, and development of new defense systems in order to preserve the qualitative superiority of the IDF and to solve pressing battlefield problems as they arise.

By the nature of its work, much of Rafael's activity is broadly diversified and highly classified. Since 1967 it has supplied the Israeli Army with over one hundred different systems developed by Rafael, some of which involve the most advanced technologies in guided weaponry and electronic warfare, electro-optics and thermal imaging, missile detection and propulsion, and a

Table 5.2. IMI Distribution Patterns.[34]

% OF SUPPLIES TO	1978	1979	1980	1981
IDF	38.0	40.6	36.4	35.9
Exports	55.6	54.4	61.2	62.3

score of other related areas. Two-thirds of its staff of approximately 6,000 are scientists, engineers, and highly trained technical personnel. A full two-thirds of its total operating budget is allocated to R & D.

Because so much of Rafael's activities are shrouded in secrecy, it is hard to guess at its direct contribution to the Israeli arms export drive. The sales turnover for 1983 was $300 million.[35] In 1982 company officials declared export earnings of only $10 million, which seems rather low.[36] Yet at the same time they offer indications of giving greater attention in the near future to overseas trade. In revealing a device designed to neutralize hollow charge anti-tank missiles, Rafael's director-general, Ze'ev Bonen, in 1983 entertained the hope, for example, that it would be sold to friendly countries.[37] The device has since been exhibited in the United States after receiving government consent in principle to such sales. In a similar vein, Rafael is engaged in joint ventures with some of the world's leading weapons manufacturers.[38] Among those few items advertised for sale to foreign armies are the David family of artillery computers and the Shafrir 2 air-to-air missile.[39] On display at the 1983 Paris Air Show were three of Rafael's newer generation of missile systems: the combat-proven Python III air-to-air missile; the ship-defense anti-missile missile, PDM (Barak); and a surface-to-air system.

Rafael's direct share of arms exports may appear to be insignificant, yet its impact upon the national economy and defense industry is quite real. On the one hand, the orders for parts placed by Rafael with some 320 small industrial manufacturers around the country contribute both to industrial production and employment.[40] In 1984, by way of further example, Rafael opened its new research and armaments production facility in the lower Galilee; another was due to open in nearby Carmiel. Part of a plan to develop that section of the country, both plants are to employ several thousand people on various projects, including ways of commercially exploiting technologies refined at Rafael and geared for export.[41] On the other hand, a number of designs originally developed by Rafael have been subcontracted to the IMI and others to be incorporated in defense items sold abroad, thus making an indirect contribution to the inventory of Israeli transfers.

Moving to the private sector, one discovers two of Israel's largest conglomerates active in defense manufacture through several of their subsidiary companies. The gigantic Koor concern, which employs 34,000 workers and whose share of Israeli industrial exports in 1983 was 15 percent, registered foreign sales of $512 million that year.[42] Koor Industries is represented in the defense area by such subsidiary companies as Soltam, Telrad, and Tadiran. In accounting for an impressive 9 percent growth in Koor's exports for 1983, officials singled out each of the three for special mention.[43]

Tadiran, employing 12,000 people, is Koor's largest exporter, and second only to IAI among all Israeli exporting firms. Although figures differ slightly, its overseas trade in 1982 was between $157 and $180 million, in 1983, an estimated $194 million;[44] Tadiran reported about $600 million worth of business in 1984, of which 40 percent — or approximately $245 million — were exports. Directing twenty-four factories and plants of its own, Tadiran is best known for its manufacture of air conditioners and radios. But the company is quite active in the military field, notably in the area of tactical communication. It produces intelligence-gathering and electronic warfare techniques, the Mastiff drone, night-sensing devices, and tank range-finders, some of which, like the HF-700 series of military radio sets, are sold abroad. Tadiran is also one of the few military suppliers to have successfully penetrated the protectionist American market.

Close cooperation with the Israeli army, now reinforced by U.S.-oriented industrial expertise and standards, has won wide recognition for Tadiran's military products. Current production embraces every type of military communications gear: radio equipment, from miniature transceivers to carrier systems, and line equipment of all kinds; field telephones, audio accessories, and mobile communication centrals; computerized command and control for air, sea and ground forces; and weapons systems simulators and complete integrated communications of COMINT/ELINT/EW complexes. Military products such as these account for a full 33 percent of the company's sales.

They also represent a major share of Tadiran's export success. Evidence of its military-export orientation includes the following: it benefits from the fact that Koor Industries, the parent group, is active on six continents with forty-five offices in major marketing centers; goods are now sold in about fifty countries, with the bulk going to the industrialized Western countries; in some of these countries, a big effort is underway to circumvent export obstacles through arranging for joint ventures; and in one case, that of the Shamir communications system, Tadiran developed a product first for an overseas customer and only then contacted the IDF in encouraging local procurement.[45] Today exports by Tadiran are 42 to 45 percent of its business, and, as reported by company executives, a full 80 percent of the company's exports are in the security or military fields.[46]

Telrad, fully owned by Koor, directs 13 percent of its turnover to the Israeli defense establishment and is judged to be the fifteenth largest company in Israel, with sales of $100 million in 1983. It specializes in telecommunications equipment and many of its systems have military application. Claiming to supply thirty countries, Telrad increased its exports by 100 percent in one year in response to the decline in IDF orders: from $15 million in 1982 to $30 million in 1983.[47] Its sister company is Soltam, whose overseas military sales in 1982–1983 make it the country's seventh largest industrial exporter. Export figures for 1982–1983 were between $60 and $67 million,[48] and included such items as the 155 mm. gun howitzer and the 81 mm. mortar.[49]

Clal Industries Ltd. is the second Israeli conglomerate with a stake in military manufacture and export. An employer of 11,000 people, Clal had export earnings of $134 million in 1983.[50] One of its subsidiaries, Urdan Industries Ltd., has the largest foundry in Israel for armored steel castings and employs 1,200 workers. It was established in support of the Merkava main battle tank program, and manufactures parts for the hull, turret, and suspension system. Successful merchandising of the Merkava abroad would, of course, increase Urdan's production, export sales, and profits. The Merkava aside, the company credits itself with contracts for millions of dollars worth of armored steel parts and kits for tank construction and upgrading won in many countries, including the American defense industry and Department of Defense. Together with IMI, Urdan is responsible for the M-47 (Rhino) tank conversion project which gives improved firepower and general performance to a tank which still forms part of the defense backbone in several countries. The Rhino is a new tank configuration whose overall performance is equal to such tanks as the M-60 in mobility, firepower, and reliability yet at a fraction of the cost of an equivalent new model, making it an acceptable solution to cost-conscious developing countries. Export sales in 1981 were valued at $11.1 million; in 1982 at $9.6 million, with 85 percent labeled military exports; and in 1983 reached $17 million.[51]

The leading growth area within the military industries complex is that of computer technology and electronic warfare devices which are a key component of today's state-of-the-art weapons systems. One of the Israeli leaders in this field is Electro-Optics Industries, Ltd. (El-Op). It advertises itself as a "science-based, defense-oriented integrated technology enterprise." Owned by Tadiran and the Federmann Group, the firm is located near the Weizmann Institute of Science and employs 1,200 people, many of them with specialized training and scientific skills. The firm specializes in passive night vision; IR thermal imaging systems; laser range finding; laser communications; tank periscopes for commander, driver and gunner; computerized fire control systems; avionic instrumentation; boresights; and intrusion detection systems.[52] Two of its more recent achievements are the Matador computerized tank fire control system, and an air-defense system for ships known commercially as Spirtas (Shipboard Passive Infra-Red Target Acquisition System) which company managers hope to sell to a number of countries.[53]

El-Op's sales policy leans heavily upon export. On the one hand, Akiva Meir, its general manager, has been outspoken in criticizing the cutback in local defense orders, cautioning that without a strong home-based defense industry "we will not be able to compete in world markets and to develop new systems that are unique. Instead we will be left with producing spare parts."[54] Presently ranked sixty-fourth among the country's industries, on the other hand, El-Op's international activities can be seen in the fact that half of its output is exported, and mainly for military use. In dollar terms, this meant approximately $15 million in 1982 and between $35 and $38 million in 1983.[55] In planning for the future, El-Op aims to preserve the balance of 50 percent production for the IDF and 50 percent for the foreign market.

Elron Electronics Industries is an industrial holding company with affiliates in the defense sector. Foremost among these is Elbit, which has grown rapidly to meet the market for advanced military electronics and which specializes in products having military as well as civilian applications. In its military trade advertisements, Elbit promotes "battle bred" weapons delivery and navigation systems, "developed in interaction with and flown by the Israel air force", of a highly technical nature, such as digital computerized multimode weapons systems. Although local sales are more than half, nevertheless, exports by Elbit in 1982–1983 reached as high as 38 percent of its entire turnover.[56] Sales figures for the year ending March 31, 1984, were $118.6 million, almost $25 million more than the previous year; of this between $42 and $50 million came from exports.[57] In February, 1984, Elbit announced it had won a $6 million order from an undisclosed European country to supply naval communication, command, and control systems.[58] Company president Uzia Galil visualizes Elbit's work as representing "a window into the worldwide electronic and defense market" and expressed confidence that its participation in defense sales would be further enhanced by complementary acquisitions overseas, thereby further stimulating export growth.[59]

The list of electronics firms includes several others active in the field of electronic warfare. Elisra Electronic Systems, formerly A.E.L. Israel Ltd., is a major supplier of early warning equipment and components to the IDF. Company sales in 1983 exceeded $50 million, and about 30 percent ($12 million) of total sales were exported to other governments.[60] Elisra works in cooperation with IAI and IMI, and was awarded the Israel Defense Prize for 1983 in recognition of its contribution to the Israeli navy and air force. Future export efforts are targeted for North America and Europe since the Third World in general is not regarded as a likely customer for most of its advanced systems. Even so, Elisra claimed foreign orders of $100 million and forecast export figures of $30 million in 1984.[61]

Another company to watch is Elta Electronics Industries Ltd., a subsidiary of IAI, which manufactures electric warning and radar systems. The company's foreign sales record is impressive, less for volume than for rate of growth: $7 million in 1977 to $25 million in 1983 and a target of $50 million for 1984.[62] If reached, it would mean that its exports, too, were approaching 50 percent of annual turnover. Motorola Israel Ltd, in addition to its nonmilitary products, manufactures electronic military equipment, some of which is included in the company's exports, $45 million in 1983.[63]

Several smaller firms have a hand in the field of metals and armor. Ramta Structures and Systems, a division of IAI, produces three types of ships — the Dvora, the Dabur, and the Shapirit — which have penetrated the international market for smaller, comparatively light patrol craft. Iscar Blades Ltd. is a manufacturer of high quality precision forged parts; it is now producing over 600,000 airfoils a year, 90 percent of which are exported.[64] Nimda Ltd. is another company specializing in retrofit and repowering programs for military vehicles, both from Eastern bloc series as well as various Western main battle tanks, including Centurions, M-4, Patton series tanks, and such light armored vehicles as AMX and M-113 personnel carriers. Also playing a part is Vulcan Foundries, since it maintains a special line in its steel foundry for military products. Early in 1984 attempts were initiated to effect a consolidation of Vulcan with its competitor, Urdan. The Carmel Forge Company, a subsidiary of Soltam, produces a range of airframe and jet engine forgings. Some 20 percent of its high quality forgings have direct military application, and it is an approved supplier of some of the largest aircraft and jet engine manufacturers in the world.[65] Ashot Ashkelon is listed here because 80 percent of its metal products are defined as military in nature, and since a large share of the $32.7 million earned from export in 1982 derived from overseas military sales, helping to make it the thirty-third biggest industry in Israel.[66]

Two other countries engaged in similar heavy defense work by right ought to be included among the large contractors. Yet they have been set aside for separate mention because of their present problematic state. Israel Shipyards, Ltd., located in Haifa, is active in the construction of naval craft, including hydrofoil patrol boats and the Saar, licensed for assembly abroad. Its most successful item is the Reshef missile and gun boat whose maneuverability, speed, and firing accuracy were demonstrated convincingly to foreign military observers in naval engagements against Soviet-built Osa and Komar missile boats in the October War of 1973. Merely to suggest the range of one company's products, Israel Shipyards over more than twenty years has built container ships, floating docks, cargo ships, dredgers, seagoing tugs, and landing craft for both Israeli and foreign flags. Bet Shemesh Engines Ltd., on the other hand, is Israel's center for developing, planning, manufacturing, overhauling, and repairing turbojet engines. Its leading export item is the Sorek 4 expendable turbojet engine used in remotely-piloted vehicles, drones, and missiles.

In their peak years both companies participated directly in the surge of defense manufacture and international sales. However they are in the midst of a crisis of several years' standing: Bet Shemesh — essentially as a result of management problems and the drop in government backing; Israel Shipyards — owing to stiffer world competition in shipbuilding and a decline in overseas orders. Bet Shemesh has accumulated financial losses which stood at $60 million by the end of 1983; its hopes for recovery depend largely upon the share it is given in the manufacture and assembly of engine components for the Lavi plane.[67] It is more likely, however, that a significant number of the engines will be built in the United States, which could mean hundreds of millions of dollars lost to the Israel economy. Israel Shipyards, which ran a deficit of $5.5 million just in the first half of 1983, has yet to find a solution to its plight, although one suggested course is to gear itself away from military construction to the servicing and repair of other countries' merchant vessels as well as naval craft.[68]

By contrast, several newer and smaller Israeli firms are in an expansionist phase, representative of those defense contractors who have responded well to the world demand for military goods. Eagle Military Gear Overseas Ltd., or *Ayit*, was formed in 1979. It offers a broad range of military and combat equipment as well as professional advice; recently, it has undertaken the production of items used for defense against chemical warfare. Eagle operates three factories in Israel, and in 1984 purchased an American firm with an annual turnover of $15 million as a means of strengthening its business dealings in the United States. Total sales for 1983 stood at $25 million — a 40 percent increase over the previous year;[69] and as further indication of Eagle's export emphasis it has purchasing officers in the United States, Europe, Central America, Southeast Asia, and the Middle East. Apart from its position as a large supplier to the Israeli army, the company claims to be a supplier to foreign armies throughout the world, and also represents the products of Elbit, El-Op, and other Israeli companies.[70] Two of its competitors in the export of military gear are *Chagor*, an affiliate of the *Histadrut*, the Israeli Labor Federation, and Rabintex, a textile manufacturer. Founded in 1951 as a small family enterprise 90 percent of whose output went to the IDF, Rabintex presently employs 360 workers. Its 1982 sales report indicates a 92 percent increase which is best explained by a conscious decision to seek overseas outlets; by 1985 the company hopes to achieve parity in the foreign versus local component of its production.[71]

Increased exports also account for the growth of Cyclone Aviation Products Ltd., established in 1969. Formerly geared to the local market, in the last few years it has sought to diversify its sales in order to lessen its dependence upon Defense Ministry orders. Exports as of 1983 comprised 30 percent of sales.[72] Drawing upon a reserve of experienced Israel air force veterans as well as professional and technical manpower, Cyclone began by assembling parts for the Mirage 5, followed by the Kfir fighter series, and then the maintenance of light planes, transport planes, and fighters. After the 1973 war the firm began to concentrate on renovating, altering, and maintaining helicopters. Manufacturing parts for the Kfir accounts for 15 to 17 percent of the firm's turnover. Future development plans are tied in part to production of the Lavi, but also to the American and the international markets as an approved supplier to General Dynamics, Corvair, Boeing, Pratt/Whitney, McDonnell Douglas, Sikorsky, and Hispano Suiza.[73]

Many more firms operating on a smaller scale also exist as part of the sprawling Israeli defense industries. Less-known yet active both in Israel and abroad are companies like Fibronics, a manufacturer of computerized communication equipment with exports of over $5 million (80 percent of its production); Astronautics C. A. Ltd.; Condor Pacific, a new company making navigational stabilizers for tanks; Achidatex Ltd., specializing in military storage units; Mechola, with a range of hydraulic equipment; and Spectronix Ltd., whose orders of $21 million at the beginning of 1984 include military fire extinguishing and explosion suppression systems.

The listing of such Israeli firms can never be fully up-to-date given their tendency to proliferate, with new companies springing up to exploit the market for specialized military technologies or services, and others which operate unnoticed and in the shadow of IAI, IMI, El-Op, and the other major defense manufacturers. The economic fair held in Jerusalem in May 1984, in addition to the periodic international military exhibitions and air shows, brought attention to these little-known companies, such as *Degem* Systems Ltd. which reports upon fifteen years of international business transactions, including military maintenance and training projects in some sixty countries.[74] The IDF itself, with some $200 million worth of surplus equipment reportedly sold in 1982–1983 outside of the country by diverse means, deserves to be included at the end of this list of domestic exporters of military goods.[75]

This profile is thus far from exhaustive. Rather, it is meant to be representative, and in support of the thesis that the defense industry in Israel is a predominant economic factor essential for national growth and stability. Organized into specialized areas and with factories dispersed throughout the country, the military industries and those private concerns indirectly geared to defense production are in the forefront of Israel's scientific, technological, and industrial progress. What began years ago in interludes of armistice or uneasy truce with the Arab states and to preserve the capacity for shifting quickly to full wartime production has since assumed an importance of its own. And in the calculations of these industries, from the smallest to the largest, their ability to maintain scientific standards, competitiveness, and growth in the future is linked intimately with the success of each one's military export program.[76] The economic prominence of these enterprises, in turn, becomes political power as sensitivity for the dollars and good business sense value of an Israeli arms transfer diplomacy enters the arms policymaking process.

NOTES

1. An Israeli economist has written recently: "In view of its large share of total industrial production, a detailed study of the defense industry is essential for research into the country's economic development, its industrial sector, and its productivity." Eitan Berglas, *Defense and the Economy: The Israeli Experience*, The Maurice Falk Institute for Economic Research in Israel, (Jerusalem, 1983), discussion paper no. 83.01, p. 36. Due in large part to the difficulty in amassing data, however, no such quantitative study has been completed. Our concern here is limited to a qualitative analysis with emphasis on the ultimate political importance of the defense industry in general, more particulary its role in the arms trade policy. The

best study of the defense industries, now outdated, is in Hebrew, Yosef Evron, *Hatassiva Habitchonit B'Yisrael* (Tel-Aviv: Eydanim, 1978). A recent effort is by Robert E. Harkavy and Stephanie G. Neuman, "Israel," in James Everett Katz, ed., *Arms Production in Developing Countries* (Lexington MA: D.C. Heath, 1984), pp. 193–223.

2. Steven Rosen, ed. *Testing the Theory of the Military-Industrial Complex* (Lexington, MA: Lexington Books, 1973), p. 24.

3. Ministry of Defense (Defense Sales), *Israel Defense Sales Directory*, 1983 (Petach Tikva: Ypoos Ltd., 1983).

4. *Haaretz*, 4 January 1984. Criticism of such competition, without naming the companies concerned, was voiced by the State Controller in his 34th Annual Report (May, 1984), p. 693.

5. *Haaretz*, 28 December 1983. The three firms were Elbit, Rada, Isra-el.

6. Quoted in a series of interviews with Israeli industrialists, *Forbes* 7 November 1983, pp. 134–142.

7. Related by Arens in an interview with *Maariv*, 27 January 1984.

8. Gidor, p. 260.

9. The open approach to weapons research and development is told in the stories of Uzi Gal (*NYT*, 7 February 1982); Yisrael Galili, designer of the Galil rifle (*Maariv*, 4 May 1984); and Al Ellis, who turned model planes into a potent intelligence weapon, persuading Tadiran to pursue his ideas (*IHT*, 12 October 1983).

10. A voice of concern lest this pioneering spirit might be fading has been sounded by Uzi Eilam, Director-General of the Israel Atomic Energy Commission. In a talk on "The Israeli Military-Industrial Complex: Technology or Faith?" at Haifa University on 15 March 1984, he wondered aloud whether perhaps this original faith of Israelis in themselves in rising to meet challenges was beginning to decline, whether because the military industries no longer had a keen alertness to IDF operational needs, because they had grown to become a marketing and export-oriented sector rather than just a defense-oriented one, or possibly because technology and profits had become ends in and of themselves.

11. A survey conducted by the Ministry for Industry and Commerce found that 85 percent of the industrial enterprises at the end of 1983 were doing some $3 billion in export business—60 percent of Israel's total industrial exports. Some of these are leaders in military production.

12. How "substitution effect" works in Pearson, p. 222.

13. Steinberg, p. 286.

14. Herbert Wulf, in Ball and Leitenberg, p. 324, lists six relevant industries: iron and steel, nonferrous metal, metal products, electrical and nonelectrical machinery, and transportation equipment. Berglas, p. 33, distinguishes three subcategories for Israel: metal products, machinery, and electronic equipment.

15. IAI development from a one-hangar operation to today's aerospace complex is traced in Schiff and Haber, pp. 543–546.

16. Gidor, p. 260.

17. Israel, *Government Yearbook*, 1982/3, p. 134.

18. *Maariv*, 27 January 1984.

19. Missile development from the Luz via the Shafrir to the Gabriel series is related in *The Israel Yearbook*, 1982, "The Israeli Missiles: First Report," pp. 264–269. In June, 1984, it was disclosed that a billion dollars worth of Gabriel missiles had been sold in recent years. *Haaretz*, 19 June 1984.

20. *Bain Galim*, an Israeli Navy Publication, no. 136 (March, 1984), p. 36.

21. Reported by company officials, *Haaretz*, 4 May 1984.

22. *Haaretz*, 14 November 1983.
23. *IHT*, 27 May 1983 and *Haaretz*, 14 November 1983.
24. *J P*, 4 May 1984, and *Maariv*, 26 April 1985. IAI claimed another $1.3 billion in future export orders.
25. The history of *Ta'as* in Schiff and Haber, pp. 542–550.
26. Information on the "Chetz" revealed in *Maariv*, 12 February 1983.
27. *Maariv*, 6 May 1984.
28. State Controller's Report, 1982, p. 719.
29. *Israel Government Yearbook*, 1981/2, p. 129.
30. State Controller's Report, 1982, p. 723.
31. *Israel Government Yearbook*, 1982/3. p. 133; *Haaretz*, 25 February 1983.
32. *Israel Government Yearbook*, 1982/3. p. 133.
33. Figures derived from Evron, p. 307 and Berglas, p. 33.
34. Israel, State Controller, 33rd *Annual Report* for fiscal year 1981 (Jerusalem, 1983), p. 510.
35. *Haaretz*, 1 April 1984.
36. *Haaretz*, 25 February 1983.
37. *J P*, 17 October 1983.
38. *Israel Economist*, January, 1984, p. 28.
39. *Israel Defense Sales Directory*, p. 171.
40. *Israel Government Yearbook*, 1981/2, p. 130, and *J P*, 8 February 1984.
41. *Israel Government Yearbook*, 1982/3, p. 134, and *J P*, 8 February 1984.
42. *Haaretz*, 13 November 1983 and *J P*, 6 February 1984. Operations are profiled in *Kesafim*, 5–11 December 1983, pp. 28–31.
43. *Maariv*, 7 February 1984.
44. *J P*, 30 August 1983, gives the $157 million figure, whereas Dun and Bradstreet (Israel), in its 1983 report on Israel's 100 top companies offers two figures of $174 million and $180 million, p. 7. Statistics for 1983 in *Haaretz*, 9 May 1984.
45. *Haaretz*. 25 May 1984, based on an interview with Yitzhak Raviv, Vice-President and Deputy Directory for Marketing and International Operations.
46. Raviv in a separate interview with the *J P*, 3 June 1984.
47. *J P*, 24 January 1984.
48. Dun and Bradstreet, pp. 8, 58.
49. On Soltam products, as well as its marketing difficulties in the U.S., see *Maariv*, 29 April 1983 and *Haaretz*, 16 March 1983. Additional material on Soltam in *J P*, 30 August 1983 and Dun and Bradstreet, p. 13.
50. *Koteret Rashit*, 16 May 1984, p. 16; *Haaretz*, 23 March 1984.
51. *Maariv*, 27 January 1983; *Israel Defense Sales Directory*, p. 183; 1982–1983 company report, *Haaretz*, 27 June 1983; 1983 figures in *Haaretz*, 24 July 1984.
52. El-Op products surveyed in *J P*, 10 May 1984.
53. *J P*, 22 May 1984.
54. *Haaretz*, 22 May 1984; also *J P*, 22 May 1984.
55. *Maariv*, 10 December 1982; Dun/Bradstreet, p. 26; *Israel Economist*, May, 1984, p. 23; *Maariv*, 22 May 1984; and *Haaretz*, 25 May 1984.
56. *Haaretz*, 18 December 1983.
57. *J P*, 22 February and 15 June 1984.
58. *Haaretz*, 22 February 1984.
59. *J P*, 17 August 1983.
60. *Haaretz*, 25 May 1984.
61. *Haaretz*, 25 May 1984.
62. *Maariv*, 6 May 1984; products description also in *Maariv*, 4 November 1983.

63. Sixty percent of exports by Motorola are to developing countries, *Haaretz*, 25 May 1984.
64. *J P*, 9 January 1984; also *Israel Economist*, January, 1984, p. 22.
65. *Israel Economist*, January, 1984, p. 23.
66. Dun and Bradstreet, p. 22.
67. *J P* feature story, 19 August 1983; also useful is a four-part series done on Bet Shemesh by Reuven Pedatsur in *Haaretz*, 16, 22, 26 April and 16 May 1984.
68. *Haaretz*, 10 November 1983.
69. *Haaretz*, 25 April and 4 June 1984.
70. *Israel Economist*, January 1984, p. 26.
71. Dun and Bradstreet, p. 37.
72. *Haaretz*, 18 May 1984.
73. *Israel Economist*, January, 1984, p. 25, and *J P*, 28 March 1984.
74. *Haaretz*, 18 May 1984.
75. *Maariv*, 12 March 1982. This 1982 estimate was made before arms caches in southern Lebanon were seized; on the assumption that some of these have found their way into the world market, the estimate must be revised upward.
76. Characteristic of this trend of thought is IMI; its export division is now seen by officials as the key to the company's prospects and future development. *Israel Government Yearbook*, 1981/2. p. 114.

6

HOW ARMS POLICY
IS MADE IN ISRAEL

The export of arms by Israel should not be misinterpreted as being merely a case of political cynicism combined with economic opportunism. The previous chapters set Israeli involvement in global weapons transfers within the context of three basic determinants. Regional strategic imperatives are one factor. Diplomatic incentives and contemporary international norms are certainly another, while serious economic, trade and industrial considerations complete the mix of interests and motives.

Whatever the impact of these situational forces, the provision of foreign military aid remains a political act by the state. Our attention is drawn, therefore, to the domestic side of Israel's arms sales diplomacy. It is the product of an internal process, the foundations of which rest upon an exceptionally broad consensus among Israelis supportive of Israel in the role of arms supplier. In this chapter we turn to look at the manner by which the policy of weapons supply and military assistance in general is made in Israel, and in addressing this internal policymaking dimension, we raise the following three questions:

1. What constitutes Israeli arms sales policy at present?
2. Who decides upon arms transactions, and by what set of procedures?
3. From where within the society does the pro-arms export policy derive its nucleus of support?

IS THERE AN ARMS POLICY?

In pondering reports of Israeli arms deals to any number of countries, one legitimately may wonder whether such sales, if true, are informed by a clear conception as to their ultimate purpose. If by policy we mean the implementation of a predetermined plan, well defined and rigorously enforced, then it is doubtful whether the term strictly applies to weapons transfers by Israel. Rather, we identify something intermediate: a sequence of low-level, ad hoc, and specific decisions taken in response to opportunities as they arise. Still, use of the term "policy" is warranted in the limited sense of a general, usually unarticulated set of principles and loose assumptions which do underline these individual transactions.

This interpretation has validity for several reasons. First, there is no documentary evidence to suggest that at any given point in Israel's past a conscious decision to elevate arms trading to a high priority in its diplomatic or economic strategy was ever taken at the highest level of government. If so, the nation's leaders have never troubled to share this conception with the Israeli public. Second, the handling of arms transfers fits perfectly into the larger mold of Israeli foreign policy. Students of the subject have observed that the conduct of external affairs in general tends to be unsystematic, with a strong emphasis upon short-term contingency planning and crisis management.[1]

As is known to happen in democratic societies, even when they are not confronted by a constant security dilemma and a hostile external environment, policies such as those governing Israeli arms trafficking tend to develop by stages in disjointed fashion and through small, modest inputs of commitment. The impression is that arms decisions — as opposed to a rational, integrated policy — were reached incrementally. As also happens in other democracies, general guidelines and restraints established by "high policy elite" tend to prove less effective than do technical or administrative decisions by bureaucratic civil servants charged with the day-to-day, technical handling of aspects relating to weapons export policy. In short, arms supply choices have been made over the years according to a disaggregated case-by-case approach which encourages greater sensitivity for immediate circumstance and momentary advantage than for those larger questions raised by arms sales and foreign military assistance.

A fourth reason is historical. The inclination to look favorably upon arms transfers developed gradually over time. The creation of an indigenous military industry with an export capability has involved a phased process the first step of which consisted of no more than acquiring the ability to service and repair weapons of World War Two vintage originally imported from abroad. Israel's arms export diplomacy is a logical extension of the growth of this local arms industry and productive capacity. For a long time it was a secondary, rather unimportant policy tool of the ambitious initiative toward the Third World in the 1960s as part of a larger technical assistance program. The tendency is often for institutional decision making to encourage continuity with the past in keeping with what might be termed "the dynamic of the going concern." Nothing succeeds in influencing policymakers and in discouraging policy reassessment or revision so much as a record of previous success. Traditional receptivity toward the use of defense sales and the record of recent accomplishments, suggesting future potential, count for a great deal. Given Israel's turnover and replacement of military equipment, plus the other incentives cited earlier, and once having reached the status of a prominent ex-

porter, the pressures to compete appear relentless and overwhelming to bureaucrats and policymakers, along the lines of "if we don't sell, someone else
will."

So strong is this tendency to stick with a successful formula and to build
upon earlier foundations that it has defied several negative experiences. Ordinarily leaders are driven by policy setbacks into looking for an alternative
policy. Yet after the stunning setback in Iran prompted by the Khomeini
revolution and the loss of other arms relationships, such as with Ethiopia and
Nicaragua, Israeli officials reached the opposite conclusion. Rather than being
deterred, and in the belief that new possibilities are inherent in a fluid international system and arms trade, they have responded instead by looking for
fresh opportunities and market replacements.

In other words, whether Israel should even be in the business of exporting
arms is not really an issue. Nor is there much evidence to suggest that it ever
was. Consequently, the conduct of arms diplomacy begins from that premise
and is confined to policy questions of a more practical nature, centering on
just how deeply Israel at any given moment ought to be involved in offering
its military goods and services to others.

From the standpoint of those engaged in making arms policy decisions there
is a substantial measure of continuity and internal coherence in Israel's approach. The logic behind defense sales can be depicted graphically, as seen
in Table 6.1. This logic is longstanding; only the relative weight and emphases
of the variables within the matrix have shifted, most notably in the recent
emergence of the economic argument as paramount.

EXPORT GUIDELINES

It has been suggested elsewhere that any of six national restraints may be
self-imposed by an arms supplier. These restrictions apply to: (1) certain types
of weapons, (2) certain volatile regions, (3) certain domestic or regime conditions, (4) quantity of arms, (5) the use, deployment, or combat role of
weapons, and (6) a so-called "end-use clause."[2] By this yardstick Israeli policy
has moved in the direction of greater permissiveness, yet not any more so than
the leading world suppliers, including the United States and the Western
Europeans.

While no formal guidelines have been announced, Jerusalem applies some
unwritten and unpublicized rules of thumb in authorizing or rejecting weapons
transfers requests. The first type of regulation, pertaining to weapons categories, also happens to be the one most strictly enforced. In January, 1983,
Gideon Patt, then minister of industry and commerce, provided a rare glimpse
into the arms export strategy by enumerating three principal considerations
governing such decisions.[3] One of these considerations is self-evident: that
no arms be sold to an enemy country and that precautions be taken to pre-

Table 6.1. The Calculus for Arms Sales.

NECESSITY	OPPORTUNITY
Domestic Inputs	
• Economic stagnation	• Industrial infrastructure
• Defense budget cuts	• Skilled manpower
• Unreliable IDF orders	• Military-industrial interest group
• Goal of full employment	• Pro-arms public consensus
• Maximum productive capacity	• Supportive governments
Regional Inputs	
• Arab-Israel conflict	• Low Arab defense manufacture
• Middle East arms race	• Battlefield experience
• Enemy numerical superiority	• Reputation of Israeli weapons
• Arab access to suppliers	
• Preserving qualitative edge	
Systemic Inputs	
• Israel's diplomatic isolation	• "Security dilemma" of all states
• Few sources of supply	• Conventional arms race
• Dependence on U.S.	• Third World rearmament
• No international safeguards	• No international constraints
	• Israeli competitiveness

vent sensitive equipment from falling into the wrong hands. As a result, under Ministry of Defense and IDF strictures roughly 80 percent of Israel's own designs, technology, and indigenous military products remain classified, and ineligible for distribution or sale overseas. In an attempt to make possible the release of additional items for sale outside of Israel, in a number of instances, including the Kfir, weapons systems have been modified by removing ultrasophisticated and secret devices.

Still in this first category of weapon types, two additional restraints exist. One is to avoid supplying arms designed specifically for use in suppressing domestic disturbances. Thus, during the reign of the late Shah, items requested by Iran clearly intended for domestic repression were denied.[4] Nevertheless, such distinctions are difficult to make, leading to numerous loopholes in their enforcement. The other restraint shown by Israel is to exclude from sale certain types of lethal or inhumane weapons known generically as "weapons of ill-repute." The same cannot always be said of the major suppliers, not even the Western ones.

The other restrictions are less stringent and effective. A second "red line" disclosed by Patt and self-imposed by Israel is intended as a way of avoiding political complications. The government will not authorize the sale of weapons to any country denied arms requests by the United States, Canada, France, and Great Britain. But if this implies that all four countries must refuse to make the sale, the reasoning could be disingenuous. Based upon previous experience, France in particular has been prone to breaking ranks and seems bent upon pursuing an independent arms course in vying for such markets as Argentina or Iraq despite U.S. and British opposition.

The marketing strategy is free of ideological ties and suggests no real political preferences. Based upon its sales record, Israel has been willing to sell to the right, the left, and the center on the international political spectrum. According to foreign sources, Israel at one time could have been supporting rebel forces in Nicaragua against the Sandinista government while aiding the government in El Salvador against insurgents supplied by Libya. Israel has avoided becoming the sole or primary supplier to any individual country. During the 1960s period of Third World independence struggles it would not sell to countries fighting to preserve existing colonial territories; in accordance with this policy the 1961 transfer of 10,000 Uzi submarine guns from licensee West Germany to Portugal was blocked.[5] As yet Israel has never faced the situation familiar to the major arms merchants of whether to limit the quantity of its arms possessed by any single country or how exactly to maintain a prescribed ratio of arms among states within a particular region.

On a regional basis Israeli policy was not to sell to states in an ongoing dispute and to stay away from volative areas of tension or of direct conflict. But like other suppliers very broad declarations of principle have permitted flexible adjustment by Israel to changing circumstances. As a result Israeli arms recently have appeared in such war zones as the South Atlantic, Central America, and the Persian Gulf, and in instances where they could end up being used for internal police action. Perhaps because Israeli negotiators realistically appreciate the impossibility of enforcing such preconditions, there are few restrictions as to end-use, sole-use, or re-transfer by the purchaser without Israel's consent. Terms of sale on the whole are attractive and competitive. As a scrambler for contracts and out of a desire to establish a diplomatic foothold, Israel offers items at competitive low cost and, where necessary, at bargain basement prices. There is some flexibility in terms of payment, too. The obvious preference is for transactions on a cash-and-carry basis. However, arms are sold on credit, and favorable terms include, as in the instance of Zaire, long-term credit. Liberal credit lines are a must, especially in dealing with less developed countries plagued by debt problems and a shortage of hard currency. In consequence, Israeli promotions will also accept extended repayment terms and provide for a deferred payments schedule.

In general Israeli arms export controls are less rather than more strict because of the way the program evolved and, in the second instance, because of recent market forces. Regarding the former, in the first stages, when sales were modest and undramatic, lower level decisions rarely required full discussion or approval at the top. And since the program has taken off dramatically in its more recent stages, the combination of a need to sell plus the temptation resulting from the comparative ease with which sales are made in peak years also works to lower criteria on what to sell, where, and to whom. The replacement of domestic military orders by foreign sales means that even though the government has full authority to control and regulate arms transfers, it has become subject to progressively heavier commercial pressures. Ever present, of course, is the desire to acquire some political and diplomatic gain through arms contracts whenever and wherever possible.

The result is an inherent tendency for Israeli leaders to support military sales in the absence of compelling counterarguments. Their bias is to see the costs as very modest compared to the importance of the objectives sought and the ends achieved. The latter continue to outweigh the risk, for example, of peripheral political involvement by so small an international supplier as Israel. The thrust of the pro-arms case is so strong at present that it threatens to override a third self-restraint imposed by Israel. Again, as presented by Minister Patt, Israeli defense transfers constitute 22 percent of total industrial exports, not including diamonds, yet would not be allowed by the government to exceed 25 percent.[6] On the other hand, a more active foreign market would weaken adherence to this restraint, too, especially at a time when Israel is confronted with a negative balance of payments and such domestic factors as unemployment and a slowdown in defense production.

Ironically, any reduction of sales that might have taken place since 1981 would appear to have resulted not so much from conscious self-limitation as from external market forces. The fact that some of Israel's best customers in the Third World have become debt ridden, for example, in effect imposes, perhaps merely temporarily, an export quota of sorts, at least in certain categories of transfers—which only goes to show that the arms diplomacy pursued by Israel is restrained more by practical calculations of moment, time, and place than by general principles. In sum, Israeli arms may flow rather liberally; however, they do not flow indiscriminately.

THE HANDLING OF ARMS POLICY

Three factors further encourage the "dynamic of the going concern" as it relates to present Israeli policy: the closed nature of the decision-making process; the existing broad consensus toward the program and strong commitment to its continuation; and the existence of a pro-arms coalition built around Israel's military and industrial sectors, centering on the defense establishment.

As part of the air of confidentiality surrounding weapons sales, little is known even by Israelis about the actual decision-making process. It is difficult to pinpoint, for example, the locus of political and administrative responsibility for directing the arms aid and sales program, or the exact procedure for dealing with issues arising from the policy, such as whether to supply certain types of assistance to a particular country and under what terms.

Within the limitations imposed on an academic and an outsider to penetrate the policy system and to understand its workings, the information suggests a composite picture, with elements of both centralization and diffusion. The system is at once less structured and less formal than in other countries but also more secretive and obscure, hence encouraging the interplay between institutions, on the one hand, and what Kissinger once described as "the accident of personality," on the other.

Centralization derives from the very nature of policymaking in Israel. Israel has had eight Prime Ministers: David Ben-Gurion, Moshe Sharett, Levi Eshkol, Golda Meir, Yitzhak Rabin, Menachem Begin, Yitzhak Shamir, and Shimon Peres. Regardless of contrasts in leadership style, each Premier has respected the practice that matters pertaining to foreign affairs and defense tend to be handled, even in noncrisis situations, by a small group of people.[7] Arms export diplomacy is most definitely one such monopoly of the select few, with membership in the circle of decision makers varying with each government, depending upon the personal preferences and leadership styles of whoever heads it. Yet only on the rarest of occasions have arms transfer questions ever been raised at the full Cabinet level. This preference for small forums is not seen as undemocratic, especially in view of the often specialized and always classified nature of the subject matter. Nonetheless, the wisdom of reconciling administrative or political necessity, on the one hand, with constitutional principles and the call for institutional controls over military-security policy on the other, was appreciated fairly early in Israel's history — toward the end of the first decade, and quite by accident, when the issue of control over arms decisions prompted a Cabinet crisis. The circumstances were that in 1959 news was leaked of Israel's intention to sell some military items to the government of West Germany, causing one partner in the coalition government to protest that the issue, so emotion-laden in the wake of European Jewry's destruction at the hands of Nazi Germany, had never been put to the Cabinet for specific approval. Note that the criticism focused even then not upon the act or principle of selling but on the identity of the purchaser. While cabinet minutes confirmed that the proposal actually had been presented and passed without debate in a deliberately vague and low-keyed statement by Prime Minister Ben-Gurion some time earlier, it was apparent that better procedures were needed. The result was the creation in 1961 of the Ministerial Committee on Defense (MCD) as a compromise between the two extremes of solitary versus collective decision-making.

To the extent that any single military grant or arms sale subsequently came up for authorization, it was within the framework of the MCD. Still, the number of people privy to information on arms relationships remained small. Even when proposals for sales or grants were before the full Cabinet, discussion tended to be perfunctory, and approval largely pro forma despite the veto power conferred upon Israeli foreign ministers. With time, the MCD fell into disuse.

In the second Begin government (1981-1983) the implications of the expanded arms export program called attention to the need for some larger body to exercise supervisory authority. The result is a compromise between the involvement of the entire government and concentrating all supervisory powers in the office of a single Cabinet member. The MCD has been reconstituted as the Ministerial Committee on Weapons Transfers, set up to oversee all aspects of the arms sales diplomacy. Membership is confined to four Cabinet-level officers: the Prime Minister, who also serves as chairman, and the Ministers for Foreign Affairs, Defense, Industry, and Commerce.[8] Its task is to review and approve on behalf of the government of Israel every single arms package for export. Underlining the difference between individual decisions and an arms policy, the Ministerial Committee on Weapons Transfers is intended, according to one of its members, first, to assure greater consistency and tighter administration for what has become in recent years a multi-faceted program, and second, to consider proposals before they are approved in terms of their political and moral implications and not only their potential economic tradeoffs.[9]

As might be expected, in small ruling circles the impact of individual ministers assumes greater significance for the emergence of policy. This certainly has been the Israeli experience beginning with Ben-Gurion himself. As witnessed in his personal advocacy of the 1959 arms deal with West Germany, Israel's first Premier had few reservations about exploiting this slight advantage of their being customers for military equipment, however modest in quantity, and converting it into political gain. Ben-Gurion's stance on weapons transfers by Israel is best expressed in his defense of the 1959 sale, when he told the Knesset:

> in anything having to do with foreign affairs we ask ourselves one simple question: "what is good for Israel?" And if it is good, then all my emotions and Jewish instincts, all my Jewish as well as human pride tell me: "do whatever is best for Israel and what is required for its security."[10]

His pragmatic approach to arms sales became institutionalized; and it continues to be a feature of each successive government down to the present one. If we confine our discussion of the arms policy consensus to the more recent period, we see that such positive attitudes were present in both the first and second Begin coalitions. Menachem Begin's hard view of world politics and strong sense of Jewish nationalism are well known.[11] The Prime Minister aside, the combination of Moshe Dayan as Foreign Minister and Ezer Weiz-

man as Defense Minister — both of them previously career military officers —
assured continued support for the accepted, longstanding practice of offering Israeli arms for sale. Their replacement respectively by Yitzhak Shamir,
a contemporary of Begin's from the days of the underground struggle against
Britain's presence in Palestine and active for many years in the Israeli secret
service, and by Ariel Sharon, the 1973 war hero, if anything only reinforced
the existing predisposition.

It was thus Sharon who in 1982 elaborated upon the reasoning for the
defense export program at present:

> We would much prefer Israeli exports consisting exclusively of flowers, avoca-
> does, tomatoes, computers and advanced medical instruments full of hope. Yet
> all these do not provide what is necessary and essential.

He went on:

> With due respect for those who wish to see the moral consideration first and
> foremost, it is impossible not to recognize the factor of sheer existence and
> survival.

Accordingly,

> It became incumbent upon Israel to develop military research and military manu-
> facture . . . Israel had no choice but to seek out and find markets for its military
> products.[12]

"Survival," "incumbent," "no choice" — in a word, necessity, stands out as the
principal compelling motive in Sharon's thinking.

The replacement of Sharon as Defense Minister by Moshe Arens at the
beginning of 1983 was hardly likely to reverse the current trend of increased
arms exports. A champion of Israel's development and independence in weapons production, an aeronautical engineer by training and a senior member
of the Israel Aircraft Industries staff prior to entering politics, Arens played
an important role in developing large-scale weapons systems, including the
Kfir, and was one of the main lobbyists for the Lavi when its fate was being
discussed.

Arens's thinking falls within the security track more broadly defined, taking in political, diplomatic, scientific, and commercial aspects in addition to
the military argument. He directly addressed the sensitive arms sales issue on
a number of occasions, elaborating at least twice on how he personally con-
ceived of their importance for Israel. In one 1983 interview he was asked whether Israel wasn't making a mistake by investing so much in building an industrial
infrastructure dependent on military exports. To which Arens replied:

> I don't think so, though logically it would be better if we were to hedge our bets
> and place our money on a number of horses. But every country should be deal-
> ing in those products in which it has a comparative advantage. That only makes
> good sense.

Confirming his reputation for rational decision making, he elaborated:

> I think Israel's largest comparative advantage is in military products, because these demand advanced technology on one hand and military experience on the other. We have both of these, and thus can do a better job than most people in the world. Our weapons systems are better and cheaper than most of the competition, and that is why Israeli military exports have been so successful.[13]

When the questioner turned next to the moral price tag Israel might be paying for its success, Defense Minister Arens offered a two-part answer. First,

> living in the Middle East is difficult. Having to stay on your guard all the time is also difficult. . . . Building up a defense industry in a small country is difficult, and one can only maintain it if you export—and that too is difficult.

Second, he insisted Israel does not approach the problem of military exports "in a totally unprincipled manner":

> In fact, we are probably more principled than most countries. I have been told more than once that the British find it difficult to understand how we could supply arms to Argentina, a totalitarian country that is in conflict with a democracy like Britain. Well, I have to remind these people that the largest single supplier of weapons to Argentina is Britain itself. I have also told these people that we would be glad to make a deal with Great Britain, whereby we will not sell weapons to totalitarian countries in conflict with Britain, if Britain does not sell weapons to totalitarian countries in conflict with Israel.

Arens returned to the subject on another occasion, offering a statement in which the different emphases attached to the triad of justifications—political, military, and economic—come to fullest expression. "We're investing a great deal of brains and resources to come up with the kind of weaponry and tactics that would be a deterrent" to Arab attack, he said. As part of this deterrence strategy,

> We have a very fine defense industry, employing a very large number of people with a combination of technological know-how and operational experience.

He continued,

> We went through a period when people said that it was crazy for a small country like Israel to try and make a missile. People said it was just nuts to make a sea-to-sea missile, the Gabriel. Israel advanced to a point where we were a little behind the Americans, and maybe a little ahead of the Russians. In certain areas we have weapon systems that are breakthroughs, and that do not exist, and will not exist, on the other side of the border.[14]

Looking ahead, Arens stressed the potential of the Lavi project which, besides discouraging Syria or any other Arab country from taking the path of war and preserving the defense industries complex at the forefront of world military manufacture, also figured in the third area: Israeli diplomacy, and particularly in Israel-American relations. "The Lavi is more than a fighter project," he concluded. "American companies will be deeply involved, and the program can also be seen as a basis for mutual cooperation."

Arens's comments are instructive for demonstrating how he personally sees Israeli armaments contributing to the nation's strength and security in the broadest sense. Not only do his remarks reflect the sentiments of those ministers comprising the highest policymaking group, the Ministerial Committee on Weapons Transfers, but they take on added importance due to his position as Minister of Defense.

Since the Ministerial Committee meets infrequently and only to oversee the arms export program, the responsibility for the daily management of the ongoing defense sales campaign lies elsewhere, and our attention shifts next from the Cabinet to the ministerial level. Appreciating the pivotal role exercised by the Ministry of Defense becomes the key to understanding the Israeli arms policy process. The reasons for its undisputed prominence in promoting and implementing the arms export program are part historical, part institutional, and part idiosyncratic and personal. Peri[15] labels the Ministry of Defense a "super-Ministry" and claims it intrudes into activities falling within the ambit of other ministries. In the specific case of foreign military sales, the ministry's salience can be traced to an expansion of its authority in two different directions: First, externally, into the sphere of foreign relations. In Ben-Gurion's conception of statecraft, foreign relations and defense policy were meant to be complementary and therefore closely integrated. But in point of actual practice the former often has served the latter.

With time the Ministry of Defense and also the Mossad (Israel's Secret Intelligence Service, operating within the Prime Minister's Office), came to be directly involved in issues logically falling within the purview of the Foreign Ministry. This involvement extended to delicate arms purchases, relations with the Third World, and between Israel and the superpowers, and since the 1960's, weapons transfers. This expanded role was contested unsuccessfully by the Ministry for Foreign Affairs, an outcome which was perhaps inevitable since as one former Israeli diplomat put it, not without a trace of jealousy, "the big battalions were with defense."[16] The result is that unlike other arms exporting countries which still see such activities as a task for professional diplomats and where, like in Brazil, foreign ministry personnel coordinate military sales, the Foreign Ministry and its departmental view of political implications arising from weapons transfers take second place to the Defense Ministry.

A second "invasion" by the ministry, as spokesman for the needs of the entire military establishment, into areas of technological modernization and private industry further strengthens its position vis-à-vis other government agencies. In the pursuit of weapons autarky in the 1950s and in the 1960s the Defense Ministry gradually took over direct responsibility for munitions, aircraft, and electronic industries whose productive capacity safeguarded IDF military preparedness.[17] When the viability of these defense industries came to depend upon foreign exports as a supplement to local orders, it seemed only natural for ministry officials to assume the limited role of advocate. But then impatience with the Foreign Ministry's modus operandi led to yet another task, namely, that of expediting the actual sale of weapons by creating outlets for the growing arms industry using the argument that only the Defense Ministry could do the job well.

This two-pronged expansion of the ministry's scope of organizational authority—horizontally, into foreign relations, and, vertically, into defense production—provides the best explanation for its entrenched position at the apex of the arms sales policy process. But personalities have been a factor, too, since successive defense ministers beginning with Ben-Gurion himself have been enthusiasts for expanding Israel's military assistance and sales activities. The role of Shimon Peres within the Defense Ministry has been mentioned earlier. Moshe Arens, who assumed the post in 1983, definitely follows in the tradition of his other predecessors, Moshe Dayan, Ezer Weizman, and Ariel Sharon, in backing defense sales in general and the Ministry's efforts in particular.[18] So does the present minister, Rabin.

Within the Ministry of Defense the responsible agency is the Defense Sales Office or, according to its Hebrew acronym, SIBAT. According to official sources the Defense Sales Office is the highest administrative agency with authority over military transfers.[19] Its mandate is "to widen the circle of contacts," "to advertise Israel overseas as a dependable source of arms," and "to deepen political and strategic ties with many states" in order to reduce the risks attendant in this most risky of all export enterprises. Headed by a deputy director-general of the Defense Ministry, SIBAT controls all export sales, from initial order to post–sales service. Its tasks, as a result, are diverse and far ranging. Besides administering government-to-government transactions, these include initiating contacts with potential clients, contracting to sell weapons systems manufactured under directions from the Ministry via Rafael or surplus IDF equipment, arranging inspection tours of plants and military displays for foreign purchasing agents, examining sales proposals, licensing, market research, and acting as an intermediary by matching prospective user requirements with IDF and local defense industry expertise.[20] SIBAT thus serves as a representative of the government of Israel, of the Israeli Army, and of the private defense industries. The present head of SIBAT is Col. (reserves) Zvi Roiter, who was appointed to the post in August, 1983, after having served as military attache in Holland, Denmark, and Norway before joining the Defense Sales Office as assistant director in 1979.

SIBAT is structured primarily on the lines of geographical regions and is reinforced in its manifold activities by a sales unit of the Ministry's Procurement and Production Administration (Figure 6.1). Its work is further facili-

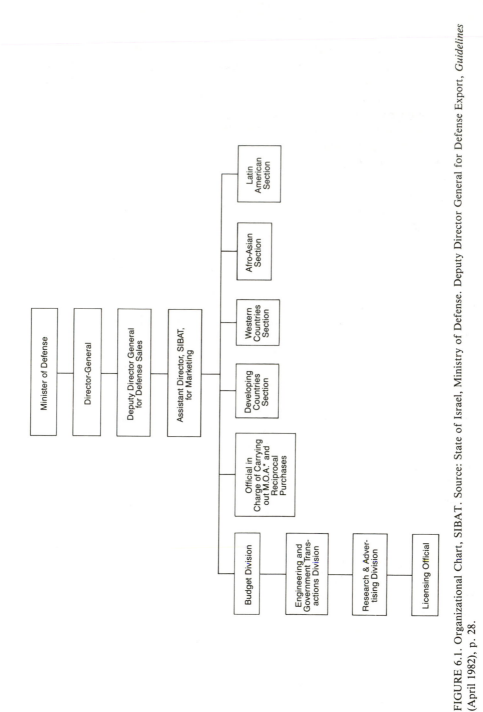

FIGURE 6.1. Organizational Chart, SIBAT. Source: State of Israel, Ministry of Defense. Deputy Director General for Defense Export, *Guidelines* (April 1982), p. 28.

*"Memorandum of Agreement"

tated by the presence of Defense Ministry missions abroad: in Europe, one mission for the United States and Canada, a representative for Venezuela, Santo Domingo, and Haiti, one for Brazil, and another covering Colombia, Panama, and Costa Rica. As the arms sales organization has enlarged and become stronger, SIBAT's task in promoting military relationships is also being performed through government-sponsored publications, advertising in military trade journals, and participation in such international exhibits as the 1984 Aerospace fair held in Singapore and periodic airshows. A recent trend is for many of the leading defense firms to station representatives abroad, which both facilitates and complicates the job of SIBAT in orchestrating efforts at the national level.

That individual Israeli companies may be competing with each other and not only with other exporting countries, and that they are prone to acting on narrow, corporate grounds in securing foreign contracts is but one of the problems SIBAT encounters. There have been failures in coordination between the government and the many export-oriented Israeli defense contractors, resulting in the loss of potential clients. SIBAT, on behalf of the government, is not always able to secure sufficient lines of credit and to provide manufacturers and exporters with financial assistance needed to bolster the export efforts. Some producers are known to rail against Defense Ministry prohibition of various items from being marketed overseas, and to object to bureaucratic red tape which hampers the prompt authorization of foreign transactions. In short, SIBAT has shown itself to be good at making policy and efficient in insisting upon strict conformity to the guidelines which have been established; however, the system tends to perform less well at the level of executing policy. Competition and duplication still exist; controls appear to be more informal than structured; and not infrequently it seems that individual companies or agents rather than the government or SIBAT set the tone for Israeli arms diplomacy.

As concerns operating procedures, arms sales negotiations authorized by the Ministerial Committee on Weapons Transfers and supervised by the Defense Ministry and SIBAT may take any of several forms, standard or unorthodox. Preparatory work and exploratory conversations with a foreign government ordinarily are handled at a lower level by members of the permanent Israeli diplomatic mission as part of exploring a range of mutual interests, or by Israeli military attaches resident in the host country.

Alternatively, the trend of late is to use state visits by Israeli leaders as opportunities for sealing weapons transactions at the level of heads of state or government. Military assistance is believed to have been one of the purposes behind Foreign Minister Yitzhak Shamir's official visits to Zaire, Costa Rica, and South America in 1982. Arms negotiations led to the personal intervention of former Defense Minister Sharon himself on at least three occasions: during an African visit in 1981, a follow-up visit to Zaire in 1982, and during a Latin American trip that same year. The presence of Sharon's national defense adviser, General Avraham Tamir, and other military personnel in the delegation to Zaire in November, 1982, suggested the importance of military cooperation, including the supply of arms, as an inducement for Kinshasa to reopen diplomatic relations and also at the direct role of the Ministry of Defense in such negotiations. Especially during Sharon's term of office the ministry confirmed the contention that it serves as "a parallel and often superior instrument for the conduct of foreign relations."[21]

Indeed, Israeli arms diplomacy is most vulnerable oftentimes to the notoriety stemming from such publicized, high-level arms negotiations. To be sure, much depends again upon the personality of Israeli officeholders; Sharon certainly has been among the least inhibited in discussing the country's arms activity and thereby drawing world attention to it. In May, 1984, for instance, his alleged comments while on a private lecture tour in the U.S. upon the Israeli sale of arms to Iran forced a spokesman for Prime Minister and Foreign Minister Shamir to issue a denial.[22] Seemingly far more effective, by contrast, is discreet diplomacy resulting in strengthened military relationships on a businesslike basis. Regarded as one of the best practitioners of the quiet approach in recent years, and therefore extremely effective in this area, is the director-general of the Foreign Ministry, David Kimche.

To repeat, the Israeli pattern is for arms sales organization and procedures to be relatively simplified. Authority is concentrated. Decisions are at the sub-Cabinet level, but always remain subject to ministerial approval. Only if the request by a client is exceptionally large, for more sophisticated items, or if authorization poses a sensitive political problem does the full Cabinet, sitting under stricter conditions of secrecy as the Ministerial Committee on Security Affairs become involved in arms sales decisions. In the past, discussion most often came after rather than before the fact, as happened in 1959, in May and, again, in September, 1982, following disclosures of arms sales to Iran and Argentina. The impact of these recent public controversies has been to further tighten government supervision and increase Cabinet involvement, especially through the Ministerial Committee on Weapons Transfers. One step further removed, a consistent voice for export authorization is available in the Defense Ministry's Defense Sales Office, through which prospective arms deals and sales applications must pass, and which also serves as the enforcement agency through its formal regulations and controls.

The process itself though seems unstructured, unlike the U.S. where arms transfers are governed by a complex network of governmental agencies, statutes, and procedures. Israeli leaders content themselves with a set of basic policy guidelines and put greater reliance upon the judgment and inherent pragmatism of officials conducting the program. Consequently the mechanisms of the process involve nuances and technicalities — what bureaucrats like to speak of as the modalities — instead of absolutes. Decisions will vary from time to time, from transfer to transfer, from client to client, and from situation to situation. Such a process discourages sweeping policy generalizations and devotes little attention to long-range planning.

There are thus few controls, even fewer inhibitions. Certainly the internal bureaucratic pressures lie in the direction of acting favorably upon sales opportunities, just as the pressures on individual ministries to sell are greater than those to prohibit sales. The presumption is that unless presented with solid political or diplomatic reasons to the contrary, requests for arms ought to be answered affirmatively.

This dominant viewpoint prompts calling attention to two other features of policymaking. The Israeli pattern is distinctive for bureaucratic consensus and interdepartmental collaboration in formulating the export policy.

As a rule supplying arms invokes competing aims and values. Resultant policy dilemmas lead one to expect to find conflict within administrative hierarchies and between rival governmental agencies. Yet official thinking in Jerusalem and Tel-Aviv is convinced of the benefits of arms transfers, suggesting that a broad governmental consensus exists on this particular issue. Multiple advocacy is not practiced institutionally since there is no single agency that challenges the basic premises of the arms diplomacy. In the absence of serious opposition within the government to foreign military assistance per se, disagreement concerns smaller details like terms of credit, the mix of arms, or the impact of a given sale upon relations with particular countries.

Even the traditional bureaucratic rivalry between the diplomatic and the military perspectives as represented by the Foreign Ministry and the Defense Ministry seems to be muted on the issue of arms. Press reports cite Foreign Ministry opposition to some of Israel's arms sales in recent years to authoritarian regimes in Central and Latin America.[23] That the sales have gone through despite the Ministry's reservations is another way of illustrating its longstanding weakness in making policy, but also how in the final analysis even the Ministry for Foreign Affairs acknowledges arms transfers to be one of the few effective tools for furthering goals abroad, thereby reinforcing the consensus.

Depending upon the nature of the specific sale under consideration the Defense Ministry has been known to work closely with other concerned agencies: the IDF, representatives of the Foreign Ministry, the intelligence community, and the special services. Periodic interdepartmental meetings are held to discuss individual sales. It is at this middle echelon of department heads of the various ministries that technical questions are settled, such as the schedule of deliveries, or the types and amounts of weapons and equipment to be supplied.

Such procedures are an improvement over the past, when the lack of coordination proved embarrassing. In one memorable instance arms sales to Nicaragua and a proposed transaction with the Dominican Republic orchestrated by Shimon Peres and the deputy director of the Defense Ministry's Armament Division prompted a formal protest by the Foreign Ministry. Its director-general wrote to Peres at the time, in 1957:

> We really put our foot in it with the Nicaraguan arms deal. All the countries of Latin America shun [Nicaragua] because of its foreign policy and domestic regime. It's a shame that you failed to consult the Foreign Ministry before going through with this deal.

He went on:

> You know as well as I do that we are very dependent on the Latin American bloc in the United Nations, which includes twenty countries. We cannot disregard their feelings. Therefore, I am asking you immediately to order that any new deal with Nicaragua be cancelled and that shipments which have not yet gone out be held up.[24]

Shortly thereafter, Peres, on his own cognizance, approved delivery of partial arms orders to the Dominican Republic, despite a negative decision by Prime Minister Ben-Gurion. This evoked formal instructions from Ben-Gurion[25]:

1. No sale of arms should be made to any country without my prior knowledge and consent;
2. The information should be provided only when one of the countries has asked to purchase arms;
3. I will not decide before consulting the Foreign Ministry;
4. . . . we must have complete co-ordination of our policy; and the sale of weapons is a diplomatic fact, not just a financial and economic one.

Ben Gurion's guidelines, issued in 1958, continue in force to the present.

Even though it is widely accepted that because of their political consequences the periodic review of conventional arms transfer policies is advisable, there are few provisions for governmental review in Israel. No known criteria have been established for assessing either the utility of arms transfers or, conversely, their irrelevance or counterproductivity for national security. Arms export diplomacy is dealt with piecemeal and has not been subjected to comprehensive study in all of its dimensions at the highest level of government. Nor does there exist a policy planning staff to bring together civilian and military perspectives, immediate circumstances with larger global patterns and trends. Arms transfers logically would be one of the proper functions of a national security council were one to be established in Israel.

Some such apparatus incorporating an adversary evaluation process becomes indispensable in order to discourage unthinking obedience to an established policy course such as has come to prevail in the field of weapons transfers and where too strong a bureaucratic consensus might at some point prove dysfunctional. Meanwhile, broad discretionary powers and bureaucratic momentum continue to fuel the overseas sales drive.

In completing this section on policymaking, one overriding observation is that the Israeli government, over time, has developed a strong interest, both political and financial, in the program. It has been drawn more intimately into sales promotion, bargaining, and even marketing. Extensive government involvement in defense industry ownership and production further increases this built-in interest in overseas defense sales. The conclusion is that the government of Israel, irrespective of its party composition, will continue, for the foreseeable future, to be deeply and directly implicated in defense-related export. Worth repeating here is the fact that the sale of military expertise by Israel is an integral, not exceptional, national practice which demonstrates remarkable constancy.

It is, moreover, bipartisan, crossing traditional party lines and standing in the mainstream of public thinking on matters of security and foreign affairs. This is best seen in the role of the Knesset.

CHECKS AND BALANCES

The question of control in Israeli defense sales policy leads us to look at the role of other domestic political factors: the Knesset, opposition parties, the media, and the Israeli public.

In the Israeli political system, adapted from the British model, there is no statutory requirement for consulting or even informing parliament about prospective or existing arms transactions. Successive governments have been sparing in the information provided the Knesset. Constrained by lack of data or staff support, the Knesset plays only a peripheral role. Unlike the United States Congress, which has become keenly interested in arms sales, and where transfers are governed by a complex structure of procedures and statutes, as well as subject to budgetary approval, the Knesset does not really fulfill the "watchdog" functions of review, oversight, and investigation. For example, there is nothing comparable in the way of explicit legislation to the 1976 International Security Assistance and Arms Export Control Act, which gives Congress the right to veto proposed arms sales.

Israeli legislators by comparison are far more tolerant of government arms practices, deferring to the military's needs and expertise as well as to the argument of national security. The fact remains that the Knesset has never been able, either in the plenum or through one of its parliamentary committees, to influence weapons transfer policies let alone to challenge basic premises. One finds only a single instance, 1959, when the arms sale to West Germany became the source for sharp parliamentary debate. It is, therefore, the exception proving the rule.

Those mechanisms available for attempting to control policy, such as legislation, questions, motions on the agenda, or proposals for a vote of no confidence, have tended to be least effective on defense matters.[26] The Knesset's Foreign Affairs and Security Committee comes closest to exercising some degree of influence, although even it falls short of overseeing national arms practices. Like its parent body, the committee succumbs to government policy under the weight of party discipline, the needs of secrecy on issues of vital national security, refusal by the Cabinet to supply sensitive testimony, and because the committee does not have an expert staff of its own. Ben-Gurion was successful in confining it to being essentially a consumer of information and a provider of public support for government policies.[27] In keeping with his practice of withholding information from the committee on most matters of national defense, he tended not to submit details of arms purchases or sales. His successors have been just as reluctant to confide in the committee, charging its members with playing partisan politics, with lacking the requisite technical knowledge, and with being "porous," that is, serving as the source of leaks to the press of classified material presented *in camera* by government officials.

Committee members, often inexperienced in industrial or defense matters, for their part also refrain from probing too closely, or from insisting upon frequent ministerial briefings. Following his appointment in 1977 as chairman of the Knesset Foreign Affairs and Security Committee, Moshe Arens set up several subcommittees, one of which was charged with overseeing arms transactions, exports as well as deliveries. The subcommittee, however, has been concerned primarily with arms procurement and appears to be neither active nor consulted on weapons sales. Thus the Ben-Gurion legacy has endured through the Begin era, with the potentially important Knesset committee neutralized, most of its deliberations leading to no definite conclusions, no decisions, opinions, or recommendations. This observation applies certainly to the entire realm of external military supplies by Israel. The role of the committee, like that of the Knesset as a whole, inclines to be general rather than specific, confirming Shimshoni's contention that by and large the Knesset has been more important in legitimating government measures by retroactive approval and in reflecting general public feelings or conscience than in initiating, controlling, or even guiding specific defense and foreign policies such as those of defense sales.[28]

It is noteworthy that in so highly politicized a country as Israel the pro-arms consensus ignores strict party lines. In a rare reference to the subject, Israeli arms initiatives in the Americas and in sub-Saharan Africa were raised in the Knesset in December, 1982. Opposition members from the Labour alignment questioned the manner in which the Begin government was pursuing negotiations or the patterns of arms deals with rightwing dictatorships. But even the political opposition did not challenge the wisdom or the principle of competing in the international arms trade. Knesset member Yossi Sarid, a leading Labour dove, was the only one who voiced objection in principle to the very act of selling arms. He charged: "We have foreseen the green route of agriculture for the red and bloody route of arms."[29]

Countering Sarid, one Knesset speaker accused the Labour socialist opposition of a double standard, recalling its pursuit of arms diplomacy when in power, and suggested that Israel could do no worse than adopt the same policy in regard to arms sales as the socialist government of France. Less partisan was the Likud's Yigal Hurvitz who said, "Sarid's speech sounds lovely, but it does not earn Israel the dollars which it sorely needs to survive in view of the hostility with which we are engulfed and the hypocrisy and one-sidedness of the seemingly enlightened world." Hurvitz, a former finance minister, added: "Selling weapons is not a nice business to be in, but Israel should sell to whichever country wants to buy on condition that the weapons we sell will not be turned against us. This is the world we live in."[30]

For our purposes this unusual Knesset exchange is important for underlining that, dissent notwithstanding, the bipartisan political consensus supporting a prudential arms transfers campaign remains strong for the present. Labour leader Shimon Peres, when challenged, defended previous arms support for both the Somoza regime and Idi Amin.[31] Gad Yaacobi, Labour's authority on economic affairs, in presenting a set of concrete proposals for strengthening the defense and industrial sectors, advocated support for penetrating overseas markets by Israeli military exports as part of political arrangements with various countries.[32] His colleague, Chaim Herzog, former ambassador to the United Nations and now president of the State, as a Labour Knesset member was even more outspoken. Referring those who would criticize the sale of military equipment to South America to the long list of other suppliers, he notes Israel is in very good company. Urging Israelis to "lower the tone of our self-criticism on this issue," Herzog reverted to the Ben-Gurion tradition, suggesting that "we must be guided in our relationships by the one criterion that has guided governments of Israel ever since the establishment of the State, namely: Is it good for the Jews?"[33]

Precisely because Israeli political figures on both sides of the Knesset aisle do not differ in their perceptions as to the arms program or its contribution to national interests, the Knesset cannot be viewed as providing any kind of safeguard. Louscher suggests seven possible arguments or types of criticism voiced by legislatures in other countries on military sales:

- complete opposition and moral indignation
- selling of arms in order to gain influence over weak states
- ceilings on arms sales
- opposition to certain countries or regimes receiving arms
- sale of certain kinds of equipment or the specific details of sales agreements
- procedures by the government for implementing arms sales
- the demand by the legislative branch to be given greater control over sales decisions[34]

Interestingly, as a closing comment upon the role, or nonrole, of the Knesset in arms policymaking, none of these seven possible lines of objection or criticism have been pursued with any degree of conviction or success.

As a further measure of the favorable domestic climate and consensus reaching down from the government and bureaucracy to the society at large, the nation's media appear to be just as marginal in the arms review process. Items about possible Israeli arms connections, often citing unofficial sources, but particularly foreign reports, both of which generally remain unconfirmed, appear quite frequently in the daily newspapers. Less frequent are editorial commentaries upon the larger issues and principles of arms diplomacy.

Israeli law requires that news filed locally or to be published abroad must pass prepublication military censorship to prevent exposes which could "endanger the defense of Israel." Less formal but equally effective is a brand of self-restraint or self-censorship practiced by Israeli journalists who are oftentimes privy to details about various aspects of the defense sales program. The author, in researching the present book, encountered this circumspection even on the part of economic reporters whose columns and analyses of Israeli export performance, for example, or of the high technology industries are illustrations of studied understatement when it comes to the place of defense production and exports in Israel's economy. Perhaps owing to the high visibility of Ariel Sharon and Yitzhak Shamir in cultivating arms ties, the number of editorials addressing the weapons policy has increased since 1982.[35] Even so, the general thrust and tenor of such newspaper commentaries would seem to aim less at the policy as a whole than at specific issues, such as those of human rights and the sale of arms to repressive regimes.

With limited access to information and with military assistance couched in patriotic terms, the attitude of the public is overwhelmingly supportive. A nation in arms, Israelis tend to be tolerant of the general policy of trading internationally in arms. The nucleus is provided by the more than 60,000 people working for the defense-exporting companies and joined by members of their households.

Despite the known unreliability of public opinion samplings, one recent survey, conducted at the beginning of 1983, is perhaps illustrative of this general approval. Of nearly 2,000 respondents 27.5 percent favored selling to any country irrespective of regime; 35 percent urged not selling to racist and dictatorial regimes, while 27.9 percent felt Israel ought to sell arms only to democracies.[36] If indicative of anything, these findings suggest that most Israelis at least are discriminating. They subscribe to the wisdom of engaging in the widespread international practice; and yet they would prefer that Israel refrain from selling to repressive governments. Still, when asked specifically about aid to Argentina, a clear majority of those interviewed expressed approval. Consequently, neither the media nor the public serves as a possible check at present against Israel's relying unduly upon arms exports in its foreign and economic relations.

However, an almost imperceptible trend does appear to be underway which may have a possible social and even political impact in the long term. Although not necessarily connected to a mood or counterculture of antimilitarism arising from such entanglements as the Lebanese war, public reactions nevertheless seem to be shifting from enthusiastic and blanket support to skepticism about the purposes and effectiveness of arms sales. More people are now beginning to ask a greater number of telling questions about reported sales and to demand to know more about the program, such as what reasons Israel might have for becoming involved in Central America.

Still, the national tendency is to support sales in the absence of compelling counterarguments. It has been suggested that in other countries as well the pressures to proceed with a weapons transfer are almost always irresistible, the arguments for going ahead almost always persuasive.[37] With Israeli arms sales booming in spite of diplomatic obstacles, the call for a reassessment of military assistance practices or a fundamental clarification and review of weapons transfers might seem superfluous to government leaders and bureaucratic enthusiasts, no less than to the military industrialists.

THE ARMS LOBBY

It is impossible to appreciate the sources of support for arms sales without emphasizing that the public, bureaucratic, and governmental consensus is itself merely one component of a powerful coalition favoring an active role in the world arms trade. Both the defense establishment and the large manufacturing concerns have a major stake in the program. Together these representatives of the military and the business sectors serve as the chief defenders of arms sales and the principal advocates of an accelerated export program. Through their shared interests and priorities, their high motivation, tremendous investment, and degree of commitment to the existing policy, as well as by their lines of communication with each other and their easy access to the decision makers, they comprise an awesome special interest group and political lobby.

The establishment of a military-industrial complex is seen as the mark of a developed armaments industry.[38] In the context of Israel the scientific community, administrators, industrialists, labor unions, and the professional military have their own set of demands upon governmental defense and economic investment decisions.

The Defense Ministry is conveniently located at the nexus of this arms policy coalition. It not only bears a large part of the responsibility for executing the sales program but is also an obvious interested party, with concerns and views of its own to promote. Responsible for Israel's defense capability and security, the ministry sees military sales as fully compatible with these goals by helping to project Israeli power and influence. The success of the program makes it easier to justify heavy defense budget outlays and vindicates the ministry's investment in local enterprises with an export capacity. And of course, success enables officials to claim credit, personal and for the ministry, by pointing up the tangible contribution of arms export diplomacy to the national collective effort, thus further consolidating the Defense Ministry's dominant place in policymaking.

In addition to promoting its own cause, however, the Ministry of Defense serves as a spokesman for others. The IDF is its principal client; and as the highest civilian authority over the military the ministry not only works closely with the general staff and is sensitive to its needs but is also a most effective representative of the armed forces in government debates. The military command also has good cause to defend recent weapons transfer practices. Arms sales are for them the "critical mass," assuring that domestic production remains at close to full capacity and possibly determining whether or not research and development can continue to be pushed vigorously. Production and research in effect combine to satisfy the IDF's primary consideration: that its own needs in conventional weapons systems be met while dependence upon external suppliers decreases except for systems obtainable only from the United States. Once those needs and supplies are met, the IDF has every reason to encourage foreign sales. The logic is simple: the IDF is dependent upon the local arms industry which is dependent, in turn, upon exports. Without sales to the Third World, it is fairly safe to assume that some of the industries at home would collapse, individual production lines would come to a halt, and projects now in the pipeline would have to be abandoned.

This affinity of interest is one of the explanations for the symbiotic relationship between the different parts, civilian and military, of the large defense establishment. Shared interests, as shown above, also extend to a third axis of the arms lobby: the military industry and the business community. For if pressure by the military to sell arms is great, so, too, have commercial pressures increased. Defense, encompassing defense sales, is, after all, the biggest business in Israel. The arms companies are anxious to sell as much as possible and feel perfectly justified in applying pressure on the government to find export outlets for weapons production. They, too, have every incentive to maximize sales. As a result, the government in effect is being asked by industrial leaders who marshal the arguments of military self-sufficiency and of economic gains to assist the defense sales promotion so that their firms might be able to export more.[39]

Interdependence between the military and the manufacturers if anything has strengthened inversely to the decline of Defense Ministry procurement from the arms companies. As a means of compensation, SIBAT and the ministry are asked at least to give their backing to foreign marketing efforts by the companies and to grant them export licenses. This is reflected poignantly in the case of The Israel Shipyards. In 1983 the Ministry of Defense preferred to purchase equipment and naval craft from a foreign manufacturer rather than from the Haifa firm despite its large stake for many years in the Israeli navy.[40] In this instance, Israel Shipyards had little recourse, since the option to sell abroad did not really exist; manufacturers of other products for which there is a demand have looked elsewhere and expect the cooperation of the Israeli authorities.

In pressuring the government, corporate representatives are backed by the scientific and technical communities as well as by the military because of their advocacy of science, technology, and innovation in every sector of industry and the economy. Employees of the military industries are another important ally with a vested interest in mounting weapons production and export sales. Their claim to wage increases combines positive and negative arguments: the contribution to Israel's economy and security made by workers and researchers, but also the danger of an exodus of brain power from the defense establishment should foreign orders decline appreciably because of government controls or lack of support. Less appreciated by the trade unions is the inevitable influence of higher wage scales upon the costs of military equipment, ultimately making Israeli arms exports less competitive and therefore less attractive to prospective clients.

The bureaucracy, the military, the business community — each exerts a major influence on public opinion and political decision makers; each is impressive in its own right. Their call for a more active Israeli arms export diplomacy, however, is all the more audible because of a mutual reinforcement which owes, in the first instance, to a web of close interpersonal relationships.

Most of the men at the top of the hierarchy within this coalition share a common military background; many are former career officers. As such they are particularly sensitive to both the IDF and the security argument; and as a result they, like an overwhelming majority of the Israeli public, can be counted upon to support any program like arms sales which has proved its worth by strengthening Israel.

Their understanding of modern Jewish history, with its themes of the Holocaust and powerlessness, reinforced by long professional military training, causes these elites to be impressed, on the one hand, by power and strength at the same time as they are inclined to be cynical, on the other hand, toward false standards of international conduct.[41] These IDF graduates are also noted for being achievement-oriented and pragmatic. The payoff in arms sales politically may only be short-term; but it is also monetary, tangible, and immediate. Just as they might interpret diplomacy — paraphrasing Clausewitz — as war by other means, and hence an extension of military preparedness, so do they perceive of arms sales as not only perfectly natural for Israel but also as adept diplomacy by other, less conventional means. They are in short, individuals for whom the argument of "dollars and sense" is a persuasive one, and the export of military hardware axiomatic.

Interestingly, we find these defense sales promoters making dual use of the dollars and sense argument and of export statistics as part of their sophisticated campaign. There is little doubt but that in private and "off the record" they present the security assistance program spearheaded by weapons transfers as both cost-effective and immensely successful. Thus, spokesmen of the defense industries, when pressing their case for undertaking new projects before Government officials, much like bureaucrats trying to impress their immediate superiors with the eventual excellent sales prospects for such products, are only too anxious to project high sales taking in foreign markets as well. In public, by contrast, they may prefer to waive self-congratulations and praise. From their standpoint it might be advisable to maintain a low profile; avoiding too much outside attention to the export program by softening the image, downplaying Israel's role in the international market, and lowering both corporate as well as aggregate national military export figures. It may be convenient therefore for them to condemn SIPRI estimates of over $1 billion worth of arms sales as politically motivated while citing embarrassingly low reports by the ACDA as being closer to the true scale of activity.

Moreover, weapons transfers possess a special symbolic appeal, confirming the image by these elites of the Jewish state held as small yet determined to survive and also enterprising. Sharing a world view in which arms sales are a fact of life and a self-image of Israel as at once resourceless and resourceful, the country's political, military, and business leaders appear confident that the demand for arms is a vacuum to be filled and that it is in Israel's interest to fill as much of it as possible. This basic predisposition toward the utility of arms and, by extension, arms sales counts heavily in decision making.

Israeli social scientists speak of "the interpenetration and interlinkage of diverse groups" in the society, facilitated by informal systems of communication and relations.[42] This would appear to be the case in the relationship among the four professional hierarchies central to arms sales: policymakers, bureaucrats, the military, and the business community.

Most notable is the tendency for retired army officers to assume positions of influence either in politics or in commerce.[43] To cite merely a few examples, three of the defense ministers active in supporting arms diplomacy in recent years, Moshe Dayan, Ezer Weizman, and Ariel Sharon, were former senior IDF commanders. At the other end of the relationship, Yeshayahu Gavish, the chairman of the large Koor concern is a retired general. The director of Elbit, Binyamin Peled, whose firm is involved in the export of military-related equipment, is a former air force commander. Upon retiring as chief of the air force at the end of 1982, David Ivri became head of the Israel Aircraft Industries; he was called back to serve in 1983 as deputy chief of staff, returning to the IAI as active chairman in April, 1985. Yaakov Shapira was for many years the head of SIBAT; he now works for the Clal concern which has subsidiaries engaged in military manufacture and exports. Iscar Blades, which sells in the United States, is headed by general manager Baruch Bahat, a retired colonel in the air force. In top management positions with Tadiran are former chief of military intelligence General Yehoshua Segui and Nati Sharoni, a top IDF commander. Maj.-Gen. (res.) Amnon Reshef, retired as commander of the tank corps and is now deputy director of Urdan Industries. The list of such former army officers presently holding high posts inside the military defense industries and their export divisions is a long and instructive one.

From their executive management posts such people serve as vigorous spokesmen for pushing arms. And a major part of their message is that, foreign relations aside, the weapons trade is essential if Israeli industry and exports are to be sustained. Other former officers can be found on the boards of interlocking corporate directorates. Still others can be found among the private arms salesmen busy seeking overseas orders. This corporate "foreign policy" and the self-interest of the arms companies and their representatives is being felt increasingly within government circles and all along the decision-making process as this community of overlapping interests continues to grow.

The policy process extends to one more stage, that of implementing the defense sales program. Success depends, therefore, on the manner in which arms emissaries proceed to market and promote Israeli military assistance. As the export program has expanded and gained official government support, a number of channels have been opened for pursuing contracts.

While the exact methods and different conduits for weapons transfers are clouded in secrecy, several can be identified. Foremost are the already mentioned overseas diplomatic and military missions whose function it is, assisted from Tel-Aviv by SIBAT, to explore possibilities for bilateral military cooperation. Taking Africa as a case in point, despite its formal exclusion from many of the countries, Israeli "interest officers" are stationed in at least five other black African countries; Israel has been able to retain an economic presence as well in Kenya, the Ivory Coast, and Nigeria, confirming that members of the Organization for African Unity desire good working relations with Israel but for political reasons stop short of diplomatic ties. For Israel, however, even this situation is satisfactory. Through this minimal presence it has succeeded in administering low-level military assistance programs in widely separated parts of the continent, from the north African Maghreb to southern Africa, just as it conducts trade relations with some seventeen African states.[44]

Second, the major arms manufacturers are themselves active in seeking out potential customers. The IAI, Soltam, IMI, Rafael and Tadiran, for example, have their own export departments and special marketing employees. Some firms maintain regional offices in key cities around the world which are used as a base of operations in establishing close, personal contacts with local military industrialists and government officials. With the support of the government they are also regular participants at international air shows and military exhibitions. A third and less known avenue is through Israeli business concerns operating in foreign countries. Clal has its own marketing outlet, "Isrex"; so, too, Koor which promotes the products of its various subsidiaries worldwide through "Koor-Sachar." Some of the preliminary work for contacts with Zaire was done by Reuven Givon, Koor's representative in Kinshasa, who succeeded in establishing personal ties with President Mobutu. A 1981 small arms deal with the Swiss army was negotiated by Israeli businessman Yekutiel Federmann, who also controls the El-Op company with an arms sales inventory of its own. The giant Eisenberg concern, with branches, agents, and expanding business contacts in east Asia, Africa, and Latin America for over twenty years, has also been instrumental in paving the way for Israeli arms contractors. Aside from his other business enterprises, which include brokering the sale of raw materials, industrial management, and the construction of nuclear power plants, Eisenberg is claimed to funnel some 10 percent of Israeli arms exports.[45]

Yet another access route to potential customers has been through members of local Jewish communities. Oftentimes local leaders and businessmen are exceptionally well placed to advise Israeli emissaries, to initiate informal feelers, and to set up meetings to discuss possible arms arrangements. Information as to the names of officials favorably disposed toward Israel and having some influence upon the selection of a preferred supplier is particularly useful in gaining a head start over other competitors.

Far more problematic is the loose network of shrewd middlemen, made up primarily of private arms dealers, who pose as Israeli arms ambassadors. Many of the 300 dealers reportedly operating from Israel are concerned with weapons procurement and represent American firms.[46] Others, however, are active in the other direction, arranging for Israeli sales. Some two-thirds of these exports are believed to be contracted for on a government-to-government level; still, as much as one-third is handled by such agents.[47] Operating on substantial commissions of from 5 to 18 percent, and relying on personal contacts in the purchasing country, their activities are secretive and unsupervised, albeit fairly effective in closing deals monetarily important to Israel.[48]

The opening for the private arms dealers and their agents is provided by the fact that Israel has a considerably narrower field of formal, regularized diplomatic activity and government-to-government relations than its rivals. Hence a good part of its arms negotiations must be conducted through these backdoor channels, most of which are officially sanctioned, although some are not. Elul Technologies Ltd., headed by David Kolitz, is reputed to be a major middleman for the export as well as import of defense products.[49] Other names prominently mentioned are Marcus Katz, a former Israeli resident in Mexico, with extensive contacts throughout South America and Levi Tsur, also active in Latin American countries. Many of these Israeli agents possess excellent credentials — close ties to government leaders in Jerusalem or, as retired army officers, familiarity with the IDF and its equipment.

Former military people are becoming increasingly prominent as private arms merchants. Representative of this trend is Brig.-Gen. (res.) Efraim Poran, former military secretary to Premiers Rabin and Begin, who specializes in exports to the Philippines, and previously served as military attaché in Singapore. Another case in point is that of Herzl Shafir, a retired IDF major-general and former chief of Israel's police, who opened an office in Nigeria as an agent of Israeli arms exporting firms, including that of Alfred Akirov, a private dealer.[50] Maj.-Gen. (res.) Avigdor ("Yanosh") Ben-Gal, former commander of the northern sector, accepted a position with the arms dealers Shlomo Eliyahu and Yechiel Fromer upon retiring from active military service.

This proliferation of private weapons salesmen aggravates the problem of coordinating the national defense sales campaign. On the one hand, their operations disguise the trail of at least some Israeli arms, which are "laundered" and resold through a maze of fictitious companies in different countries. The further removed they are, however, from government control, the greater is their private motivation and insensitivity to the larger interests at issue in such arms transactions. Representative of this attitude are the comments of one enterprising seller who insisted the policy was "to sell without being too inquisitive about the purchasing states or their regimes" since "beggars can't be choosers." Reacting sharply to criticism, he equated the cessation of arms activity with devastating Israeli industry and destroying the state, and countered that "this is a sacred mission, export pure and simple of which we are proud."[51] Leaving this judgment aside, in operative terms SIBAT has no real mechanism for preventing Israeli companies or private agents from competing against each other for markets in the United States as well as elsewhere.

With so many representatives in the field and such large quantities of Israeli conventional weapons circulating, the policy threatens to get out of hand and to inflict damage upon Israel. Nor is Israel's image as a reputable supplier enhanced by such news items as the one alleging German war criminal Klaus Barbie had secured large amounts of Uzis and Galil rifles for Bolivia;[52] or periodic reports of illicit arms shipments being traced to Israeli ports of origin.[53] This failure or inability to control weapons flows and to assure closer coordination from policy formulation to execution and ultimate destination reflects negatively upon the policymaking process as a whole. It makes Israel vulnerable to the charge that some of its arms practices are inefficient to the point of cancelling some of the initial gains attainable through foreign military assistance.

NOTES

1. For a discussion of Israeli foreign policy, see Brecher's two-volume study, *The Foreign Policy System of Israel* (New Haven: Yale University Press, 1972) and *Decisions in Israel's Foreign Policy* (London: Oxford University Press, 1974). The

latter is a book of case studies strongly oriented toward crisis decisions. Also useful is Lewis Brownstein, "Decision-Making in Israeli Foreign Policy: An Unplanned Process," *Political Science Quarterly* 92 (Summer 1977):259–279. Another critique is volunteered by Stanley Hoffmann, "A New Policy for Israel," *Foreign Affairs* 53 (April 1975):405–431.

2. Helga Haftendorn, "The Proliferation of Conventional Arms," in Wolfram F. Hanreider, ed., *Arms Control and Security: Current Issues* (Boulder: Westview Press, 1979), p. 316.

3. *Maariv*, 11 January 1983; *Newsview*, 25 January 1983.

4. On the insatiable desire of the Shah for weapons, see Barry Rubin, *Paved with Good Intentions* (New York: Penguin Books, 1981), esp. Ch. 6, "Arms and the Shah." The best treatment thus far of the Israeli-Iranian relationship is Shmuel Segev, *"Hamishulash Ha-Irani"* (Tel-Aviv: Sifriat Maariv, 1981).

5. Frank, p. 127.

6. *Maariv*, 11 January 1983. The newspaper report added that Commerce Ministry economists in a working paper argued for a less strict cautionary "red-line," maintaining military exports might be permitted to reach, although not surpass, 30 to 35 percent of industrial exports, *Maariv*, 11 January 1983.

7. In his work Brecher refers to such actors as "the High Policy Elite."

8. With the resignation of Premier Begin on 15 September 1983, the forum was reduced in effect to three people, since Shamir retained his post as Foreign Minister.

9. Disclosed by Minister Patt in *Maariv*, 11 January, 1983.

10. Ben-Gurion's statement in the Knesset on 1 July 1959 is quoted in Shmuel Shichor, *1958–1961. A Diary of Events* (Jerusalem: Haaretz Publishers, n.d.), p. 42, which also provides a chronology of the government crisis.

11. Daniel Shimshoni, *Israeli Democracy: The Middle of the Journey* (New York: The Free Press, 1982), p. 207.

12. Dov Goldstein, "Interview with Defense Minister Ariel Sharon," *Maariv*, 17 December 1982, supplemented in a second interview on 28 January 1983 in which the political-diplomatic argument is prominent due to renewed ties with Zaire and other African states.

13. *J P*, 7 September 1983.

14. *J P*, 6 April 1984. Arens elaborated on the theme in *Maariv*, 19 August 1983, emphasizing the contribution made by sales of the Gabriel to the national economy.

15. Yoram Peri, *Between Battles and Ballots. Israeli Military in Politics* (Cambridge, England: Cambridge University Press, 1983), p. 194.

16. Gideon Rafael, *Destination Peace. Three Decades of Israeli Foreign Policy* (London: Weidenfeld & Nicolson, 1981), p. 378. The Defense Ministry's expanded scope of operation is traced in Brecher, pp. 134–137, and in Peri, pp. 193–231.

17. Amos Perlmutter, *Military and Politics in Israel* (London: Frank Cass and Co., 1969), p. 74.

18. Beyond this shared tradition, however, different emphases are apparent. Under Sharon a global strategic conception governed his support for a forward arms transfer policy. As reflected in some of Arens' early statements backing the Lavi project, the aerospace industry, and indigenous military production, the technological and economic arguments carry more weight owing to his scientific background.

19. *Israel Government Yearbook*, 5741, 1980–1981, p. 124.

20. *Israel Government Yearbook*, 5741, pp. 100–101; *Defense Sales Directory*, 1983. See also, Israel, Ministry of Defense, Deputy Director-General for Defense Exports, "Guidelines for Coordination Between Exporters of Military Products and Defense Technology and the Defense Sales Office" (Hebrew), (April, 1982).

21. Peri, p. 194.
22. *J P*, 17 May 1984.
23. See, for example, *J P*, 1 June 1982.
24. Walter Eytan to Shimon Peres, 5 July 1957. Golan, pp. 81–82.
25. Ben-Gurion to Peres, 5 March, 1958. Golan, p. 84.
26. For an analysis of the Knesset's role in policymaking, see Daniel Shimshoni, pp. 205–207.
27. Peri, p. 184. Gad Yaacobi. *The Government of Israel* (New York: Praeger Publishers, 1982), pp. 62–67.
28. Shimshoni, p. 207.
29. *J P*, 14 December 1982.
30. *Haaretz*, 14 December 1982.
31. *Haaretz*, 17 December 1982.
32. *Maariv*, 17 May 1983.
33. Chaim Herzog, M.K., "South African Visits," *Maariv*, 17 December 1982. Another prominent member of the "dovish" school in the Labour Party, Abba Eban, when asked whether arms to Third World authoritarian rulers troubled him, insisted that Israel had no real choice but to develop and to market arms, although it was his impression that in the days of the Labour governments there had been greater hesitancy, *Koteret Rashit*, 23 September 1983.
34. David J. Louscher, "The Rise of Military Sales as a U.S. Foreign Assistance Instrument," *Orbis* **20** (Winter 1977):933–964.
35. Contrary to the journalist's craft and quest for newsworthy stories, most of the Israeli press editorials object to the penchant of the government to make figures on arms deals public and point out the political damage to the country's interests and image. See, for example, *Haaretz's* lead editorial on 18 May 1984, "Sharon: Declassifier of Classified Information."
36. Modi'in Ezrachi Research Institute survey, *J P*, 2 February 1983.
37. Michael Moodie, "Arms Transfers Policy: A National Dilemma," *Washington Quarterly* **5** (Spring 1982):111.
38. Neuman and Harkavy, p. 17. Also useful is Jacques S. Gansler, *The Defense Industry* (Cambridge: MIT Press, 1980).
39. See Jacques S. Gansler, "The Defense Industry's Role in Military R & D Decision Making," in Long and Reppy, pp. 39–135.
40. *Haaretz*, 22 November 1983.
41. Brecher argues for combining a number of these attitudes, arriving at what he calls "a Tzahal View of the Outer World," pp. 335–339. Of late one finds references in the press to the existence of an identifiable complex; see, for example, Yehuda Shaari, "The Military Power Elite," *Haaretz*, 3 January 1983.
42. Shimshoni, p. 216.
43. For earlier statistics on subsequent occupation patterns of retired senior IDF officers, see Perlmutter, p. 76 and Peri, pp. 108–109, on the surge of demobilizations in the post-1967 period; see also Reich, in Kolodziej and Harkavy, p. 219.
44. Peri, pp. 240–241, suggests Israel in the early 1960s helped train Moroccan security forces as part of what Rafael, p. 81, alludes to as "cooperation in other fields."
45. Eisenberg, with headquarters in Tokyo as well as Tel-Aviv, has companies registered in Vaduz, Liberia, and Panama, and is reputed to have excellent connections in China, *Haaretz*, 30 March 1984 and *Haolam Hazeh*, the Israeli weekly magazine, 3 August 1983, pp. 22–23.
46. *Newsview*, 12 January 1982.
47. *Maariv*, 12 March 1982, quoting Defense Ministry sources.
48. The subject of improper commission fees surfaced briefly in 1982, *J P*, 1 October

1982; *Maariv*, 12 March 1982; also in *Globes*, an economic digest, on 7 December 1983, p. 5. The most extensive list to date of these companies and their agents appeared in *Monitin*, No. 59 (July 1983), pp. 86-96.

49. *IHT*, 27 May 1983.
50. *Haaretz*, 7 February 1983.
51. Quoted in *Maariv's* weekend magazine, 12 August 1983, pp. 7-9.
52. *Haaretz*, 2 February 1984, citing sources in London.
53. In March, 1984 the episode of the "Viking" briefly captured public attention. A ship with Panamanian registry but owned by two former officials of the Zim shipping line and carrying a cargo of arms and ammunition was apprehended by Italian officials in Italy. The owners claimed the shipment was destined for Brazil although speculation centered upon the Red Brigades or possibly a Middle Eastern port, *Haaretz*, 21-23 March 1984.

7

THE WORLDWIDE SALES CAMPAIGN

The essence of Israeli foreign military assistance lies in a single concept — diversification. It finds expression in present international military relationships in two ways: first, by a diversified inventory of marketable defense services and products of increasing sophistication, and second, by the global dimensions of the export campaign, with an extensive list of countries who have been or are presently recipients of aid from Israel. This dual marketing strategy further explains why a small and developing country like Israel has succeeded rather remarkably in penetrating the international arms trade and in remaining competitive.

FORMS OF ISRAELI AID

No one has yet come up with a satisfactory definition of what is included in direct military assistance. Like Pearson, most students and research centers prefer a narrower application, focusing upon conventional military equipment, i.e., "non-nuclear weapons of war, spare parts, ammunition, support equipment, or other primarily military commodities."[1] We find this definition too confining and incomplete for our purpose; if applied to Israel it would hide its full range of military activity.

The sale of actual arms and ammunition undoubtedly captures the most attention, whereas in our analysis this entire area, broad as it may be, constitutes merely one of three forms of Israeli defense goods and services. Aside from these conventional weapons transfers which involve finished products, Israel supplies two other less direct kinds of aid: advice and training, and military technologies.

Direct Weapons

Direct weapons are the primary component of Israeli defense exports. This military hardware — "combat consumables" — includes the standard inventory: aircraft, naval vessels, armored and non-armored vehicles, missiles and rockets, artillery, infantry weapons, small arms ammunition and other ordnance, para-chutes and uniforms, military communications and electronic equipment, and spare parts.[2] A second classification involves the choice offered a client be-tween second-hand, redesigned or refurbished, and brand new weapons. A third category, cutting across the first two, is the origin and source of the par-ticular item or system sold by Israel. Four possibilities exist which in them-selves suggest Israel's distinctiveness: arms of United States, Western Euro-pean, or Communist bloc manufacture, or Israeli "blue-and-white" products. Israel may be the only country in the world with so mixed an inventory on the basis of point of origin and also the only country in the world that develops defenses for both Western and Soviet weapons systems. What is established fact is that Israel has had possession of advanced arms from both sides and that it has successfully introduced modifications in these systems before put-ting them up for resale on the international market.

Combining the three classifications strengthens the impression of diversi-ty. Israel's trade in spare parts, obsolete arms, and older generations of weap-ons merely scratches the surface. These, like the American A-4E Skyhawk and the French-made Mirage, are constantly being phased out as part of the accelerated IDF replacement schedule forced by the unrelenting Middle East arms race; they are then simply passed on to others.

Related to these are reconditioned weapons. Israel has earned a reputation worldwide for excelling in modernizing other countries' existing weapons sys-tems. Designers and technicians have succeeded in the servicing, recondition-ing, and enhancement of such Western weapons as the Patton and Centurion tanks. The latter, for example, has been revived in Israeli factories with the addition of a 105-millimeter gun and a fire-control system that includes a digi-tal computer and laser range-finder.[3] The IAI is reported to have upgraded 15 Mirage-5S planes for Colombia closer to the lines of the Kfir.[4] When re-converted and upgraded, the life span of these items becomes lengthened con-siderably, making their repurchase worthwhile. Once reassembled in Israel they are then passed on to Third World customers. To poor but defense-conscious countries, such hybrid systems suit their needs better than being forced to buy a newer but more expensive system.

In a fourth class by itself are Eastern bloc weapons captured from Syria, Egypt, or the P.L.O. This source of surplus weapons first emerged in 1956 when Egyptian troops fleeing the Sinai left newly acquired arms behind; the 1967 fighting led to staggering amounts of such arms caches and again posed the challenge of how they might be used for both political and commercial advantage. Again, after the 1973 Yom Kippur War, Israel capitalized on its seizure of additional quantities of Soviet arms and ammunition. Operation "Peace for Galilee" in 1982 provided yet a fourth wave of Communist hard-ware: over 1,320 vehicles, including T-34, T-55, and T-62 tanks; more than 30,000 Kalashnikov AK-47 rifles, submachine guns and other light arms; and

200 anti-aircraft pieces, not to mention countless hand grenades, mortar rounds, and artillery shells.[5]

Testifying to Israeli ingenuity, different ways have been found to employ these stockpiles in offsetting part of Israel's war costs. Some have been upgraded, many have been sold and still others just given away for political rather than commercial motives. After each campaign any number of useful items were automatically introduced directly into the IDF, with units specially set up and equipped with Soviet models. In addition, captured equipment has been passed on to Western allies. Quantities have been sent in the past to the United States for testing, analysis, and training in keeping with Israel's strategic value to the West.[6] NATO training schools in Western Germany also are reported to have whole platoons of Russian tanks and batteries of artillery that are used for making training exercises more realistic. Still a third use is the export of Russian-built equipment to Third World countries in the market for such items. In September, 1984, IDF military sources for the first time spoke of the program for refurbishing some 600 captured T-54, T-55 and T-62 Soviet tanks and then putting them up for sale.

A final category of weaponry are systems originating in Israel. The model for this was the Uzi. Since then items designed and produced almost exclusively at home, ranging from the Galil assault rifle through the Gabriel missile to the Kfir plane, compare favorably to Western and Soviet equivalents and have found customers abroad. It was hoped by its planners that the Merkava tank also would follow suit. The manufacture of such high precision components and systems calls attention to yet another feature of Israel's arms supplier role: while it merchandises inexpensive and pedestrian mass market items, it is also included among the select group of sophisticates producing state-of-the-art technologies.

This prompts a fourth classification of military hardware: by degree of sophistication as well as in terms of weapon type, age, and origin. Israel initially started manufacturing ammunition and conventional equipment; much later, toward the end of the 1960s and increasingly during the seventies, its aspirations vaulted all the way up to the level of designing and manufacturing *major* weapons and entire systems, including warships, fighter planes, and tanks. Solely from the standpoint of marketability abroad, the utility of such major systems is open to question.

So expensive is the manufacture of such major land, sea, and air weapons systems that their added value is often considerably less than one might imagine, especially for so small a country as Israel. Their sheer size and visibility can also deter politically sensitive clients who are perfectly willing to buy less conspicuous arms or equipment. In addition, the Israeli version almost invariably suffers from the competition since there are too many larger manufacturers offering comparable systems and at less cost. Lastly, despite the impressive effort by Israel, these elaborate systems are not quite wholly "blue-

and-white" products. Witness the need for foreign-manufactured engines with end-use restrictions in both the Kfir and the Lavi planes, making their resale abroad hinge on consent by the foreign supplier, in both instances the American government.

Fortunately, Israeli defense specialists had the wisdom and foresight to spread out into a third, intermediate and more promising field. In between conventional small arms, on the one hand, and the complete, elaborate weapons systems on the other, is the research, development, and production of components. Military technologies are in increasing demand, especially those subsystems providing for greater accuracy and more rapid delivery. Military trade journals devote considerable space to "smart weapons," to precision-guided munitions and to the new technology of electronic warfare.

On the frontiers of this technology are to be found such specialized and refined areas as computers, optics, communications, and microelectronics. For a number of years Israel has been actively engaged in research and development programs in each of these areas. Moreover, it enjoys a good reputation; commenting upon the lessons of the 1982 fighting over the Falkland Islands and in Lebanon, a British general admitted: "We fought yesterday's war," whereas "the Israelis fought tomorrow's war."[7] Because military strategists tend to concur in the assessment that the outcome of future battles will hinge upon these emerging electronic warfare technologies no less than on how many tanks, ships, or aircraft are deployed, an international market already exists for such components which is worth millions of dollars.

Israel's sales prospects are enhanced by two or three advantages at least. For one thing it enjoys a headstart. Not only are Israeli firms producing such items now in demand by both developed and developing countries, but subsystems have been tested in actual combat. Second, production costs often are lower. A third factor is that many of the Western defense contractors, and the United States in particular, are rather reluctant to share their technological know-how with other countries, even friendly ones. Thus, American law and policy ordinarily stress the sale of completed weapons systems rather than of the technology to produce them. Israel generally has shown less reluctance. These advantages can be seen in the wide interest shown in the two Israeli versions, the Scout and the Mastiff, of remotely-piloted vehicles (RPVs); and also in the foreign sales figures of companies like Tadiran and El-Op, which have staked their corporate success on sustained development of electronic warfare measures and countermeasures in what promises to be the most dynamic area of military technology.

Services

Supplying military hardware, as stated at the beginning of this chapter, represents only one of the three forms which Israeli defense assistance presently takes. The second form is of a more advisory and technical nature. The distinction is that in contrast to the direct provision of arms, Israel goes beyond the mere transfer of weapons and aids others to better utilize, operate, and maintain their own military arsenals, which may or may not feature Israeli weapons. This type of assistance often goes under such euphemisms as the "transfer of skills and erection of service infrastructures" and encompasses a number of defense-related projects and activities, for example, the training of local personnel in the operation and maintenance of weapons systems familiar to, or furnished by, Israel. Related to this is the instruction of local officers, at Israeli bases or in the host country, in staff and operational units. Military courses such as these, often conducted by the IDF in Israel but also by army advisers seconded to the recipient country, were particularly emphasized during the 1960s and are an important component of Israel's renewed military cooperation with Zaire. A similar situation in the military relationship with Sri Lanka came to light in 1984 when government officials in Colombo confirmed that specialized Israeli consulting services were being solicited in combating Tamil separatist terrorism on the island.[8] Also in this category are backup equipment like electronic warning fences, transport, surveillance and support capabilities; and construction and technical services. Delivery, assembly, and maintenance fees are a part of what Israeli suppliers promote in "turn-key" arrangements, whereby complete systems — everything from freightage to access roads, storage facilities, and full operationalization of the weapons systems contracted for — are carried out under Israeli supervision and responsibility. It is the need for such services by Third World customers which further accounts for the large numbers of Israeli advisers, training personnel, and technicians reportedly working abroad.

Know-how

To complete this picture of diversified Israeli products and services, one would have to add a third and final category: the export of military expertise and technologies. This type of aid goes beyond strengthening a recipient's "force posture" — the arsenal, armed forces, and military infrastructure (air bases, fortifications, etc.) at its disposal — and is directed toward helping to strengthen that country's own military-industrial base. Taken together, Israel's range of assistance covers the acquisition, better use, and actual making of arms.

We are witnessing a notable growth on a worldwide scale in the transfer not only of arms but also of defense-related technologies through collaborative ventures among two or more nations. Today many states seek more than military hardware alone. Their priorities call for importing software as well, meaning the technical know-how necessary for the indigenous production of arms. This proliferation of conventional arms-making technologies is in fact part of the expanding global flow of three sorts of technology: nonmilitary, explicitly military, and "dual-use" — communications and transportation equipment that can also be adapted to military projects.

This recent trend poses a serious problem for the international system. On the one hand, the exchange and sale of scientific data as well as products with both civilian and military uses, such as computers, microprocessors, semiconductor manufacturing equipment, and machine tools fits the pattern of interstate collaboration encouraged by functionalists, integrationists, and advocates of interdependence and multilateralism. But on the other hand, of course, it is a dysfunctional type of cooperation, leading to an arms buildup and the spread of dangerous military know-how, thus posing yet another challenge to arms control.[9]

Klare refers to such transfers of technology as the "unnoticed arms trade" and includes under this rubric a wide variety of transactions: the sale of blueprints and technical data for the production of complete weapons by another country; the sale of components, machine tools, and manufacturing know-how for the assembly of such items; the sale of training and technical assistance in the introduction of new production processes; and the sale of complete factories or production lines with all the parts and machines needed to operate them.[10]

Military and "dual-use" technology transfers are emphasized here because if arms production increasingly is becoming a multinational affair, Israel has been quicker than most in perceiving this trend and capitalizing on it.[11] Furthermore, if Israel is able to preserve its technological lead in the military sciences, this form of defense sales will in all likelihood become progressively more prominent in the mix of assistance, arms, and know-how, at least until such time as the dominant actors in the international system succeed in devising an effective arms restraint policy.

The export of military technology is known to be carried out through a variety of mechanisms leading to codevelopment, coproduction, or both. More than two dozen developing countries are reportedly participating in such joint ventures,[12] suggesting that there is a large, growing, and constant market for the kinds of skills, know-how, and experience Israel has to offer. Some of these countries might feel compelled to decline Israel's invitation to supply a particular item or weapons system directly, either due to diplomatic complications arising from open identification with Israel or to internal priorities, the foremost being to expand local military production. Yet from their standpoint as well as from Israel's, licensing and coproduction arrangements provide an excellent alternative.

For Israel's partners the technical assistance affords a chance to escape from the two-fold danger of high cost and political high risk. The production of basic weapons and the incorporation of marginal improvements can be a cheap, simple, and effective counter to the overly sophisticated hardware offered by the larger suppliers which not only absorb precious funds and are difficult to handle but may not necessarily increase a developing country's military effectiveness.[13] Even more important, by such means as licensing, comanufacture, and similar joint ventures, a Third World country can pursue indigenous arms production in order not to become dependent on foreign military supply nor to link itself irrevocably to one of the superpowers.[14]

The benefits for Israel are also readily apparent. Licensing adds to the profit margin of companies marketing their military technologies once they have been fully developed. Tadiran, for example, presently is claimed to have outlets in twenty-two countries; about ten of them are actual plants which manufacture goods on a joint basis, often with 40 percent of the components shipped from Israel.[15] Other firms as well produce sub-systems which cannot be produced economically in Israel in other countries, where the assembly work is also done.

Coproduction and other mutually beneficial arrangements, in other words, provide shared learning experience and, important for Israel, help in finding badly needed investment capital for its own military projects. Joint R & D projects are especially prized as an excellent way of lowering the shared cost of systems development. As two examples, SIPRI reports that in 1977, Israel approved licensing and coproduction agreements for Reshef class boats to be built in Durban in addition to six previously acquired by the South African Navy; also for Gabriel-2 missiles to be assembled in Taiwan.[16] In 1984 it was revealed that an unnamed foreign government had been willing to finance the development in Israel of an engine for a medium range artillery rocket which is now operational and in use by the IDF.[17]

Diversification, reflected in the several forms of direct or indirect military assistance offered by Israel as well as in its extensive weapons inventories, carries over as well into Israeli military relationships with regional and individual country clients. We look next at defense exports by region.

GEOGRAPHIC CONFIGURATIONS

In regional terms the Israeli marketing pattern suggests the absence of any single priority. Other arms suppliers, by contrast, concentrate their sales efforts on a particular target area, sometimes on a solitary customer; cornering a large share of the Saudi Arabian arms market, for instance, is enough to catapult any Western country into major supplier status. Certainly Israel's situation is unlike that of Britain, France, or even the Soviet Union which have concentrated on the Middle East in boosting respective national arms sales.

Indeed, the first thing illustrated by a market analysis is the number of regional outlets virtually written off by Israeli arms salesmen. For obvious reasons the Arab Middle East is automatically excluded; so, too, the outlying Muslim countries like Pakistan which do not qualify as commercial trading partners, let alone candidates for military assistance. To make the point more forcefully, not one of the six leading arms importing states (Libya, Iraq, Syria, Iran, Vietnam, Saudi Arabia) possibly aside from Iran — and even that more for its political than its economic significance — has been a customer of Israel's.[18] Another bloc of countries closed to Israel are those within the Communist camp, especially the Eastern European states, although a small qualification is required. Over the years rumors have circulated, although without any confirmation, that Israeli arms have actually reached behind the Iron Curtain. Thus, in 1968 it was reported that Romania and Yugoslavia were buying Soviet-made tanks from Israel;[19] again, as recently as 1984, American sources claimed Israel had sold some captured P.L.O. armored vehicles to Romania.[20]

Western Europe and North America pose problems of a different sort for Israel. Theoretically nothing prohibits an arms relationship with NATO countries, and in fact Israeli arms contractors do have access. In practice, however, this market has been peripheral for the most part; by every criteria it has yet to even approximate its potential. The reasons are several. France, Great Britain, Italy, and West Germany, but especially the United States, have grown increasingly exclusive and protectionist. They seek military self-sufficiency either through local manufacture or through the adoption of interlocking, complementary weapons systems as part of NATO policy. Current industrial unemployment and export drives directed to the Arab states are further disincentives to buying what might even be acknowledged as superior Israeli systems or components. Besides producing for their own armed forces, these same countries are major weapons exporters in their own right, and thus Israel's competitors. They have little desire, therefore, to indirectly strengthen Israel's military industrial capability by importing Israeli defense products.

Nevertheless, despite these obstacles, some individual successes have been recorded. IMI is able to sell scientific military data to Western European countries; and Israeli transfers of technology to NATO countries amount to millions of dollars annually.[21] The Uzi submachine gun is standard equipment for the West German and Dutch armies.[22] In 1981 Israel was able to conclude a $40 million sale with Switzerland for tank ammunition.[23] Negotiations began in 1983 to provide Canada's Navy with advanced navigational and fire control systems for frigates under construction.[24] In 1984 the Belgian Navy took delivery of a data center for monitoring battle conditions to be used aboard its warships.[25] Similarly, the relationship with West Germany has deepened despite such points of friction as Bonn's desire to sell its Leopard tank to the Saudis. West Germany sends raw materials needed in Israeli arms manufacture; is known to buy from Israel military goods ranging from flak jackets to 105 mm. cannon shells; and has expressed a willingness to trade military technologies.[26] While obviously encouraging, such transactions or the availability of quality Israeli products of themselves are not enough to overcome the obstacles, mostly economic but also political, involved in bidding for contracts in the Western industrialized countries.

Consequently, the Third World has become Israel's principal target for conventional weapons transfers, and it is here that the brand of arms export diplomacy practiced by Israel has been most successful, at least until recently. This concentration derives in part from a shift in Israel's own diplomatic orientation. In the early period of Israel's history, a primary consideration in Israeli foreign policy was a country's ability to *provide* arms, hence the strong Western bias. That predisposition toward United States and European trading partners remains, but there is also an interest in the non-Western world because some of the emphasis now is upon the ability of a target country to import and *absorb* military transfers *from* Israel.

The reasons for this shift have to do mostly with conditions in the Third World. The developing areas, also referred to as the "less developed countries" or LDCs, as a whole constitute a zone of growing armament and militarization. In the past decade the volume of major weapons to the Third World countries has risen by more than 300 percent.[27] Arms imports jumped from $6.2 billion at the end of the 1960s to $15.5 billion (in constant dollars) in 1978.[28] Statistics indicate that in 1979 alone Third World countries imported $19.3 billion worth of arms as part of their defense effort;[29] this accounted for 81 percent of the world arms trade that year.[30] A breakdown of this figure by principal region and share of the trade shows the Middle East leading ($7.3 billion, or 34 percent), followed by Africa ($4.2 billion, or 19 percent) and Latin America ($1.5 billion, or 7 percent).[31] Altogether, the Third World's share of total arms imports for the period 1979–1981 remained in the vicinity of 62 percent.

The result is a steady expansion of military capabilities and appetites, causing Third World countries to commit as great an allocation of resources for defense as for social programs.[32] Those with military governments are even more inclined to stress military readiness and budget. For all of them, the effect of foreclosing the nuclear option is to spur their interest in conventional weapons readily available on the open market. Similarly, the effect of the Falklands war was to embolden Third World countries to move up the technological scale in their arms purchases. More and more LDCs are choosing to diversify their own sources of arms supply, as evidenced statistically.[33]

The unsettled politics of these regions, both internal and interstate, lies behind the rush to arms procurement. Political factors include: the multiplication of new states; more nations wanting more arms; internal instability, matched in many cases by tense external relationships; weapons levels commonly interpreted as a symbol of national status and strength; and rapid attrition of weaponry which creates the incentives for acquiring newer and larger arsenals. These general characteristics are true throughout the Third World, and suggest why Israel, in offering a cost-effective alternative, is qualified to meet their needs. Since relatively few of these countries possess either the resources or the skilled manpower to support large quantities of advanced technology weapons a substantial market for traditional weapons is virtually assured.[34] Therefore, relatively cheap, highly mobile, easily operable conventional weapons will continue to represent the core of Israel's sales to the LDCs.

THE AMERICAS

Taken as a region Latin America looms quite large in the Israeli arms sales picture. Here Israel appears to enjoy some distinct advantages. For one thing, Latin American weapons imports from all sources were up 608 percent in a decade.[35] Second, it is the only area of the Third World where the majority of states — twenty-one — maintain diplomatic and trade relations with Israel.[36] Total trade with the Americas (excluding the United States) stood at $290.4 million in 1980 and at $316 million in 1981, of which Israeli exports amounted to $161.3 million and $157.5 million in each of the respective years.[37] Weapons transfers may not be fully reflected in these figures since Latin America is alleged to buy anywhere from one-third to one-half of Israel's arms exports,[38] which may also explain why the directory of Israeli military factories and their products circulated among overseas clients by the government is published in two editions — English and Spanish.

Israel's efforts in Central and South America owe to more than momentary openings. Indeed, nowhere is the full mix of incentives for Israel to engage in arms diplomacy better reflected than in the case of the Americas. First, Israel is not a newcomer to the region, having been a supplier of military assistance to South American countries since the 1950s. Second, these countries provide an open market, encouraging a greater diversity of suppliers than in any other region. Third, their rush to arm is traceable to a relatively low state of military preparedness; the profusion of military and authoritarian regimes; and the range of contingencies for intraregional conflict, whether due to subversive movements, border disputes, or traditional territorial claims.

Fourth, from Israel's standpoint the incentives to satisfy this urge by Latin American governments to modernize their armed forces are, first and foremost, political. Israel has no vital strategic or military interests in Latin America, yet is concerned about both the East-West regional balance and P.L.O.-Arab penetration. And while it is certainly true that military sales provide Israel with an entree into civilian markets, they have figured in the past more importantly in preserving ties with Jewish communities in Latin America. Statistically, whether coincidental or not, it is noteworthy that some of Israel's largest regional arms clients are also those with substantial Jewish populations: 140,000 in Brazil, 30,000 in Chile, 50,000 in Uruguay, 12,000 in both Colombia and Venezuela, 5,000 in Peru and 300,000 Jews in Argentina.[39]

Their well-being is one obvious source of concern. But Jerusalem is equally sensitive to the diplomatic dimension, employing this valuable military relationship to wage a campaign against possible anti-Jewish and anti-Israel influences, including the resident Arab communities, Arab League representatives and, on an institutional level, clergy whose impact on the attitudes and political belief systems of the predominantly Roman Catholic population is considerable.

CENTRAL AMERICA

The Caribbean basin, too, has become a zone of accelerated militarization in the 1980s under the combined weight of Marxist revolution, terrorism, and subversion. Israel entered the Central American arms market already in the 1950s when it furnished small arms to the Somoza regime in Nicaragua. Such aid owed nothing to affinity for the regime but arose primarily from the traditional friendship and support at the state level for Israel in world forums shown by countries like Nicaragua, Costa Rica, and the Dominican Republic ever since the historic 1947 U.N. General Assembly resolution in favor of Jewish statehood. Israel's involvement deepened in the late 1970s when it moved into markets vacated by the United States, becoming the largest supplier of infantry equipment to El Salvador and Guatemala.[40] It also filled a comparable role for human rights non-violators such as Costa Rica and Honduras, which made effective use of the Arava transport aircraft in counterinsurgency actions against guerrilla forces in densely forested areas.

If Israeli transfers clashed with the U.S. policy of denying aid to suspected human rights violators during that period, today there is a greater identity of interests following a restatement of America's position by President Reagan:

> When countries must divert their scarce resources from economic development in order to fight imported terrorism or guerrilla warfare . . . security assistance, therefore, is an integral part of our aid policy with respect to Latin America and the developing world in general.[41]

This policy is also reflected by the strong recommendation of the Kissinger Commission on Central America calling for a significant increase in military assistance for the region. Both countries presently are engaged in a parallel effort to strengthen conservative forces in Central America through a combination of fostering economic development and assisting with security concerns.

The shift in American thinking since the Carter administration is much closer to Israel's own policy toward the Americas for many years, and makes it easier for Israel to operate in the area. As part of its enlarged military training missions and role as a supplier of arms to Central America, Israel has offered to share stocks of arms captured in Lebanon, assisted intelligence activities in Costa Rica and Guatemala, and reportedly trained government forces in both of those countries as well as in Honduras and El Salvador to combat antigovernment insurgents.[42]

Israel reportedly is among the largest secondary suppliers to Central America. This is partly the result of longstanding military relationships, and partly the result of more recent developments in the area as well as an expanded Israeli conception of its security interests. The latter was best reflected perhaps by the arrival in December, 1982, of then Defense Minister Sharon for talks with Honduran government officials and military leaders; his visit led to considerable speculation as to future military cooperation between Israel and the governments of Central America, possibly with the U.S. brokering and indirectly supporting this stronger Israeli presence.

The choice of Honduras may have been made for more than symbolic reasons. Although most of Honduran military needs are filled by the United States, arms deals of a modest nature had been concluded with Israel in previous years; its leaders are vitally concerned at the inability of the United States to contain revolutionary forces backed by Nicaragua and Cuba in the arc of instability surrounding Honduras; and they therefore are permitting the country to serve as a Western base for counterinsurgents, training, prepositioning supplies, and intelligence activities while at the same time seeking to diversify their own sources of supply.[43]

Should Israel continue to deepen its military commitment in the Caribbean, Costa Rica is a logical candidate as a second base of operations. Israel enjoys warm relations with Costa Rica, as seen by the decision in 1983 to acknowledge Jerusalem as Israel's official capital and by the cordial reception given Foreign Minister Shamir in San Jose in October, 1982. More important is the anxiety of tiny Costa Rica at the political intentions of Nicaragua, with which it shares a long border. Lacking a regular army, Costa Rica has been seeking the help of other countries in improving the defense capabilities of its small internal security force.[44] These arms needs, however, are quite modest.

El Salvador's, by contrast, are much greater, and it is apparently the largest consumer of Israeli arms and aid in Central America — 6 percent of Israel's military exports, 80 percent of El Salvador's defense imports.[45] The bilateral military relationship, prominent in the mid-1970s, has become increasingly so, again due to regional developments stemming from the Sandinista seizure of power in July, 1979, which not only changed Nicaragua internally but upset the regional balance and threatens the regimes of countries like El Salvador in immediate or close proximity to Nicaragua. In coping with this dual security threat, fighting a prolonged civil war, and at the same time bolstering external defenses, military officials in El Salvador have openly expressed confidence that Israel, among other friendly nations, would volunteer military assistance.[46]

Other Central American countries with which Israel at one time or another has had small-scale arms supply relationships include the Dominican Republic, Guatemala, Haiti, Mexico, and Panama. Nicaragua, prior to the 1979 overthrow of the Somoza dynasty by the Sandinistas, provided Israel with its best opportunity in the region. Since then, even though that outlet has been shut, the threat posed by the new regime in Managua to other countries in the area indirectly has served to provide Israel with new and unprecedented potential opportunities (Table 7.1).

Table 7.1. Arms Deliveries to Central America, 1970–1983.

Costa Rica		National guard training
		Small arms
Dominican Republic		Uzi submachine guns
El Salvador	11–25	Arava (STOL) transports
	24	Fouga Magister trainers and Ouregan fighters
		80-mm. rocket launchers
		Uzi submachine guns
		Ammunition, spare parts (including captured stores)
Guatemala	10–17	Arava (STOL) transports
		Armored cars
	10,000	Galil assault rifles
	5	Mobile field kitchens
		Intelligence and training
		Helmets and infantry equipment
		Kfir fighter planes
Haiti		Light arms and ammunition
Honduras	12	Kfir fighter planes
		Uzi and Galil guns
	6	Arava (STOL) transports
		Westwind reconnaissance plane
	5	Coastal patrol boats
	16	Super Mystere planes
	14	Armored cars
		Mortars
Mexico	10	Arava (STOL) transports
		Armored cars and troop carriers
Nicaragua	2	Arava (STOL) transports
		Rifles, ammunition
		Patrol boats
		Radio equipment
		T-54 and T-55 tanks
Panama		Radar and communications systems
	1	Westwind reconnaissance plane

Derived from SIPRI Yearbook, 1980, 1981, 1982; IISS, *The Military Balance*, 1979–1980 through 1983–1984; Jane's; *International Defense Review*; *Defense and Foreign Affairs*; *The New York Times*; *Washington Post*; Cynthia Arnson, "Israel and Central America," *New Outlook*, vol. 27, no. 3–4 (March/April 1984), pp. 19–22; *Khadashot*, 8 June 1984, pp. 56–57.

For all of their apparent success, however, military relationships with the Central American republics have recently begun to pose challenges for Israeli arms diplomacy. Briefly, these center on political and economic assumptions. In previous years, with few exceptions, Israel held to the principle of selling only to legitimate regimes and avoiding involvement in internal struggles in countries with which it maintains normal relations. The civil war in El Salvador, for instance, or reported Israeli support of the Contras fighting the Sandinista regime in Nicaragua sorely test such principles. Such persistent rumors regarding covert activity and arms supplies, moreover, serve to put Israel on the defensive in terms of its image and international standing.[47] Third, the Central American market conceivably could dry up as quickly as it surfaced, especially if efforts at peace mediation such as those by the Contadora group were to succeed in putting a freeze on arms shipments and in negotiating the withdrawal of all foreign troops and military advisers from the region. Fourth, the United States, when it wants to, effectively dominates this arms market in its backyard. Lastly, as clients, the Central American states share one final characteristic: their arms needs are on a modest scale. Costa Rica in 1983, for example, decided to increase military spending by 30 percent: $3 million in aid from the United States, plus another $1 million in purchases from five other nations.[48] Therefore, while Jerusalem can claim to see political dividends from its military relationships with Central America, the region's imports of services rather than direct arms hardware suggest that the economic reward for Israel is quite marginal.

SOUTH AMERICA

The southern tier of Latin American states presents a somewhat different configuration: the military relationship stresses Israeli aid of the more direct and material kind, and is characterized by large weapons transfers. Recent openings were made possible because of a reorientation in U.S. policy. On the one hand, Jerusalem explains its arms transfers as serving the larger American goal of containing Communist subversion in the southern hemisphere; at the same time Israel has jumped in to fill some of the void caused by a drop in the U.S. share of the Latin American arms market in the late 1970s from 70 to 20 percent.[49]

Argentina is by far the largest South American customer, absorbing nearly 30 percent of Israeli weapons transfers during the 1970s,[50] and has been set aside for separate analysis. But, again, diversification has ensured more or less regularized military relationships with a number of other South American countries (Table 7.2).

Contrary to the generally accepted view that the shared status of Brazil and Israel as the two leading suppliers of arms to the Third World precludes their having any supply relationship of their own, in March, 1984, the Brazilian

Table 7.2. Arms Deliveries to South America, 1970–1983.

Argentina		Gabriel missiles
		Military uniforms and gear
	48	Nesher ("Dagger", or Mirage III) combat aircraft
		Shafrir missiles
	4	Coastal patrol boats
	30	Skyhawk jet fighters
		Fire control systems
		Parachutes
		Mobile field hospitals
Bolivia	6	Arava (STOL) transports
	24	Kfir fighter planes
Brazil		Helicopters
		Gabriel missiles
Chile	6	Reshef class fast patrol boats
		Shafrir air-to-air missiles
		Radar systems
		Light arms and ammunition
		Mobile field hospitals
		Fire control systems
Colombia	3	Arava (STOL) transports
	12	Kfir fighter planes
		Gabriel missiles
		Field artillery pieces
		Tanks
		Airplane maintenance equipment
Ecuador		Barak anti-missile missiles
		Rockets, explosives, ammunition
	12–24	Kfir fighter planes
		Field kitchens
		Armored personnel carriers
	9–10	Arava (STOL) transports
Paraguay	6	Arava (STOL) transports
Peru		Small arms and ammunition
		Radio equipment
Venezuela	24	Kfir fighter planes
	3	Arava (STOL) transports
		Rubber boats
		Multiple rocket launchers
		Tactical communications equipment

Derived from SIPRI Yearbooks; IIIS, *Defense and Foreign Affairs; Khadashot*, 8 June 1984; Steinberg, in Ball and Leitenberg, p. 296.

naval command announced its intention to purchase Gabriel missiles from Israel, in addition to eight helicopters bought in 1982 from Israeli surplus stocks.[51] The following month it was reported that Ecuador would be buying Barak missiles for its navy.[52] Also in 1984 defense contractors like the IAI joined other Israeli industrialists in pressing the government to conclude negotiations with Colombia whereby the latter would agree to oil shipments in exchange for a variety of military as well as nonmilitary Israeli goods and services.[53]

In terms of the future, however, Israel's prospects for further arms sales to South America are dependent on the ability of these regional customers to put their economic houses in order. The current international banking and debt crises are centered in Latin America; and some of Israel's biggest arms clients have been unable to manage the burden of paying interest on existing international loans (Table 7.3). Most of these countries must undertake severe remedial measures, either voluntarily or in the face of international pressures, if they are to improve their economic performance. A logical budget item for trimming is defense expenditure, which would necessitate cancelling arms buildup programs and foreign defense imports.

It is harder to deal in regional characteristics or patterns when referring to Africa or Asia. One distinction between Africa, on the one hand, as opposed to Latin America and Asia, on the other, is the geographical factor. Only in the case of the former does geographic proximity argue for military aid as a cushion against the diplomatic isolation caused by Arab and Muslim pressures within the narrower context of the Arab-Israeli conflict, whereas in the latter regions these considerations take second place to the larger, systemic struggle. There Israel becomes a participant in the East-West confrontation and justifies its arms transfers accordingly.

AFRICA

In the instance of Africa defense ties with Israel were already deep and rather significant in the 1960s. Those inroads were attributable to a combination of factors: revolutionary changes in the map and politics of the continent plus Israel's accurate as well as early perception of the opportunities these changes posed. But then followed more than a decade of strained ties during which Israel's presence fell to eight diplomatic missions on the continent when African leaders abandoned Israel as the condition for Arab monetary aid. The situation in the 1980s would seem to present Israeli military sales diplomacy with renewed opportunities. Aside from African disillusionment with Arab performance as opposed to verbal pledges, sub-Saharan Africa remains the least heavily armed region of the world.

This has begun to change, however. Africa as a whole registered the largest average annual rate of increase (33.37 percent) in arms imports as compared to the other regions between 1971–1980.[54] Postcolonial insecurities, unresolved boundary disputes, and ethnic irredentism are but a few of the causes for the current trend toward increased military expenditures by each of the African nations. It is a response to deeper regional problems, marked by the rise of intervention and a decaying security system. Other symptoms include: eco-

Table 7.3. Leading Debtor Nations in South America.

COUNTRY	TOTAL EXTERNAL DEBT ($ BILLION)
Brazil	92
Mexico	87
Argentina	43.6
Venezuela	34.5
Chile	17.9
Peru	12.6
Colombia	11.8
Ecuador	6.7
Bolivia	4.4

From *Jerusalem Post*, 3 May 1984. Reprinted with permission.

nomic stagnation, political fragmentation, growing disparities in military power, the accelerating import of arms, the erosion of regional norms, and the manifest incapacity of the Organization of African Unity to cope with threats to regional stability, all of which encourage resort to force.[55]

In terms of individual countries, South Africa stands out as the single largest customer. It is thought to have been the purchaser of 35 percent of all Israeli arms sold in the years 1970–1979.[56] The arms flow is one explanation for the balance of trade between the two countries — in 1981 Israeli imports were $104.2 million, exports $101.2 million.[57] Both because of its distinctiveness within African politics and its salience for Israeli arms diplomacy, South Africa has been selected for separate analysis in the following chapter.

Sub-Saharan Africa lends itself to Israel's preferred strategy of market diversification. The Central African Republic, Ethiopia, Ghana, the Ivory Coast, Kenya, Nigeria, Tanzania, Uganda, Zaire, and Zambia are regarded as having been recipients at one time or another of military assistance from Israel. Other clients are said to include Gabon, possibly Chad. With a resumption of ties, Liberia is added to the list (Table 7.4). The listing is a partial one and not fully reflective since it mentions only identifiable transfers and omits military aid other than direct hardware, as in the instance of Uganda perhaps; nor does it include South Africa.

Neither can the listing as yet give tangible expression to the emerging military relationships begun recently, such as with Zaire (also to be dealt with

Table 7.4. Arms Deliveries to Africa, 1970–1983.

Ciskei	1	Westwind reconnaissance plane
Ethiopia		Light weapons, mortars, ammunition
Ghana		Uniforms
		Fire-fighting equipment
Kenya	2	Missile boats
		Sea-to-sea Gabriel missiles
		Uniforms and military gear
		Mobile field kitchens and hospitals
		Airplane maintenance equipment
Liberia	4	Arava (STOL) transports
Morocco		Armored personnel carriers
		AMX tanks
Nigeria		Oil tanker trucks
		Fire-fighting trucks
		Uniforms, infantry equipment
		Field kitchens and hospitals
Swaziland	1	Arava (STOL) transport
Tanzania		Field kitchens and hospitals
Uganda	10	Sherman tanks
Zaire		Galil, Uzi, M-16, Kalachnikov rifles
		Tents and sleeping bags
		Rifle and artillery shells
		T-54 tanks
Zimbabwe	11–15	Bell helicopters

From *Jerusalem Post*, 3 May 1984. Reprinted with permission.

separately in the next chapter) or with Liberia. At the time of writing, the only confirmed transaction was agreed upon in September, 1983, whereby Liberia contracted to pay $10 million to IAI for 4 Arava transport planes.[58] That Liberia is greatly interested in Israel's defense products can be inferred from President Samuel Doe's tour of several military plants and army facilities during a state visit to Israel in August, 1983, at which time Israeli-Liberian ties were renewed.[59] On that occasion Foreign Minister Shamir assured Doe that Israel is ready to help African friends protect their security against aggressors.

Tangible evidence of this commitment in the past may help to explain Israel's unique military relationships with countries like Morocco and Ethiopia. In the case of the former, the secret transfer some years ago of armor no longer used by the IDF may have been carried out in accordance with Israeli goals of: (a) seeing a moderate Arab, pro-Western monarchy remain stable in the face of such external threats as Nasserist Egypt, Algeria, Libya, or the

Polisario movement; (b) assuring the continued liberal policy toward the emigration of Jews from Morocco maintained for many years by King Hassan.[60]

The same interests governed the Israeli arms supply policy toward Ethiopia during the final years of Emperor Haile Selassie's reign. Dictated by larger strategic concerns in the Red Sea–Horn of Africa area (freedom of navigation, containing both Soviet and Egyptian expansion southward), this policy persisted despite the fact that Ethiopia broke relations during the 1973 war. Israel continued to provide weapons and advisers to Addis Ababa in its struggles against Eritrea and in the Ogaden War with Somalia. As late as 1977 Israel supplied bombs and ammunition; Israeli mechanics kept U.S.-made F-5 fighter planes in service, enabling the Ethiopian airforce to combat Somalia's advantage in armor.[61] A similar desire to ensure against Libyan domination in North Africa at least would make reports from foreign sources of Israeli arms and even technical advisers in Chad on the side of the constituted government in N'djamena comprehensible.[62]

ASIA

One step further removed, Asia poses both opportunity and challenge to Israel. So great is the geographical spread of nations that it fits perfectly the Israeli formula of diversificiation. At the same time so distinctive is each of the Asian countries in terms of political and security concerns that it is impossible to speak of an integrated regional approach by Jerusalem. Rather, arms sales continue to be made, as they have since the fifties, when, for example, two frigates were sold to Ceylon, on a country-by-country basis. Asian countries — both trading partners and reported recipients of military aid in the past — include Indonesia, Malaysia, the Philippines, Singapore, South Korea, Taiwan, and Thailand. Israeli exports (of which arms are a probable component) to some of these countries are substantial: $47.4 million in the case of Singapore, $25.6 million in the case of Taiwan.[63] In the absence of separate figures for classified arms sales such statistics on total exports serve as an important indicator of probability, although they may be inconclusive and even misleading. Thus Israeli exports in 1981 to Hong Kong ($216.8 million) and to Japan ($206 million) — two Asian trade partners not known to have a weapons transfer relationship with Israel — were the highest of all regionally.

One pattern, however, which can be extracted from this listing is Israel's success with countries of the Association of Southeast Asian Nations (ASEAN): the Philippines, Singapore, Indonesia, Malaysia, and Thailand. This five-nation ASEAN area is in many ways a natural target for commercial ties due to its economic growth rate and interest in high technology.[64] Close trade relations, and the presence of seven diplomatic missions in Asia, also provide the opening for some form of security assistance relationship, as well.[65] Appreciative of such opportunities, a number of Israeli companies have shown a growing desire to tap Far Eastern markets. One of these is Tadiran, three of whose five export categories are described as being in the security field and given as representing 70 to 80 percent of the company's total exports. Due in large part to export difficulties experienced in 1982, Tadiran hoped to improve its 1983 sales performance by stressing the Far Eastern market, with exports there expected to reach $60 million, or some 30 percent of all its foreign sales.[66]

Unlike Central America or Africa, arms procurement policies by these Asian countries owe much less to immediate conflict situations than to efforts to guarantee a constant state of preparedness (Table 7.5).

Israel stands to benefit from several advantages in dealing with Asia: Arab and P.L.O. influence is not so prominent, and the governments of the region attempt to maintain a balanced position vis-à-vis Israel and the Middle East conflict; their dependence on Arab oil is lessening; they share a respect for Israel's national determination and view it as a role model in defense readiness; finally, these countries are in the market for military technologies even more than for arms themselves.[67] Foreign Ministry officials appear altert to these

Table 7.5. Arms Deliveries to Asia, 1970–1983.

Australia		Airplane parts
		Computer and communication systems
Indonesia	18	Skyhawk planes
Malaysia		Gabriel missiles
		Skyhawk planes
		Mirage jet fighters
New Zealand		Military communications equipment
		Parachutes
		Rubber boats
Papua-New Guinea		3 Arava planes
Philippines		Military gear
		Mobile field kitchens and hospitals
		Surveillance and radio equipment
Singapore		155-mm. howitzers
		AMX light tanks
		Gabriel missiles
		Military and infantry gear
		Troop carriers
Taiwan		Gabriel missiles
		Shafrir missiles
Thailand		Gabriel missiles
		Armored vehicles
	3	Arava (STOL) planes

From *Jerusalem Post*, 3 May 1984, and international edition of *JP*, week ending 16 February 1985. Reprinted with permission.

opportunities for broadening trade, military, and technical cooperation with the Far East, and to strengthen Israel's position among the countries of the region. This led the Ministry's director-general, David Kimche, to visit the area in early 1984, with stopovers in Australia, Singapore, Thailand, and Japan. Returning from this mission, he expressed the opinion there was still insufficient awareness in Israel, especially in the business community, of potential markets for quality Israeli exports in Southeast Asia.[68]

A COMPOSITE CUSTOMER PROFILE

The sheer number of recipients of Israeli military arms and assistance is in itself quite striking when one considers Israel's formal diplomatic isolation. Estimates of countries dealing either openly or covertly with Israel vary. One local magazine has Israel selling arms to twenty-nine countries;[69] another unofficial tabulation claims as many as fifty-one clients.[70] Each of the two government-controlled defense manufacturers, IAI and IMI, admit to marketing their products to more than forty countries, but without specifying which ones.[71] These are conservative estimates given the unlikelihood of both lists being exactly identical.[72] Nevertheless, assuming the actual number to be close to fifty, the figure compares most favorably with other suppliers, falling between the U.S., with sixty-seven arms clients, and the Soviet Union, with twenty-eight confirmed recipients.[73]

The numbers by themselves are insufficient. Despite the differences, geographic and otherwise, among the customer countries, analysis of the data does provide a composite description of the type of client most conducive to Israeli marketing efforts.

A typical purchaser is likely to be:

- a Third World nation committed to development,
- a government in power rather than dissident or rebel forces,
- rightist in its political orientation,
- not prominent within the Arab-Muslim bloc,
- pursuing nonalignment although more inclined toward the U.S. and the West,
- under a defense-conscious government.

This latter attribute is in all probability linked to:

- the local military being either the actual or proximate locus of power,
- high defense expenditure,[74]
- an existing domestic arms-manufacturing capacity, or else plans to establish one with outside assistance.

Strong emphasis upon defense and a military buildup are the result of:

- that country's strategic value,

- the existence of a perceived security threat originating domestically or, if external, posed by a menacing neighbor country or an expansionist superpower,
- the need for military aid in a hurry,
- international criticism or isolation,
- difficulties encountered in meeting its arms needs,
- reluctance to become dependent upon a single source of supply, hence willing to do business with Israel and Israeli firms.[75]

From Israel's standpoint the prospects for a meaningful military bilateral relationship are that much better if the country possesses any of several reinforcing traits:

- preferably if it has no cash flow problem,
- alternatively, if it has and is prepared to exchange a strategic raw material vital for Israel's own industrial and military needs.

Nor would it hurt if, in addition, that country shares Israel's concern at the power of an Arab, possibly Muslim, state or coalition of states. Also advantageous, though certainly not mandatory:

- the Jewish factor, in the person of an active and influential local Jewish community, or a foreign policy seeking preferential treatment by American public opinion,
- previous satisfactory experience with Israeli military assistance.

A conservative foreign policy orientation and some degree of regional prominence would seem to be the characteristics shared by Israel's principal clients. The highest frequency of convergent interests appears where the arms recipient, in addition to its poor international standing, is an inherently status quo country. Also noticeable is the success Israel has had in affiliating itself through defense sales with at least one rising regional power that can exercise considerable local and international influence on security issues affecting Israel. These have included West Germany in Europe, Iran in the Middle East, Argentina in South America, and South Africa and Zaire in the southern and central African subsystems. To a lesser extent this is true of South Korea and Taiwan in East Asia as well.

We believe Argentina and South Africa can serve as instructive case studies for profiling Israel's supply relationships. They reflect some of the attributes sought by Jerusalem in prospective clients. Moreover, SIPRI listed them as the largest recipients of Israeli arms in the 1970s: 35 and 29 percent, respectively.[76]

Straddling the major sea lanes and ocean resources in the Southern Cone between Cape Horn and the Cape of Good Hope, Argentina and South Africa are geopolitically and strategically vital to Western economic and security planning toward the end of this century. Israel regards itself as part of this global defense system.

In the author's opinion, both Argentina and South Africa in the 1980s share other arms diplomacy prerequisites. Both give high priority to military preparedness against external threat and thus are in the market for fighter craft, missiles, and patrol boats, which are Israeli specialties. Both have presented no real problem in negotiating payment, perhaps because of their urgency or dependence and the difficulties in securing outside sources. Both have large and prosperous Jewish communities, members of which appear able to immigrate to Israel with relatively few restrictions. In the case of Argentinian Jews, the government there tends to treat them, at Israel's urging, as a relatively protected minority. Also, neither has shown any special affinity toward the Arab position on issues relating to the Arab-Israeli conflict. Nor has either country had cause to complain over the performance of weapons systems purchased from Israel. Lastly, both countries are defensive under the three-fold challenges of an internal threat, continental rivals, and international ostracism.

NOTES

1. Frederic S. Pearson, "U.S. Arms Transfer Policy: The Feasibility of Restraint," *Arms Control* 2 (May 1981):25–65, 48. Cf. the broader usage of "security assistance" in order to include grants for military materiel, grants for military training, funds for credits and guarantees for foreign military sales, and grants to foreign governments for support of their security programs. Philip J. Farley, Stephen S. Kaplan, William H. Lewis. *Arms Across the Sea* (Washington, D.C.: The Brookings Institution, 1978), p. 26.
2. The listing conforms to the definition used by the U.S. Arms Control and Disarmament Agency, *World Military Expenditures and Arms Transfers, 1967–1978*, (Washington, D.C.: U.S. Government Printing Office, December, 1980), p. 28. A partial yet extensive list of military products produced by Israel is in Merrill Simon, *Middle East: At the Brink* (Washington, D.C.: The Center for International Security, 1982) pp. 80–81.
3. *NYT*, 16 March 1982. An interesting piece on Israeli upgrading is Gerald Steinberg, "Recycled Weapons," *Technology Review* (April, 1985): 28–38.
4. *Flight International* figures quoted in *Haaretz*, 11 May 1983.
5. *IHT*, 31 July–1 August 1982; *Haaretz*, 25 October 1982; W. Seth Carus, "The Bekaa Valley Campaign," *The Washington Quarterly* (Autumn 1982): 34–41; *Haaretz*, 22 July 1983.
6. *The Economist*, "Foreign Report," 23 September 1982, p. 3.
7. Quoted in *Business Week*, 20 September 1982, p. 104.
8. *J P* and *Haaretz*, 27 May 1984.
9. Bjorn Hagelin, "International Cooperation in Conventional Arms Acquisition: A Threat to Armaments Control?", *Bulletin of Peace Proposals* 9 (1978): 144–155.
10. Michael T. Klare, "The Unnoticed Arms Trade," *International Security* 8 (Fall 1983): 68–88.
11. Neuman, p. 193, concludes "offset arrangements in various guises will be the future currency of the arms transfer system."
12. Pierre, *The Global Politics of Arms Sales*, p. 11. Also relevant is Augusto Varas and Fernando Bustamante, "The Effect of R & D on the Transfer of Military Technology to the Third World," *International Social Science Journal* (1983), pp.

141–162. From the supplier perspective the discussion of multinational arms production in SIPRI, 1982, is useful, pp. 124–126.

13. That most countries are bent upon making or securing increasingly elaborate and ornamental systems of only marginally greater effectiveness is the central thesis presented by Mary Kaldor in her book, *The Baroque Arsenal*.

14. Saadia Amiel, "Defense Technologies for Small States: A Perspective," in Louis Williams, ed., *Military Aspects of the Israel-Arab Conflict* (Tel-Aviv: University Publishing Projects, 1975), pp. 16–22.

15. *J P*, 3 June 1984. Tadiran company officials would not volunteer specific locations for these plants but indicated they were in the U.S., West Germany, South America, and the Far East.

16. SIPRI, 1984, p. 278 on both South Africa and Taiwan.

17. *J P*, 6 May 1984.

18. ACDA, p. 9. Of the nineteen largest Third World customers in 1981 no less than twelve are closed to Israel, SIPRI 1982, p. 186.

19. *Newsweek*, 23 September 1968, and cited in Eliyahu Kanovsky, *The Economic Impact of the Six-Day War* (New York: Praeger, 1970), p. 49.

20. *NYT*, 28 August 1983. Drew Middleton, "Small Nations Crack Arms Market," quoting the U.S. General Accounting Office.

21. *Israel Government Yearbook*, 5742, p. 129.

22. Thayer, p. 286.

23. SIPRI, 1982, p. 188.

24. *Haaretz*, 7 June 1983.

25. *Haaretz*, 21 May 1984.

26. *Maariv*, 18 May 1984. SIPRI, 1984, p. 221, shows 4 Westwinds ordered in 1980.

27. SIPRI 1980, p. xxvii; *IHT*, 28 May 1982.

28. Pierre, p. 13.

29. *WSJ*, 29 June 1982.

30. ACDA, 1982, p. 5.

31. Ibid., pp. 8–9.

32. "Table of Expenditure Upon Military, Education and Health," *NYT*, 20 September 1981.

33. Neuman, p. 195, presents data confirming that the number of LDCs receiving arms from four or more suppliers tripled between 1972–1973 and 1981–1982, rising from ten to thirty-two. In doing so they sought as suppliers other fellow Third World and "minor European" states.

34. On Third World requirements, see James L. Foster, "The 'Revolution' in Conventional Arms: Implications for Great Powers, Middle Powers, and Others," in Milton Leitenberg and Gabriel Sheffer, eds., *Great Power Intervention in the Middle East* (Elmsford, N.Y.: Pergamon Press, 1979), pp. 188–204.

35. *WSJ*, 29 June 1982.

36. *The Israel Economist*, August, 1982, p. 11.

37. Israel, Central Bureau of Statistics, *Foreign Trade Statistics Quarterly* 32 (October–December 1981): 19.

38. *The Israel Economist*, August, 1982, p. 12.

39. Statistics in Edy Kaufman, Yoram Shapira, and Joel Barromi, *Israel-Latin American Relations* (New Brunswick: Transaction Books, 1979), p. 34.

40. *IHT*, 18–19 December, 1982.

41. Address to American Legion Convention, 23 February 1983; text courtesy of U.S. Information Agency, Tel-Aviv.

42. *Maariv*, 17 December 1982, citing undisclosed U.S. sources; *J P*, 10 December

1982 and *Haaretz*, 8, 13 December 1982 following a publicized visit by Sharon to Honduras. Sharon would only say officials had discussed "general areas of cooperation" while Hondurans claimed an arms sales agreement had been signed; see also *Yediot Achronot*, 31 March 1983; *Time*, 18 March 1983. On the Contras, see *Haaretz* reports, 16, 18 April 1984; see also "Israel Dabbles in a Distant War," *The Sunday Times*, 28 August 1983.

43. On Israel-Honduras, see Cynthia Arnson, "Israel and Central America," *New Outlook* **27** (March/April, 1984): 19, 21; Eric Hooglund, *Israel's Arms Exports* (Washington D.C.: American-Arab Anti-Discrimination Committee, n.d.). ADC Background Paper no. 8, p. 13.

44. *IHT*, 7 May 1984.

45. On El Salvador, see SIPRI, 1980, p. 86; SIPRI, 1982, pp. 213, 400; *The Israel Economist*, August 1982, p. 12.

46. See, for example, comments by El Salvadoran leaders describing prospective aid requests as a quid pro quo for their opening of the embassy in Jerusalem, *Haaretz*, 22 April 1984.

47. Rumors and denials printed in *Haaretz* and *J P*, 25 April 1984.

48. *IHT*, 24 August 1983.

49. Richard Betts, "The Tragicomedy of Arms Trade Control," *International Security* **5** (Summer 1980): 100. While the United States unilaterally maintained restrictions on sales and credits for several years, the West Europeans sold $1.3 billion worth of arms between 1968 and 1972, which represented 84 percent of Latin American arms purchases, Pierre, p. 234.

50. SIPRI, 1980, p. 86.

51. *Haaretz*, 18 March 1984. Supply of helicopters identified in SIPRI, 1983, p. 309.

52. *Yediot Achronot*, 9 April 1984.

53. *Haaretz*, 4 January 1984. Sources in Bogota spoke of the possibility of arming the police force with the Galil rifle, confirmed that IAI was working on upgrading Colombia's air force planes and saw prospects for buying the Kfir fighter plane, *Maariv*, 21 October 1983.

54. ACDA, 1983, p. 29. A regional analysis is Bruce E. Arlinghaus, ed., *Arms for Africa: Military Assistance and Foreign Policy in the Developing World* (Lexington, Mass.: Lexington Books, 1983).

55. These trends are surveyed in two excellent articles by S.N. MacFarlane: "Intervention and Security in Africa," *International Affairs* **60** (Winter 1983/4): 53–73; "Africa's Decaying Security System and the Rise of Intervention," *International Security* **8** (Spring, 1984): 127–151.

56. SIPRI, 1980, p. 86.

57. *Haaretz*, 10 December 1982.

58. *Maariv*, 16 September 1983.

59. *Haaretz*, 25 August 1983, with a photograph of Doe inspecting the Galil rifle; see also *J P*, 28 August 1983.

60. This remarkable relationship is discussed publicly for the first time and in considerable detail by Shmuel Segev, *Operation "Yachin"* (Tel-Aviv: Ministry of Defense Publishing House, 1984).

61. Aspects of military cooperation with Ethiopia in Halliday and Molyneux, pp. 232–233; see also, Robert F. Gorman, *Political Conflict on the Horn of Africa* (New York: Praeger, 1981), pp. 121, 137–138.

62. *Haaretz*, 14 August 1983, relying upon British sources.

63. *J P*, 29 June 1983. Exports to Singapore declined in the first three years of the decade from $80 million in 1980 to $53 million in 1981, and down to a mere $35

million in 1982. One suspects this decline is partly due to a weakening bilateral military supply relationship as Singapore reaches self-sufficiency in a number of specific areas.

64. *IHT*, 14 February 1983. Anticipated economic growth rates for the ASEAN countries run from between 3 to 5 percent; *IHT* 5 July 1983. *Haaretz*, 1 July 1983, reports an agreement to supply Indonesia with Skyhawks in a follow-up to the transfer in 1979 of eighteen planes. In 1982 ASEAN as a whole spent more than $8 billion on armed forces; *Economist*, 24 December 1983.

65. In 1982 some thirty-five economic projects of cooperation between Israel and Thailand were carried out, testifying to a significant presence in that country. Thailand sees itself as part of the Western free world.

66. *Haaretz*, 17 January 1983.

67. Prime Minister Lee Kuan Yew in 1967 stated:

> We made a study of what smaller countries surrounded by large neighbors with big populations do for their own survival. The study eventually led us to compare three such tightly-knit communities — Switzerland, Finland and Israel. In the end, Singapore opted for the Israeli pattern, for in our situation it appears necessary not only to train every boy but also every girl to be a disciplined and effective digit in the defence of their country.

Quoted in Adam Roberts, *Nations in Arms* (London: Chatto & Windus, 1976), p. 33.

68. *J P*, 22 February 1984.

69. *Ha'olam Hazeh*'s list mentions: Brazil, Argentina, Chile, Peru, Ecuador, Colombia, Venezuela, Nicaragua, Honduras, Haiti, Guatemala, El Salvador, Costa Rica, The United States, Canada, Switzerland, West Germany, Lebanon, Iran, Ethiopia, Chad, Kenya, Zaire, South Africa, Liberia, Indonesia, Philippines, Taiwan, China. 3 August 1983, pp. 22–23.

70. *Khadashot*'s report includes: Argentina, Australia, Austria, Belgium, Bolivia, Brazil, Canada, Chad, Chile, Ciskei, Colombia, Denmark, Ecuador, El Salvador, Ethiopia, Finland, France, Germany, Ghana, Great Britain, Guatemala, Haiti, Holland, Honduras, Indonesia, Iran, Italy, Kenya, Liberia, Malaysia, Mexico, Morocco, New Zealand, Nicaragua, Nigeria, Norway, Panama, Philippines, Singapore, South Africa, Spain, Swaziland, Sweden, Switzerland, Taiwan, Tanzania, Thailand, U.S.A., Venezuela, Zaire, Zimbabwe.

71. Evron, p. 289.

72. SIPRI, 1980, claims Tadiran sales to sixty countries.

73. U.S. and U.S.S.R. figures in SIPRI, 1982, p. xxvi.

74. Within ASEAN, Indonesia is the biggest defense spender, Singapore the biggest per capita, Malaysia the biggest in percentage of GNP, *The Economist*, p. 24, December 1983.

75. Two examples: Sri Lanka reportedly turned to Israel when other friendly countries declined, *Maariv*, 15 June 1984; the Philippines have experienced some degree of delay in pledged American assistance, *IHT*, 15 March 1984.

76. *SIPRI Yearbook*, 1981, p. 116.

8
SPECIAL MILITARY RELATIONSHIPS

So extensive and subject to change is the list of countries reached by Israeli military transfers that trying to identify them all is futile. Such compilations, then, are less than exhaustive; ultimately they are also misleading since in some instances arms dealings with a given client state proved brief, politically and economically marginal, or both. Nor do the listings tell us anything qualitative about Israel's more lasting and serious bilateral military relationships.

The following two chapters emphasize two types of exceptional clients: the pariah state and the patron. The former alludes to a loose grouping of countries on the very fringe of the international community; the latter, to the United States, occupying the center of world politics. These fringe states are presently Israel's largest arms outlet; the American defense market (to be explored in the next chapter) and the mounting demand in the United States for sophisticated military technologies are seen as the key to the question of whether Israel in fact will remain a supplier of substance in the future as well.

THE PARIAH NATIONS

The pariah state is a reference to small and diplomatically weak nations the legitimacy of whose government or very sovereign state existence remains open to question. Such a state is perceived of by others, but also perceives of itself, as an international outcast. This sense of forced isolation determines its national security policy in several important ways: the pariah state is unlikely to be welcomed — at least not openly — as a valued ally. Nor does it take comfort from any permanent alliance willing to guarantee its security. Even should such a possibility arise, the pariah is reluctant to entrust vital interests to the goodwill of others, preferring to conduct diplomacy through temporary relationships with other pariahs based upon immediate, shared, concrete and mutual interests arising from common estrangement.

References to the existence of this unique alignment of "pariah" states comprising the "Sixth World" have begun to appear recently in the literature.[1] Among the other characteristics of "pariahtude," we find the following supplementary definition:

> A nation with precarious, perhaps sole, sources of conventional-arms supply and which is too small or underdeveloped to provide a significant portion of its arms needs through indigenous production; also, very vulnerable in a crisis to cutoffs of spare parts or to denial of weapons resupply.[2]

In other words, in keeping with political realism, the pariah nation will accept military aid, when offered, from any quarter. Even then, such procurement is meant to gain time during which the isolated and threatened country strives to the maximum to assure its safety by enhancing its own defense capabilities. The error lies in considering the development of "weapons of mass destruction" as the sole "equalizer,"[3] whereas the redoubled efforts of such countries to rapidly expand local manufacture of conventional weapons are overlooked.

It is here that Israel enters the picture by providing a model for others in similar circumstances. For all of its modern history the Jewish state has been part of this heterogeneous yet distinct group of countries thrown together by accident because of international or regional ostracism.[4] And its willingness to share some of this military knowledge and experience has paved the way for military relationships with most of the pariah countries.

Their shared isolation provides the foundation for a general mutual assistance framework which supersedes ideological differences. Encountering serious difficulties in obtaining assured and unconditional arms supplies because of their common diplomatic ostracism, the bloc of pariah countries have formed a floating coalition of sorts, with membership optional, nonbinding and, in the case of some, even temporary. This network of military supply and cooperation transcends both regional and political distinctions, and at the systemic level represents the seeds of a truly international defense productive process. For Israel especially this network affords a unique opportunity to strengthen itself commercially as well as diplomatically by adjusting to political configurations as they emerge.

Countries like Argentina, Chile, and El Salvador owe their recent membership in this grouping of pariah states to charges of authoritarian rule, repression, and human rights violations. Despite their pro-Western orientation, they have had to face an arms embargo by such traditional suppliers as the United States and Great Britain. Iran, in its continuing war with Iraq, finds itself cut off from all the Muslim Arab states except for Libya and Syria, and from the United States. Its desperate quest for replacements and spare parts is the basis for rumors of clandestine orders from the Zionist enemy.

Another pariah state with an arms procurement problem is Taiwan, which felt threatened by the U.S. decision in August, 1982 to phase out arms sales as part of Washington's policy of rapprochement toward the People's Republic of China.[5] Taiwanese public reaction at the time included threats to seek arms aid from other sources, although observers doubted whether other potential suppliers would risk Chinese anger by making major sales arrangements with Taiwan.

Western sensitivities toward Beijing explained their hesitancy to fill Taiwan's defense orders. Israel, not having formal ties with the PRC, was under no such restraint. Once Taiwan decided to respond by buying U.S. spare parts and by diversifying its outside sources, while at the same time using its economic strength to develop local arms production facilities, Israel can be of assistance in all three regards.[6] Again there was the element of precedent. Israel had established military ties with Taiwan in 1977, licensing production of its Gabriel-2 missiles.[7] Since then the Taiwanese authorities have bought the Shafrir air-to-air missile and are reported by SIPRI to exchange information on conventional weapons with Israel and South Africa.[8] Subnational groups like the Kurds in Iraq and the Maronites in Lebanon have also been armed in part by Israel; of late, United States officials cited $100 million in covert military aid provided in 1983 to Afghan insurgents by Saudi Arabia and other Arab countries, China and Israel.[9] Here again, the need for arms as part of their local political struggle and the fact of diplomatic nonrecognition provided the basis for short-term assistance.

Perhaps a final general note on the informal relationship among pariah states is the prospect of an even more complicated relationship: trilateral and even multilateral, deriving from claims of the existence of circuituitous supply routes in order to avoid embarrassing diplomatic complications and possible detection. Thus the use of third countries for resupply purposes, as in the instance of a reported contract by Argentina for six Corvettes to be constructed under Israeli supervision but secured from South Africa.[10] Similarly, *The Economist* claims that arms sent by Israel to Iran on at least one occasion were routed via Argentina.[11] That the transregional axis has the potential for cooperation of global dimensions owes to still other reports such as in the *Middle East*, involving Israel, South Africa, and Taiwan in a project to produce Cruise-type missiles.[12]

As in most cases the "rules of the game" require that references in the press or elsewhere to such bilateral or trilateral relationships be played down by officials. Yet they are an important and fascinating aspect of present day world politics in general and of Israel's weapons transfer connections in particular.

Four countries falling within this loose coalition have been singled out for separate comment: South Africa, Argentina, Iran, and Zaire.

South Africa

In attempting meaningful yet guarded relations with the Republic of South Africa, one of the first countries to extend it recognition in 1948, Israel is forced often to walk a political tightrope. For example, in 1961 Israel voted on behalf of a U.N. resolution involving sanctions against South Africa only to have Pretoria retaliate by revoking Israeli exemption from commodity and transfer restrictions. Five years of quiet diplomacy were needed before the preferential status was reinstated, and political fences mended.

Relations have since improved owing to what appears to be a two-tiered understanding between Jerusalem and Pretoria. Israel remains on record as dissociating itself from the apartheid practices. But at the same time Israeli leaders have sought constructive engagement with South Africa, in the belief that gradual liberalization is best encouraged from outside by persuasive rather than punitive measures. A second motivation are vital national interests coming under the twin heading of bilateral commerce and strategic cooperation.

This is affirmed in Israel-South Africa trade which grew, according to the NY Times, in 1983 to $250 million.[13] The Israeli daily, Haaretz, puts 1983–1984 investment in South African enterprises second only to that of Taiwan.[14] SIPRI analysts claim broader trade is accompanied by military ties, with South Africa having accounted for some 35 percent of Israeli defense sales before 1980.[15] Relations intensified following a visit to Israel by Premier John Vorster in 1976.[16] The Economist suggests it was then that a wide-ranging agreement entered into effect which provided for economic, scientific, and industrial collaboration, with a joint committee set up to promote the program and to administer it.[17] One plausible explanation for this renewed interest in Israel by Pretoria was its own increased sense of isolation during the 1970s.

South African vulnerability derived then as now from its minority white status at home and on the continent, leaving the country estranged from much of Africa. Insecurity was heightened by Soviet influence in nearby Angola, and by the arms boycott leveled against the regime in 1963 and again in 1977. In its favor, though, South Africa remains of immense value because of its mineral wealth. Indeed, much of the free world is dependent on Pretoria for assured supplies of such strategic items as chromium, manganese, nickel, uranium, diamonds, and gold, as well as copper, lead, zinc, tin, iron ore, and asbestos.[18] All of these are necessary in high technology fields and without exception are not found in any appreciable quantity within Israel.

This served the South Africans as leverage in fulfilling pressing arms requirements, as did the readiness of other countries to compete for contracts in defiance of international sanctions. Thus at various times France, Britain, the United States, and West Germany reportedly have stepped in as direct suppliers of conventional arms; at one stage France is identified as having supplied 53 percent of major arms transfers to South Africa.[19] Pierre includes Israel in this list but only as a secondary supplier.[20] SIPRI likewise gives South African purchases from Israel as limited to several missile boats, Gabriel missiles and small arms.[21]

However, efforts by the Republic to circumvent the international ban on direct weapons transfers go beyond acquiring equipment abroad. The larger strategy aims at self-sufficiency through military industrialization, with construction of defense plants inside the country facilitated by foreign licensing arrangements providing for coproduction of weapons locally. South Africa appears to have been remarkably successful. After reducing the proportion of its defense budget spent on imported arms from 70 percent in 1966 to a mere 15 percent in 1982, it now possesses the world's tenth largest arms industry.[22]

Changes in the Republic's strategic doctrine might also be judged fortuitous for Israel. One of the more important would seem to be an appreciation for the kind of pocket navies and electronic warfare favored by Israel. Following termination of the Simonstown defense agreement with Britain and France's cancellation of a contract for the supply of combat vessels, South African naval planners decided to shift their emphasis away from large blue-water ships deemed vulnerable to missile attacks. No longer willing to accept primary responsibility for defending the strategic Cape route on behalf of the West, they began to concentrate instead on protecting the country's harbors and long coast line.[23] To achieve this aim the building of a fleet of small, versatile, high-speed craft was authorized. Israeli military contractors, as confirmed by the official South African publication, *Panorama*, successfully competed for some of the navy bids and have assisted both the state-owned Armscor as well as the Sandock-Austral shipyards in Durban.[24]

Nevertheless, officials on both sides deny the existence of a deeper military relationship. At the end of 1984 Foreign Minister Shamir would only describe Israel-South African relations as "normal," while his counterpart, Roelof F. Botha, termed them "realistic" and cautioned against creating the impression they are very close "because it is not true."[25] Yet in the face of studied silence and the absence of anything more authoritative either from Jerusalem or Pretoria, reports continue to circulate in the Western media of cooperation in a range of defense areas.[26]

Were only a fraction of the persistent reports valid, it would still suffice to suggest several deeper insights into the South African connection. First, it is the dissimilarities between Israel and South Africa as much as their shared features which help to explain any ongoing relationship. Beginning with the latter, both societies preserve a strong sense of nationhood just as both feel themselves threatened within a hostile environment. Still, in our opinion it is the contrast which makes whatever security understanding as does exist both logical and reciprocal. Israel is geographically small, has scant material assets, and yet possesses a degree of sophistication in arms technology. South Africa, for its part, has a vast interior rich in natural resources, yet still has certain defense needs obtainable only from external sources.

A second insight is the staying power of "pariah" states in the face of adversity. Arms restraints selectively applied are only likely to have the opposite effect. Rather than compellence, such boycotts are the single most influential stimulant for intensified weapons production. Confirmed by the separate experience of Israel and then South Africa, embargoes have been catalytic, encouraging the development of indigenous arms-making capabilities.[27] Were it not for the French cutoff of aid to Israel or the half-hearted embargoes enforced against South Africa, their respective emergence as arms manufacturers and then as arms exporters arguably would have been retarded. Third and directly related is the type of military assistance possibly rendered by Israel. What seems to work best is not the outright sale of large weapons systems, but rather: (a) provision of the building blocks of modern weaponry — components, unfinished assemblies and dual-use technologies; (b) licensing and coproduction. Thus, for example, SIPRI mentions the building in South Africa of at least 9 Reshef-class vessels in recent years under license, while other reports refer to participation by Israeli firms in a variety of joint ventures.[28] Common to all such references is the assumed contribution of funding and materials by Pretoria, and of scientific know-how and practical experience by Israel.

A fourth insight lies in the diplomatic sphere and Israel's place in African politics. The objective is to maintain a balanced policy of commercial trade and limited security assistance with South Africa and with the independent black African countries. That this may be feasible is encouraged by improved ties with Liberia. An even more instructive case perhaps is the emerging relationship with Zaire.

Zaire

Israel's relationship with Zaire illustrates both the potential for Israeli defense assistance to the less developed countries and the integration of arms diplomacy into Israel's larger national interests. Zaire is the first black African country to have resumed diplomatic ties with Israel, exchanging ambassadors in May, 1982. Even before, commercial exports to Zaire had reached $4.5 million in 1981. Despite its serious economic problems, Zaire has achieved a measure of political stability under President Mobutu. And yet it is badly in need of external assistance. American capital for the exploitation of its vast copper and cobalt resources is seen in Kinshasa as one of the best prospects, and one possibly to be fostered via Israel and the latter's links to what Zairian officials apparently perceive of as Jewish banking houses within the international financial community. Consequently, as viewed in turn from Jerusalem, Zaire is attractive on at least three counts. It is rich in gold, diamonds, oil, copper, uranium, and cobalt. If cultivated properly it could serve as both precedent and test case, providing the stimulus for a restoration of relations with other African states as well. Zaire offers an opportunity for the kinds of projects which Israel over the last twenty years has tended to do best in the developing countries: agriculture and arms aid.

In an official visit to Zaire late in 1982, Foreign Minister Shamir proposed that Israeli experts help direct a number of large agricultural estates to be followed, at a second stage, the opening of branches and plants by Israeli industrial firms in Zaire to handle the processing, packaging, and marketing of the produce. Three firms reported at the time to be making such plans were Koor, Solel Boneh, and Tahal which are remembered as having been active in the days of combined economic and military assistance to Iran.

Israel became active again in Zaire in the military field in 1982. As early as March of that year, and without waiting for a formal announcement of a restoration of diplomatic ties, Israeli officers began instructing units of the army and training Mobutu's own presidential guard; also it was confirmed that in 1982 Israel had sold $10 million in military supplies to Zaire.[29] An Israeli team has completed a survey of Zaire's defense needs for the next five years; its recommendations will serve as a guideline for arms purchases under the assumption that many of these needs will be secured from Israel.[30]

The Israeli-Zairian military relationship deepened early in 1983 in an exchange of visits by Ariel Sharon and his counterpart in Kinshasa, Admiral Lomponda. That Zaire sought to diversify its range of acquisitions by involving Israel most prominently in training and supplying the Zaire armed forces was revealed by Mobutu himself who, in January, said that Jerusalem would provide artillery, mortars, and communication equipment. Numerous reports circulated to the effect that the series of bilateral military accords included purchase of patrol boats, pilotless planes, a warning system for monitoring border incursions and air defenses, as well as equipment captured in Lebanon.[31] The unique Israeli formula of combining agricultural and military programs is demonstrated again in the approved plan for strengthening security in Zaire's mineral rich southern Shaba province on the border with Angola by establishing a line of farming settlements similar to IDF paramilitary pioneering youth Nahal units to be manned by the elite Camaniola division armed and trained by Israeli officers.

These efforts, in turn, smoothed the way for a significant diplomatic triumph for Israel when in January, 1984, Chaim Herzog paid an official state visit to Zaire, thus symbolizing his country's renewed presence in Africa.[32] Besides showing the flag and countering the image of Israel as diplomatically isolated, should the emerging relationship with Zaire deepen and extend into nonmilitary related areas an example can be provided to other African and Third World countries of the security benefits for them of renewing ties with Israel. The next relationship, with Argentina, demonstrates, among other things, Israeli reliability.

Argentina

Argentina is regarded, along with South Africa and Brazil, as one of the three leading states in the South Atlantic with the potential for achieving Great Power status by the turn of the next century. Yet despite this chance at regional primacy and its longstanding disputes with neighboring countries, Argentina's security problem is much more immediate and acute, deriving as it does from the 1982 confrontation with Great Britain over the Falkland (Malvinas) Islands.

That defeat by superior British forces is a source of genuine embarrassment to Argentina, the more so as the military does not despair of eventually regaining control over the contested islands. In the aftermath of the crisis, Argentina has undertaken a major arms buildup, placing defense orders with several suppliers. Some reports indicated that the country's leaders promptly committed themselves in 1982–1983 to more than $1 billion in arms purchases, with Israel, France, and West Germany cited as principal suppliers.[33]

Israel's military ties with Argentina extend through each of the three phases: before, during and since the war. While Argentina had secured some of its needs in earlier years from Israel, the latter's value became most apparent at the height of the crisis when the Argentinian armed forces experienced serious shortages in many defense items. Even worse, traditional political allies like Peru, Venezuela, and Brazil were slow in responding.[34]

During that critical time Israel's response appears to have been both substantial and comprehensive, to such an extent that it became the first small Third World arms manufacturer to act as a primary supplier of major and sophisticated weapons systems to a belligerent party during a military engagement, taking over a role heretofore the sole province of the major arms producers.[35] Discretion, the suitability of the products required, and the fact of a pre-existing supply relationship, plus a willingness by both sides to expand these ties, served to enhance Israel's chances of meeting Argentinian needs for the prompt replacement of aircraft and missile systems.

Among the items supplied by Israel during the crisis were quantities of Barak, Gabriel, and Shafrir missile systems.[36] But its primary function was to help the Argentinian air force maintain a credible strike capability. In replacing lost aircraft, Israel is variously reported to have transferred from twenty to twenty-five Dagger planes (the Israeli version of the Mirage-III),[37] along with some twenty-four to thirty American-built A-4 Skyhawk fighters.[38] Spare parts and technical advisers appear to have been included as part of these transactions.[39]

These arms transfer actions involved considerable risk, for Israel effectively challenged the Western alliance's embargo against Argentina, caused friction with Britain, and ran counter to American policy during the Falklands war. What might have been Israeli motives? The least charitable explanation is that the flow of arms corresponded to the aggressive export-oriented character of

Israel's general arms diplomacy with the emphasis upon seizing market opportunities as they arise.

Less commented upon, however, are other possible considerations. One is that through an expanding arms relationship the welfare of the local Argentinian Jewish community might be better ensured, although some Israelis and Argentinian Jews whose relatives apparently died at the hands of the military junta criticized this approach.[40] Nevertheless, weapons transfers were reportedly linked to the fate of Argentina's Jews by Foreign Minister Shamir in the discussions he held in Buenos Aires in December, 1982. Second, Israeli aid may have served Western and American interests by preventing Argentina from turning in desperation to the Soviet Union.[41] Third, Jerusalem may have tended to be more partial to the Argentinian position regarding the adjacent islands simply on the merits of the case.

Fourth, aid to Argentina fits into the context of the pariah state floating coalition. Whatever transfers as were made in 1982 might have been undertaken for reasons other than the single military objective of aiding Argentina. For by going through with the arms deal, Israel did nothing so much as confirm its reputation as a dependable military ally and supplier. Instructive in this regard were explanations of Israel's position which stressed that while Israel would not undertake any new sales agreements while the fighting lasted, by the same token it would honor signed contracts for weapons. Lastly, Israeli-Argentinian military relations may possibly permit the network of isolated countries to pursue indirect and third party conduits. Two fairly recent possibilities are suggested by intimations that Argentina acted as a supplier to Honduras and the antiSandinista rebels, and, as a transit point for arms to Iran;[42] in neither instance was it clear which country served as the supplier of origin.

Iran

The crash of a plane loaded with arms over the Soviet Union under mysterious circumstances in July, 1981, led to speculation that it contained Israeli-supplied military equipment destined for Iran. On the surface such a Jerusalem-Tehran connection defied logic and even bordered on the absurd when one recalls statements at the time by Ayatollah Khomeini condemning Zionism and encouraging his followers in the war effort against Iraq as "the road to liberating Jerusalem." A closer look, however, does suggest reasons why a continuing relationship between the two countries might be plausible.

One factor is circumstantial. The military invasion launched by Iraq in 1980 found the Iranian regular army in a dangerously low state of preparedness as a result of the revolutionary purge of its ranks. Intensification of the protracted Gulf war only increased Tehran's rather desperate quest for arms suppliers. Its self-imposed isolation from traditional regional and superpower allies thus qualifies revolutionary Iran, with its pro-P.L.O. and anti-Zionist stance, as both an international outcast and a candidate for arms from any quarter, including Israel.

However, prior to 1979–1980 the basis for Israeli-Iranian military ties had depended on neither Tehran's diplomatic isolation nor its sense of desperation. The origins of their relationship rather, had been positive and rested upon permanent geopolitical foundations. Under the Shah, Iran's legitimacy and political orientation were unquestioned. The strategic interests of Washington, Tehran, and Jerusalem essentially paralleled each other. The goals held in common during the decade of the seventies centered on resisting Soviet encroachment in the area, frustrating Iraqi expansionism, checking radical terrorism threatening both Israel and Iran, and bolstering moderate Arab regimes like those in Egypt and Jordan. American policy pledged itself to raising the status of Iran to that of a predominant power in the Persian Gulf area. As a result, Iran, its purchasing power multiplied several times over by oil revenues, became the single largest purchaser of American arms; of the $11.4 billion worth of arms sold by the United States in 1977, Iran accounted for $5.5 billion.[43] In a sense, Israel came in on American coattails, riding the crest of Iran's military expansion program.

Still, Israel had succeeded in establishing a special tacit relationship with Iran by its own efforts some years earlier due to the fact that the Shah and his government shared Jerusalem's concern about the spread of Nasserist influence. The Shah also appreciated Israel's qualifications for assisting primarily in Iran's modernization and also in meeting some of its military needs. Israeli exports to Iran stood at $33 million in 1973; a year later they rose to $63 million and in 1975–1976 passed the $100 million mark. Trade statistics, which included military exports, presented a figure of nearly $200 million by 1976–1977. These figures give some indication of just how important an arms market Iran had become for Israel at the time of the Shah's downfall; another indication immediately thereafter was the forced layoff of workers and lower export sales by firms like Urdan previously engaged in producing for the Iranian army and air force.

Commercial considerations aside, although weighty in themselves, the political benefits for Israel were profound, beginning with a leap over the wall of Arab hostility, a breakthrough in regional ties, and the services of Iran as a listening post as well as counter to Egyptian, Syrian, and Iraqi radicalism. Not widely known was the fact that Israeli prime ministers from Ben-Gurion to Begin paid secret visits to Tehran for consultations with Iranian officials, including the Shah himself;[44] and the Israeli government enforced strict censorship in preserving the tacit nature of these ties.[45] The Israeli mission in Tehran supervised the ongoing bilateral relationship in its military and nonmilitary aspects. When integrated with economic and developmental assistance, military aid helped gain access for Israel to an assured, conveniently-placed supplier of oil, while preserving a no less important access route to the Jews of Iran. Not to be overlooked, finally, is that friendship with Iran also contributed indirectly to an improved U.S.-Israeli understanding on the Middle East regional power balance.

But fortunes were quickly reversed, and Israeli-Iranian relations reached their nadir immediately following the return of the Ayatollah Khomeini and the expulsion of Israeli personnel. The United States arms embargo imposed during the seizure of the American embassy and its staff, the purging by the Islamic tribunals of the country's officer corps on the charge of loyalty to the Shah, together with the outbreak of fighting against Iraq in September, 1980, and subsequent military defeats, provided evidence as to the deteriorated state of the Iranian armed forces and their poor maintenance of the American planes, tanks, and other equipment received previously. Here again desperation, isolation from traditional suppliers, and the need for urgent re-supplying to prevent military defeat, as in the case of Argentina, force Iran's new rulers to eschew ideology in favor of the pragmatism associated with the international arms trade.

In October, 1980, in the second month of the Gulf war, the Begin government had already agreed to sell several hundred thousand dollars worth of spare tires for F-4 fighter planes.[46] In 1981, after the release of the American hostages, Israel is reported by SIPRI to have transferred to Iran, through indirect channels, quantities of ammunition, refurbished jet engines, spare parts for U.S.-built M-48 tanks, and additional aircraft tires.[47] In 1983 rumors persisted of ongoing supplies from Israel, valued at over $100 million.[48] This, at a time when the most generous estimates showed Iran possessing as few as thirty to forty operational aircraft while facing opposing Iraqi forces amply supplied by countries like France.[49] In 1984, reports, emanating primarily from West German sources, referred to Israeli plans to deliver badly-needed supplies of anti-tank weapons; these same sources estimated that Israeli aid since the outbreak of the fighting may have amounted to nearly half a billion dollars by the end of 1983.[50]

The accuracy of such reports and the extent of Israeli help are but two of the questions which remain unverified. A third item of controversy is the extent to which clandestine supply activity by Israel is undertaken with the knowledge and prior consent of Washington. According to one credible account, the United States protested when, belatedly, it was informed of the initial transactions, causing a temporary cessation in the arms flow while the Islamic revolutionary guards continued to hold the Americans hostage; but once they were released in January, 1981, the weapons trade between Israel and Iran was resumed.[51] When Ariel Sharon made public reference, and in the United States, to this recent arms relationship with the Khomeini regime, insisting in the process that it was done with American approval, he was criticized in Israel for seeking headlines and for exaggerating.[52] A spokesman for Prime Minister Shamir denied that Israel is "selling arms nowadays to Iran."[53] Yet other local sources were prepared to confirm that in the past, as opposed to "nowadays," "inconsequential" material did reach Iran through indirect channels.[54]

What might be Israel's motivation in aiding Khomeini's Iran? First, there is one opinion which says that the weapons deliveries indeed have been small scale and that they were handled by small firms and by private or foreign arms dealers acting independently of the Israeli government and for particularistic rather than national interests. The thesis is difficult either to prove or disprove, and depends upon both specific information — quantities as well as quality of weapons — and one's subjective impression of how successful bureaucracies are in closely coordinating and enforcing any given foreign policy decision.

In any case the more cogent pro-arms-for-Iran argument lies in the realm of national interest and political realism. It begins by distinguishing between Iran the geopolitical fact and its regime. Israelis view Iran as strategically vital in two regards: (a) within the global context, in order to prevent Soviet southward expansion and breakthrough to the Gulf; (b) in terms of the Arab zone, in keeping not only Iraq but the Arab countries in general in a high state of alert. Arab-Persian centuries-old animosities coupled with the Islamic schism between Shi'a and Sunni branches force the Arab countries, particularly those with Sunni regimes, to turn their attention from Israel, on the western perimeter of the Arab world, to Iran on the east. Over time, the fanaticism of individual leaders must yield to transcendant historical, geographic and political circumstances.

From both a systemic and a regional perspective, therefore, it may be in Israel's strategic interest to have the Iran-Iraq war of attrition continue on a low flame indefinitely, thereby blunting Tehran's fundamentalist revolutionary fervor while at the same time distracting Baghdad, even if only temporarily, from the anti-Israel "resistance front." Clearly, victory for either side would upset all such neat and rational calculations, although arms, especially spare parts from Israel, can hardly provide Iran with the military means for a breakthrough. Such assistance, though, can enable the Iranians to defend themselves against both the Soviet and the Iraqi threat. Iran has a genuine need for defensive weapons and its present sources are limited; and, so the argument goes, better Israel as an arms source than anti-Western or anti-Zionist suppliers seeking to use this leverage to exercise a negative, as opposed to a moderating and stabilizing, influence over Iran.[55]

Furthermore, it can be argued of the Tehran government as well as of the Reagan administration that they "protesteth too much." Ideological fervor and rhetoric aside, Khomeini and his people early on showed the cold realism which is the hallmark of pariah states no less than of great powers in consenting to accept arms from Israel. Similarly, there are surely those in Washington who, even as they tilt toward Iraq's Sadam Husayn, can see the logic of Israel's strategic view. And as a result they might be prepared to countenance clandestine weapons transfers, even of U.S.-made equipment, channeled by Israel as a hedge against losing Iran entirely or exposing a devastated, demoralized Iran to Communist pressure.

In sum, Iran, for all its recent upheavals, retains its geopolitical and strategic importance for Israel. Nor have those earlier foundations which made an initial Israeli-Iranian political and military relationship possible been dislodged. A convergence of interests exists, with each still needing the other. So long as the Persian Gulf conflict remains stalemated, in itself satisfying Israel's overall strategic position, and the Iranians are compelled to keep on a war footing through such means as large-scale arms imports, the supply relationship with Israel, however incongruous on the surface, could endure. If so, it will not depend on goodwill but on the larger and permanent interests which hopefully will outlast Khomeini, his revolution, and regime, at which time there will be a possibility for Israeli statecraft to enlarge the existing minimal relationship with Iran and renew it at a strategic and ongoing level.

The Potential Market

Like international affairs, customers for Israeli arms are subject to political change and realignment. Renewed diplomatic, commercial, and military exchanges with Zaire, should they actually materialize and encourage other black neighboring countries to do likewise, could signal improved prospects for Israel among the nations of Africa.[56] If regional isolation and arms procurement problems earmark a country for pariah status while leading it to view Israel and others like it as serious suppliers, then Zimbabwe could qualify, following the 1983 decision by the United States government to cut aid to that country by almost half.[57]

Taiwan becomes a logical candidate for intensified military trade and cooperation. At the end of 1983, for example, Taipei government officials suffered two successive military procurement setbacks. In November, Switzerland refused two Swiss companies permission to deliver fifty tanks and air defense systems worth about $200 million;[58] then the following month the Dutch government denied permits for the export of six conventional submarines contracted for by Taiwan.[59] These actions stemmed from the wish of both Western European suppliers to improve political and trade relations with China, even if accomplished at the expense of Taiwan. Such reverses only strengthened Taipei's resolve to increasingly develop its own arms manufacturing capability; in 1982 an initial $150 million had already been allocated for research and development to produce a high-technology fighter within a decade, also advanced fighter aircraft engines. Such plans obviously implied interim arms suppliers of certain needed systems, particularly acquiring sophisticated technologies from abroad. This was as much as admitted by Taiwan's defense minister who gave as an estimate the figure of approximately $1 billion which would be required to import high technology for use in advanced weaponry.[60] Clearly, Israel would have both the interest and ability to secure part of this market for itself.

The Philippines, belatedly recognizing the threat of Communist insurgence, has a need for basic logistical and communication equipment, including trucks, uniforms, ammunition, radio sets and spare parts for ground combat systems. Japan, were it to become less dependent on Middle East oil and less sensitive to OPEC pressures, might be a prospective customer for modest transactions with Israeli manufacturers. In 1984 Japan's Prime Minister Nakasone announced a plan to spend $13 billion in 1985 on new military equipment in order to improve its defenses against air and sea attacks.[61]

There are signs of increased aid to Honduras arising from American and French hesitancy in supplying Honduran arms requests because of the latter's quarrel with Nicaragua. Already equipped with Galil rifles and Uzis as well as Arava and Super-Mystere planes from Israel, the Honduran Army would like to acquire fighter aircraft and is believed to have discussed an intensified supply relationship with Israel at the time of a visit by former Defense Minister Sharon to Tegucigalpa in December, 1982.[62] Haiti, as part of its modernization program, is considering further orders from Israel's inventory in the hope of long-term credits.[63]

Consistent with this theme of fluidity in weapons transfer partnerships were reports early in 1983 of Israeli success in pursuing limited cooperation with one of its earlier clients, Ethiopia.[64] Such reports are prompted by the failure of Ethiopian troops armed and trained by Soviet Russia in campaigns against the Eritrean rebels. Should Israel in fact be invited by the Marxist regime of General Mengistu to replace some of the Soviet advisers, the results would not only improve Israel's own position (a Tel-Aviv–Addis Ababa air route, the Falashan Jews) but could affect the strategic balance in the Horn of Africa in favor of the West. Mutuality of interests should not even preclude exploration of some of India's defense requirements.

Nor is it beyond the realm of possibility, given repeated references of late about deals concluded, for Israel to gain a share of the huge market for military hardware and technologies on mainland China.[65] Indeed, usually authoritative sources like *Janes Defense Weekly* estimated that the trade might already be as high as $3 billion.[66] China would appear to possess most if not all of the requisites and characteristics sought for by Israel in a client. The plight of the PRC derives from: a 1950s arsenal; lack of capital to buy quantities of the latest state-of-the-art systems; determination not to become dependent on foreign military supply nor to tie itself irrevocably to one superpower; industrialization programs, including indigenous arms manufacture; during the transition stage a need for parts used in both Soviet and Western armaments.[67] Again, propaganda and politics aside, Israel answers most of these needs.

These examples of possible military relationships are offered merely as indicative of Israel's potential. Success with any one of these countries might help not only to sustain its arms industry but would also further confirm the validity of Israel's market diversification policy in creating new opportunities and new clients. Voice was given to this strategy by Prime Minister Peres in September, 1984. Upon presenting his National Unity Government, he pledged; "We shall work for closer ties with the European continent; we shall open wider the windows [of opportunity] created in Africa; we shall intensify the dialogue with Latin America, and we shall once again knock on great China's door."[68] But when Defense Minister Yitzhak Rabin was asked in more specific terms about the existence of an arms supply relationship in January, 1985, he replied rather disingenuously: "We don't talk about any arms deals with countries that prefer not to agree to that. When it comes to China, well, of course, I deny it."[69]

By right the United States ought to be included in the list of potential customers. But to treat the U.S. as simply another purchaser would touch only the surface of a far more complex relationship. The truth is that Washington exercises a disproportionate influence on various aspects of current Israeli arms export diplomacy. Moreover, its stance — ranging from tolerance to determined opposition — will have considerable bearing on Israel's future prospects in the conventional arms arena. It is for this reason that the role of the United States is reserved for separate discussion in the following chapter.

NOTES

1. Only recently are these states and their ability to colloborate with each other being taken seriously as a factor in world affairs. Robert E. Harkavy, "The Pariah State Syndrome," *Orbis*, 21 (Fall, 1977): 623–649; Efraim Inbar, "The Emergence of Pariah States in World Politics," in *Korean Journal of International Studies* 15 (Winter 1983/84):55–83.
2. Harkavy, p. 627.
3. Harkavy, p. 627.
4. This interesting comment upon Jewish statehood is made by Irving Louis Horowitz, "From Pariah People to Pariah Nation: Jews, Israelis and the Third World," in Curtis and Gitelson, pp. 361–391.
5. *J P*, 18 August 1982.
6. On Taiwan's plans, see *IHT*, 2 November 1982.
7. SIPRI Yearbook, 1983, p. 350.
8. SIPRI Yearbook, 1983, p. 275.
9. *The Economist's* "Foreign Report" of 23 September 1982, citing American intelligence reports, claims Israel provided military aid worth at least $400 million to the Phalangist forces between 1978–1982. Further reference in Ze'ev Schiff and Ehud Ya'ari. *Israel's Lebanon War* (New York: Simon and Schuster, 1984), pp. 18, 28, 85. The authors cite an investment by the Rabin Government of some $150 million in military aid from 1974 to 1977 in building up the Maronite forces. Administration references to Afghanis reported in the *New York Times*, 28 November 1984.
10. *The Middle East*, May, 1983, p. 32. *The Defense & Foreign Affairs Handbook* lists a May, 1982 delivery to Argentina by South Africa of Gabriel missiles and Mirage III parts, p. 922.
11. *The Economist*, "Foreign Report," 28 October 1982.
12. *The Middle East*, May 1983, p. 32.
13. *NYT*, 6 November 1984.
14. *Haaretz*, 20 June 1984. Three Israeli firms in 1982–1983 invested 2.3 million rand,

while ten firms are reported to be investing 20.3 million rand in developing areas of South Africa, including near Durban and in steel production enterprises.

15. SIPRI, 1981, p. 116. Also *Haaretz*, 17 July 1983; *J P*, 28 June 1983; *IHT*, 16–17 July 1983.
16. The visit and its significance are recalled in James Adams. *The Unnatural Alliance* (London: Quartet Books, 1984).
17. According to *The Economist* (5 November 1977), pp. 90–91, the 1976 cooperation agreement provided:

If Israel will. . . . fill South African needs for naval equipment including six Reshef-class fast patrol boats armed with Gabriel surface-to-surface missiles, automatic guns, anti-submarine torpedoes, submarine detection systems and electronic counter-measures plus train the South African crews in Israeli naval bases; . . . supply armoured equipment including 105 mm self-propelled howitzers, air-to-air rockets and portable anti-tank missiles; electronic and counter-insurgency equipment including radar stations, electronic fences, anti-guerilla infiltration alarm systems, communication systems, computers and night vision devices, . . . modernise 150 South African Centurion tanks. South Africa will . . . . put up money for the next generation of the Reshef-boats, ... offer Israel a rare type of steel to be used in the Israeli Chariot tank plus advanced technology in steel manufacture, . . . also supply Israel with 40,000 tons of coal a month to operate the Hadera dual-fuel power station in case of an oil embargo. In time of war the coal convoys will be escorted to their destination by joint South African-Israeli naval forces.

Further reference is in Russell Warren Howe, *The International Game of Arms, Money and Diplomacy* (Garden City: Doubleday & Co., 1980), pp. 724–725.

18. Robert S. McNamara, "South Africa: The Middle East of the 1990's?", *NYT*, 24 October 1982, see also, South Africa, Department of Foreign Affairs and Information, "South Africa's Strategic Metals," *Panorama* **27** (August 1982):1–9. More than three-fourths of the chromium vital for aircraft engines and stainless steel used in the United States in 1983 was imported, most of it from South Africa. "South Africa and U.S. Allied Through Trade and Diplomacy," *WP*, 28 January 1985.
19. The ability of South Africa to circumvent the U.N. boycott through illicit means, including from American suppliers, is traced in Michael T. Klare, "Evading the Embargo: Illicit U.S. Arms Transfers to South Africa," *Journal of International Affairs* (Spring/Summer, 1981): 15–28. Israel's commercial relations, as well as those of West European Soviet bloc, black African and U.S. ties to South Africa in circumvention of U.N. embargos are described in Kunirum Osia. *Israel, South Africa and Black Africa* (Lanham, MD: University Press of America, 1981). Data on French supplies in SIPRI, 1980, p. 112.
20. Pierre, pp. 266–267.
21. SIPRI, 1980, p. 112.
22. Progress at converting from arms imports to indigenous production is presented in Richard Leonard, *South Africa at War* (Westport: Lawrence Hill, 1984).
23. South African military thinking is presented in the Institute for Strategic Studies of the University of Pretoria *Strategic Review* monograph of June, 1983.
24. *Panorama* (December 1982), "The Ship-Building Industry," pp. 1–7.
25. Remarks by Foreign Ministers Shamir and Botha on the occasion of a private brief visit by the latter to Israel in November, 1984. *NYT*, 6 November 1984.
26. Some details of the military relationship are reported in *The Middle East* (May, 1983): 30–32, and in *J P*, 3 June 1983. An exaggerated account of the military relationship since 1976 can be found in Azim Husain, "The West, South Africa

and Israel: A Strategic Triangle," *Third World Quarterly* **4** (January 1982):61–73; another attempt, containing a number of inaccuracies, is Olusola Ojo, "Israeli-South African Connections and Afro-Israeli Relations," *International Studies* **21** (January–March, 1982): 37–51. Perhaps the most balanced survey is in Barry M. Blackman and Edward N. Luttwack (eds.). *International Security Yearbook*, 1983/84 (New York: St. Martin's Press, 1984), pp. 297–299. Israeli Ambassador to South Africa, Eliahu Lankin, responding to accounts of such cooperation offered by the *Sunday Times* defense correspondent, James Adams, in his book, *The Unnatural Alliance* (London: Quartet Books, 1984) and in the *Sunday Times* on 15 April 1984, called them "tendentious; a fantasy that I have no doubt is not objective; a distorted picture," *J P*, 16 April 1984. Adams, however, provides an extremely detailed account of the bilateral relationship, with frequent references to Israeli officials in Tel-Aviv as the source for his information.

27. South Africa and Israel support Peleg's hypothesis that the correlation between weapons self-production and the degree to which a nation was exposed to arms supply limitations in the past should be strong and positive, Peleg, p. 220.
28. SIPRI, 1982, p. 278.
29. *Haaretz*, 11 February 1983.
30. *Newsview*, 14 December 1982; *J, P*, 30 November 1982.
31. *J P*, 20 and 21 January 1983; *Haaretz*, 19 January, 11 February 1983. Sources in Zaire in January, 1984 claimed that Israel has supplied the army with light weapons, recoilless guns, half-tracks, artillery and trucks, *J P*, 22 January 1984.
32. President Herzog's visit was given elaborate coverage, both in Zaire and in the Israeli media, *Haaretz*, 19 January 1984; *Maariv*, 22 January and 27 January 1984. During his stay Herzog made a point of visiting military installations to see training programs under IDF sponsorship.
33. *IHT*, 17 December 1982.
34. Argentina's efforts at breaking the arms boycott are described in Ronald L. Slaughter, "The Politics and Nature of the Conventional Arms Transfer Process During a Military Engagement: The Falklands-Malvinas Case," *Arms Control* **3** (May 1983):16–29.
35. This claim is made for Israel by Slaughter, p. 23.
36. *Haaretz*, 15 February 1983; *J P*, 13 June 1983.
37. Argentinian press reports claim as many as seventy Daggers; the lower figure is cited in *Aviation Week* and reported in *Haaretz*, 14 August 1983. Some thirty-five of these planes are alleged to have been sold even before the outbreak of fighting, *IHT*, 22–23 January 1983.
38. Slaughter, p. 19; *Haaretz*, 9 April 1984.
39. Former Argentinian President Leopold Galtieri since has claimed that Israel volunteered to dispatch pilots along with the twenty-two Daggers rushed to Argentina.
40. Objection to Israeli supplies is expressed in *Maariv*'s weekly supplement, 29 June 1984.
41. The point is made by Slaughter, p. 27.
42. Trilateral flows are hinted at in *Maariv*, 8 June 1984 and *IHT*, 11 June 1984.
43. Pierre, p. 33; Segev, especially pp. 75–93, 213–222.
44. Insight into the cooperative effort is provided by Michael Ledeen and William Lewis, *Debacle. The American Failure in Iran* (New York: Knopf, 1981), esp. pp. 107–108.
45. When a story on the impending visit by Premier Levi Eshkol in June, 1966 was filed, the chief censor hurried to prevent its reaching print, Bar-On, p. 188.
46. *Time*, 25 July 1983, p. 19.
47. SIPRI, 1982, p. xxviii; *The Economist* 29 August 1981, p. 42.

48. *J P*, 13 July 1983; *Haaretz*, 13 and 18 July 1983; in addition, see: SIPRI, 1982, p. 188, quoting the *Financial Times*, 12 November 1981; *Haaretz*, 5 November 1982. Leslie Gelb refers to documents proving that $100 to 200 million in arms, spare parts, and ammunition were delivered to Iran from Western Europe in the previous eighteen months, half of it supplied or arranged by Israel. "Israel Said to Be Key To Iran's Arms Supply," *IHT*, 9 March 1982.

49. *Aviation Week and Space Technology*, 11 April 1983, pp. 16–18; *IHT*, 19 July 1983.

50. *IHT*, 19 March 1984.

51. *The Economist*, 29 August 1981, p. 42.

52. *Haaretz*, 17 and 18 May 1984.

53. *J P*, 17 May 1984.

54. *Haaretz*, 18 May 1984 and *J P*, 17 May 1984.

55. An interesting presentation of positive reasons for Israel pursuing a relationship with Iran is A. Schweitzer, "The Hidden Ally," *Haaretz*, 11 June 1984. Israel's interest, like that of the United States, requires a restrained, not an impotent, Iran. See Henry A. Kissinger, "Pressure Points in the Gulf" *Washington Post* 5 February 1985.

56. *IHT*, 16–17 July 1983.

57. *IHT*, 21 December 1983.

58. *IHT*, 24 November 1983.

59. *IHT*, 23 December 1983.

60. *Aviation Week and Space Technology*, 12 April 1982, p. 46.

61. *WP*, 30 December 1984; see also Ken Ishii, "In Japan the Buildup is Moderate," *IHT*, 7 December 1982. On Japan see Kent E. Calder, "The Rise of Japan's Military-Industrial Base," *Asia Pacific Community* 17 (Summer 182):26–41; and Rajaram Panda, "Security Concerns and Militarism in Japan," *Asia Pacific Community* 20 (Spring 1983):20–33. The revised 1984 defense budget is $12.3 billion, *IHT*, 13 July 1983.

62. *Haaretz*, 8 December 1982.

63. *NYT*, 27 March 1983. *Defense & Foreign Affairs* (February, 1985): 24, reports a deal involving TCM-20 anti-aircraft guns ordered from the Ramta Company. SIPRI, 1984, p. 238, mentions an unconfirmed supply of 24 Kfir planes to Haiti.

64. Unconfirmed reports to this effect in *WP*, 19 October 1984, 2 January 1985.

65. In November, 1980, *Newsweek* magazine reported that Israel was selling significant amounts of arms to China; both Israel and China denied the report. In September, 1982, the Israeli press contained reports of an impending visit to China by representatives of Tadiran to display advanced electronic tank equipment to military officials there, *Maariv*, 10 September 1982; *J P*, 10 September 1982. French press speculation on the presence of two hundred Israeli military personnel on the mainland was picked up by the Israeli newspapers as well, *Haaretz*, 22 July 1983, *Maariv*, 22 July 1983, *J P*, 24 July 1983. Reports picked up again toward the end of 1984 when military observers noted tank cannon remarkably similar to Israeli designs during a military parade on 10 October in Beijing. *Maariv*, 19 October 1984 and *Haaretz*, 15 October 1984.

66. A *Washington Times* report on 24 January 1985, quoting State Department sources, believed Israel to be filling arms orders worth more than $1 billion, which the Israeli Embassy spokesman neither confirmed nor denied.

67. Outlines of China's military supply problem in Paul H. Kreisberg, "The Limits on U.S.-Chinese Military Cooperation," *IHT*, 28 December 1983.

68. 13 September 1984. Text courtesy of the Embassy of Israel, Washington, D.C.

69. The *New York Times*, 30 January 1985.

9

THE UNTAPPED U.S. MARKET

Since trading in arms is a recognized form of politics among nations and is regarded therefore as an expression of sovereign will, Israel would very much wish to see itself as a free agent in the international arms market. Yet the more ambitious and sophisticated its defense sales have become the less freedom of maneuver and liberty of action does Israel possess on the key operational choices of what items to sell and to which clients. By having to secure prior consent from a second party, the United States, for the sale or transfer of weapons systems containing American components, Israel increasingly must contend with a special kind of restraint not found, certainly not to such an extent, in the weapons transfers policies of the other prominent suppliers. Indeed, it can be argued that no other element of Israeli external affairs calls into question its claim to independent action or underscores the serious extent of Israel's dependence on the United States.

In analyzing the impact of the United States on Israel's program of foreign military assistance and arms sales, one observation needs to be made at the outset. Whether in fact the U.S. government approves or disapproves of Israeli arms export diplomacy will depend upon two things: (a) the general state of relations between Jerusalem and Washington; (b) respective weapons transfer policies of the two countries, which can either parallel each other or sharply diverge.

Arms sales practices by Israel, like the supply by the United States to Israel of advanced weapon systems, are but one aspect of the far larger, multifaceted and delicate Israeli-American relationship.[1] Strains have been known to surface at times over broad policy matters, such as the Arab-Israeli conflict, the 1982 Lebanon intervention and Middle East peacemaking procedures. The 1973 arms airlift, the 1975 "reassessment," refusal by Jimmy Carter in 1977 to sanction an Israeli sale of planes with U.S. components to Ecuador, the AWACs controversy, and the unprecedented suspension of arms already contracted for by Israel as a means of exerting political leverage on Jerusalem following the destruction of the Iraqi nuclear reactor in 1981 are other recent reminders of the close linkage between arms and policy, between Israel as a recipient and as a supplier. A further reminder, should it materialize, would be the political struggle over the proposed sale by Washington of mobile, improved Hawk missiles, Stinger anti-aircraft missiles or fighter aircraft to Jordan.

The official U.S. attitude toward any particular Israeli mission or arms deal consequently could have as much to do with the prevailing atmosphere of general bilateral ties as with the actual merits of the case. It should be recalled in this connection that both the Carter and Reagan administrations chose to signal U.S. displeasure at independent moves on the part of Israel (settlement policy, Lebanon) by demonstrating America's capacity for obstructing Israeli weapons transfer activities.[2] The result is to make Israeli arms diplomacy hostage to the larger questions of Israel's place in American foreign policy and the nature of relationships between superior-subordinate states.

Yet no small amount of friction over Israeli arms exports is the product of narrower differences with the United States in this specialized field of activity. It is these specific differences vis-à-vis the international arms trade which draw our attention in this chapter.

Over the years Israel's association with the United States has proven both an asset and a liability in terms of Israeli arms diplomacy. There are instances where identification with the United States and the West gave Israel a relative advantage. Weapons transfers to the Kurds and to Iran in the era of the Shah were expedited with the encouragement as well as the knowledge of officials in Washington because these flows of arms were regarded as fully consistent with America's long-term regional strategy. The same was true of arms to the anti-Communist Somoza regime at a time of threatened Cuban activity in Central America, and is just as much a factor in the strategy of containing the Sandinistas.

Similarly, the image enjoyed by Israel as a friend of the United States may have worked to improve its stature in the eyes of would-be clients who turned to Jerusalem as a conduit for the resale and re-export of American arms, and possibly as a source of influence on American congressional and public opinion in their quest for U.S. economic or military aid. The record, however, also suggests other cases where the American connection, and more specifically Israel's dependence on the United States, have been a drawback in attempts at pursuing and widening an independent course of arms export diplomacy.

The United States enters the calculus of Israeli weapons transfer policy at essentially five sensitive points. The first instance is in the role of enthusiast, when, for a variety of reasons, policymakers in Washington may welcome Israel's assuming arms relationships with certain select countries.

THE UNITED STATES AS PROMOTER

Acting through Israel as the immediate supplier of conventional arms provides the U.S. with the type of "middle option" sought by bureaucrats and strategists in Washington in the post-Vietnam era under the Nixon doctrine who find themselves subject to congressional restrictions. While they may not like to express appreciation of Israel's role as such, operating essentially in concert with, and through, Israel represents the preferred choice between keeping a low profile and perhaps relying solely upon local forces usually ill-equipped and unprepared for the assignment, or, at the other extreme, becoming directly involved.

When asked on one occasion whether the Reagan administration looked kindly on Israeli arms activities in the Americas, a high State Department official commented: "Absolutely. We've indicated we're not unhappy they are helping out. But I wouldn't say we and the Israelis have figured out together what to do."[3] Here the degree of tactical coordination matters less than the approval in principle. From an American standpoint this amounts to a minimal commitment. There is no direct U.S. involvement, and all that is required is a go-ahead, explicit or implicit, to Israeli leaders. Given this green light, Israeli military experts have been able to assist in combatting antigovernment insurgency in countries of concern for the United States as Costa Rica, El Salvador, Guatemala, and Honduras, where the press noted the activities of American and Israeli operatives.[4]

This is most apt to happen when both sides are in basic accord and the pending transaction satisfies their mutual interest, meeting Israel's short-term diplomatic, security, or commercial needs while strengthening America's regional or global position. The advantages to the United States are appreciable since tacit arrangements permit the U.S. to keep at a safe distance from Israel publicly; yet, the United States stands to benefit geopolitically: pro-Western states bolstered militarily and inflicting defeats upon Soviet-armed clients, the assurance that American equipment will be employed more effectively under Israeli supervision, etc.

That American military specialists are cognizant of the contribution made by Israel's own distinctive program of arms and assistance can be derived from a letter written in February, 1983, to President Reagan by more than 130 retired generals and admirals. The text, as published in *The New York Times*, cautioned: "If the free world doubts the actuality or the significance of these startling [Israeli] advances in weaponry and tactics, Moscow cannot afford to. . . . "[5] Whatever the effect upon White House and Pentagon policy, such praise for Israel amounts to a free advertisement, and one likely to attract interested foreign customers.

Nor does there appear presently to be any lack of situations or of customers for indirect American assistance via, or together with, Israel. The Americas, and the Caribbean in particular, are a premier case in point where the United States comes up against the limits of its own power. In 1982 and 1983 the Administration deepened its resolve to support friendly regimes in El Salvador, Guatemala, and Honduras, pledging emergency economic and military aid. Kissinger argued the need for a firm U.S. response, including the use of covert operations in order to retain America's credibility elsewhere.[6] Congress, however, expressed opposition to the unrestricted flow of arms, fearing this would be the first step, along with providing military advisers, toward direct military intervention by the United States.[7] Further limiting American freedom of action was the refusal of its Western European allies to help in countering stepped-up arms deliveries by the Soviet Union to Cuba and Nicaragua;[8] indeed, high administration officials expressed strong disappointment at France's unilateral decision early in 1982 to sell arms to the Sandinistas in contrast to attempts by the United States to isolate them because of their alleged support for leftist guerrillas in El Salvador.[9]

Perhaps due in part to these frustrations in supplementing American security assistance to friendly governments, senior Reagan administration officials let it be known in July, 1983, that at the request of the United States Israel had agreed to send weapons captured from the P.L.O. to Honduras for eventual use by Nicaraguan rebels.[10] Such confirmation of Israel in the role of proxy supplier is extremely rare. Yet it offers a glimpse into what may be other instances as well: Argentina, at least until the United States agreed to the resumption of arms sales; Chad, countering Libya; Taiwan, where the United States is torn by a predicament between planned sales of arms and the repercussions for Chinese-American relations of what Beijing warns would be a violation of an earlier 1982 agreement whereby sales to Taiwan would see progressive yearly reductions;[11] and Iran, where the question of whether America in fact privately condoned Israel's re-export of U.S.-made equipment remains a matter of conjecture.

American approval, admiration and encouragement for Israeli military assistance in support of larger U.S. and Western interests needs to be seen as a double-edged sword. To many, U.S.-Israeli global cooperation only further vindicates American assistance from 1948 to 1984 of over $30 billion as a worthwhile investment, while similarly demonstrating the "special relationship" between the two countries and their potential for working together on the basis of a strategic understanding covering shared interests and common goals.[12] Unquestionably, a positive attitude in Washington toward Israeli military and scientific development leading to an active arms export program, whether to the United States or only to third countries, constitutes a major boost for the defense industries in Israel.

The danger, however, lies in a possible excess of approval and encouragement. In other words, a United States paralyzed by a constitutional struggle between the executive and congressional branches, defensive in foreign affairs, fearing overseas entanglements yet no less fearful of Communist successes in Third World "arcs of crisis," its conventional forces overextended, might feel itself called upon to press Israel to act as a proxy and surrogate arms supplier. At such a point U.S. encouragement might work negatively by, in turn, encouraging Israeli policymakers to throw caution to the winds and to abandon those few restraints on weapons transfers as presently exist.

Should it be so inclined, the United States, as the principal economic and diplomatic patron, certainly is not lacking leverage; the challenge for Israel, therefore, will be in navigating between the Scylla of too warm an American response to arms sales by Israel and the Charybdis of Washington's principled or selective disapproval.

THE UNITED STATES AS CRITIC

Israel and the United States have not always seen eye to eye on particular military sales, or, for that matter, on general principles governing conventional arms transfers. At such moments the United States impinges on Israel's freedom to pursue an active arms diplomacy through its ability to pass judgment on Israeli actions.

In this second capacity of critic of Israeli policy, the United States tends to set itself up as an arbiter of international arms conduct, judging not only Israel—although at times it seems *particularly* Israel—but other weapons suppliers as well by American standards. Here the emphasis shifts from commonalities and shared interests to fundamental differences: of scale, of outlook, of behavior patterns.

Military transfers, however small in global terms, are regarded as vital by Israel; the United States, sometimes in the past has treated its own activities as secondary: important but something less than a national priority. Israel is driven more by immediate circumstance and short-term, concrete advantage; the United States, adopting a strategic and global frame of reference, sees the flow of arms in balance of power terms. Israel as an arms supplier appears clear-minded, consistent; the United States, ambivalent and not always consistent. Israel's sales policy shows continuity, being maintained through changes of government; that of the U.S. reflects the change from one administration to another. Israel long since has made its peace with the contradictions between moral precepts and the realities of power. Students of U.S. foreign relations insist that the American people and their leaders have yet to accomplish this reconciliation of values.

Aspects of the contemporary moral dilemma in trafficking in arms were resolved earlier for Israel. "When a country friendly to Israel asks for help," explained one unnamed Israeli official, "we don't ask whether it is democratic or nondemocratic and we don't ask about its motives."[13] Far from being callous, cynical or amoral, such statements represent the collective insight garnered from over three decades of a precarious existence as a small, Jewish state in a hostile environment.

In founding the state Ben-Gurion expressed Israel's intention to maintain close ties of all kinds with other states irrespective of ideological differences and without sitting in judgment of their domestic forms of government. It was Ben-Gurion who again offered future leaders a second maxim of statecraft relevant to arms diplomacy as well by pledging to do whatever necessary to ensure the survival of the Jewish people and the security of the Jewish State. In justifying the 1952 agreement to accept reparations from West Germany, Ben-Gurion drew a clear moral line. He was proposing "neither forgiveness nor wiping the slate clean." Rather, his decision was "the final injunction of the inarticulate six million, the victims of Nazism whose very murder was a ringing cry for Israel to rise, to be strong and prosperous, to safeguard her peace and security, and so prevent such a disaster from ever again overwhelming the Jewish people."[14] The security of the Jewish people is itself a moral imperative. This, for Israelis, has remained the highest moral and ethical principle.

A third pillar of Israel's moral stand on arms sales is offered in a comment attributed to Moshe Sharett, Israel's first foreign minister, a critic of many of Ben-Gurion's actions and someone identified with a moderate, more moral approach to foreign affairs. Sharett made the following ethical distinction: "A scattered and defenseless people can and, perhaps, must live only in the memories of the past . . . "

But, continued Sharett,

a people which exercises political sovereignty over a territory of its own is in a very different category. . . . It must follow every shift in the balance of forces around it and in the world at large; it dare not neglect any opportunity of increasing its strength.[15]

As a result, Israel has achieved greater clarity as to ends and means.

Whatever else its merits or demerits, this rationale for a fundamental pro-arms sales consensus is an attempt by Israel at rising above expediency and forging an approach rooted in practical morality and prudence. Statecraft consists of making careful, prudential judgments about lesser evil and greater good. Like any other country striving to uphold moral values in conducting foreign policy, Israel cannot avoid grappling with the same dilemmas of ends and means. Offering arms and military aid to countries charged with abusing human rights is regrettable, and not only because it may strain ties with the United States and damage Israel's image abroad. Yet Israel's weapons transfers are far from being indiscriminate. Sound reasons must exist politically, militarily, or economically for transferring the arms, despite the acknowledged negative side effects.

The normalcy of the Jewish State, in short, cuts both ways. Israeli policies may disappoint those who from afar deal in moral absolutes. Such people, on the one hand, insist that Israel be strengthened, but on the other hand require that it keep its hands spotlessly clean.[16] Israeli political and military leaders, in facing the present challenges, must confront both political necessity and moral precepts. It is unrealistic if not unfair to ask them to unilaterally forego one of Israel's principal advantages. Despite enemies, detractors, or stern judges, Jerusalem has been willing to bear the responsibilities of arms export diplomacy as the price for increasing its presence and influence in the world. Moreover, practical Israeli salesmen remain capable of distinguishing between influence and interference.

To Israelis today arms are the hard currency of foreign relations. They are part of the price Israel as a small state has to pay in moral currency, too, for the primacy of national security. Weapons, arrangements for their sale when feasible and where judged consistent with the national objective, and the types of military-political relationships they tend to foster may be one of modern Israel's best answers to its moral, and political, imperative: not to submit to others in the determination and realization of vital interests.

Supplementary justifications vary with the specific circumstances. Transfers to Argentina have been defended as a channel for interceding on behalf of the Jewish *desaparecidos* without compromising the already precarious condition of Argentine Jewry; also by noting that if Israel ceased selling to Buenos Aires its place would quickly be taken by other countries. As a result, successive Israeli governments have not viewed military assistance and weapons transfers as either morally reprehensible or politically unacceptable. Israeli arms diplomacy thus reflects none of the oscillations of American arms policy during the Nixon-Carter-Reagan administrations.

The divergence of Israeli and American views was widest perhaps during the Carter presidency especially following his announcement on 19 May, 1977, that conventional arms transfers would be regarded as an "exceptional" foreign policy implement. The Carter policy of limiting the sale of American arms overseas, of urging unilateral restraint, of tying military aid to human rights performance, and of attempting to reduce international arms traffic met with mixed success. But as long as these guidelines remained official policy and reflected the president's own position, they put Israel and the United States on a collision course, especially as the end of the seventies coincided with a dramatic rise in arms exports by Israel, not to mention larger policy differences with the Begin government following the Sadat initiative.

In contrast to attempts by President Carter to control U.S. arms sales abroad, and in some cases to pressure other suppliers to do likewise, the emphasis under the Reagan administration underlines flexibility in weapons transfer practices and accepts the use of arms as a key foreign policy instrument. As Ronald Reagan himself explained in his landmark presidential directive of 8 July 1981, which reinstated arms sales as a major instrument of U.S. foreign policy:

> The realities of today's world demand that we pursue a sober, responsible, and balanced arms transfer policy, a policy that will advance our national security interests and those of the free world. Both in addressing decisions as to specific transfers and opportunities for restraint among producers, we will be guided by principle as well as practical necessity. We will deal with the world as it is, rather than as we would like it to be.[17]

As long as this statement continues to be the official American stand it moves the United States appreciably closer to the established position firmly held to by Israel. Arms sales may be employed by the United States to counter the Soviet global challenge, by Israel to cope with the Arab regional threat but also to counter Soviet expansionism.

This is not to suggest an end to friction or that Washington will no longer take a dim view of specific Israeli sales, merely that such differences as do arise in the near future will owe to other than alternative approaches to the proper ordering of ethical and political principles. Proof that the potential still exists for disagreement at the governmental level over specific arms dealings by Israel is seen from the following recent misunderstandings. In the Falklands much was made of the fact that American policy supported Britain while its ally, Israel, rushed to aid the Argentinian military. In December, 1983, the story that U.S. customs agents in Florida had impounded 12,000 illegally imported Israeli-made rifles destined for Guatemala made national headlines.[18] Israel's role in Central America similarly was blown out of proportion and exploited by both sides at the height of the 1983 contest of presidential versus congressional wills over military assistance to the Caribbean basin.[19] Descriptions of Israel as an arms mercenary and as a subordinate of the United States made their way into the American media and became part of the public debate; it was then that for some unexplained reason accounts picturing Israel as one of the top ranking world arms merchants began to appear, further putting Israel in an unfavorable light. Still later, prominence was given to reports of arms funneled to Khomeini by Israel while the role of other allies — Switzerland, Brazil, Great Britain, South Korea, and West Germany — went virtually ignored. So, too, it was leaked from within the administration that pressure was being applied to Israel to refrain from any further transactions with Iran.[20]

These episodes suffice to show that the United States has in its power the capacity for embarrassing Israel and Israeli arms diplomacy. In the role of critic, Washington's means of influence go beyond planted leaks and media exposure and include various practical measures. One such measure might be the withholding of military technologies needed by Israel for its further growth.

THE UNITED STATES AS COPARTNER

A third pressure point owes to the fact that America remains the chief supplier of military and scientific data of a type crucial for Israel if it is to preserve its status in the front rank of weapons developers. The policies of the United States can further reduce the latitude presently enjoyed by Israel as an autonomous supplier of arms. For the truth is that despite its best efforts Israel is not self-sufficient in weaponry or weapons technology.

Licensing procedures and the application of export controls to high technology are a sensitive issue in American politics evidenced, for example, in the debates over embargoing American technology and equipment for the Soviet gas pipeline to Western Europe. This problem has touched Israel in the case of the Kfir aircraft, with its American engine. A program to sell M-1 Abrams tanks to Saudi Arabia has led the Pentagon to deny Israel technical information on the tank, data wanted by Israeli researchers in order to design antitank weapons and tactics. Certain military and business circles have gone on record also as being reluctant to allow Israel to coproduce the F-16 planes lest Israeli scientists become too familiar with the latest American technologies.

Both sides, in other words, are fully aware of the implications of U.S. scientific aid. The Americans have made virtually all their most advanced weaponry and technology—meaning the best fighter aircraft, missiles, radar, armor, and artillery—available to Israel. Israel, in turn, has utilized this knowledge, adapting American equipment to increase its own technological sophistication, reflected tangibly in Israeli defense offerings. As has been noted in an official U.S. government report, these Israeli military exports "could adversely impact on the U.S. economy and can affect U.S. ability to control proliferation of these technologies."[21] In effect, by doing business with Israeli counterparts, U.S. companies are concerned that they might find themselves competing with their own technology and designs in the international market.

Using various arguments—Israeli self-reliance, that U.S. and Israeli research efforts are complementary rather than competitive, that revenue from arms sales makes Israel more viable and hence is far preferable to annual increases in American financial aid—Israeli negotiators have managed by and large to persuade Washington to contribute a sizeable proportion of the research and development money and some of the technology needed in the past to undertake such ambitious weapons systems programs as the Kfir plane and the Merkava tank.[22] Not to be overlooked is the fact that in return the United States benefits from three Israeli advantages in R & D: innovativeness of applications, faster turnaround time, and, often, lower cost.

Data-sharing has come to figure prominently in the Lavi project, which depends upon U.S. financial, but particularly scientific, assistance. American participation, however, has fallen prey to political considerations, and questions about Israeli competitiveness have been raised by administration, corporate, and congressional advocates of a tough stance on exporting valuable know-how to the Israeli military industry.

At least in the initial stages, Israeli spokesmen would appear to have been successful in overcoming reluctance in Washington. Almost $1 billion in federal funding for the Lavi system has already been authorized as foreign military credits.[23] On the technical side, the Israel request had been for U.S. export licenses on twenty-five items extending to fabrication technologies for the plane's wing and tail structures, high strength graphite composites, and a computerized flight control system. United States defense firms, led by Northrop, tried to defeat the measure in Congress but in effect were neutralized by other lobbyists, including Grumman, which won the contract to develop the wing assemblies for the Lavi. Objections by the Defense Department were also overridden, so that finally in early 1984 licenses for all twenty-five data packages were approved by the U.S. government.[24]

Equally encouraging is the willingness of the U.S. government to join with Israeli scientists in new military research and development programs. This found expression in the Memorandum of Agreement (MOA) signed by Moshe Arens and Secretary of Defense Caspar Weinberger on 14 March 1984, which refers to agreed principles governing mutual cooperation in R & D, and an exchange of scientists and engineers, as well as procurement and logistic support of selected defense equipment. There was also the offer in 1985 for Israel to participate in "Star Wars" research. Yet there is little question but that Israeli data requests in the future will face greater scrutiny and perhaps more determined opposition within the United States the more American companies and defense contractors feel threatened by high technology transfers to arms-exporting allies.

THE UNITED STATES AS MARKET

Israel seeks more than moral support for its arms diplomacy from Washington. The United States enters the picture, therefore, in a fourth role: as purchaser and market for Israeli defense exports. If technology transfers present a problem, so, too, does the opening up of the U.S. defense industrial base to Israeli competition. Israel's arms manufacturers have long sought to capture a share of this market, but with only limited success. Indeed, no other single market has the potential for preserving, elevating or deflating the status of Israel as an international supplier of arms and defense-related equipment. Noteworthy here is that spending for military hardware and research in the United States has almost doubled in the last five years, growing to $123.5 billion in fiscal year 1984.

Part of the problem why Israel thus far has enjoyed only modest success owes less to Israel than to traditional American reluctance to encourage any foreign competition in the defense sector and to grant the local defense industry considerable protection. In preventing what is seen as the "erosive impact"[25] of foreign competition, legislation has been enacted to discourage outside bids; the Buy American Act, for example, provides that only materials and articles substantially of U.S. origin may be acquired for public and defense use. Such barriers are seen as discriminatory by America's Western trading partners who find defense imports from the United States constantly rising. Thus the existence of the "one-way street" is a problem for other allies of the United States, and not for Israel alone.

Israeli efforts at overcoming the problem began as early as 1975 in the negotiations over the U.S.-Israel Memorandum of Agreement and are a testimony to persistence and will. In it the United States government offered assurances that every effort would be made to be "fully responsive" on an "on-going and long-term" basis to Israel's military equipment and other defense requirements, to its energy requirements, and economic needs.[26]

The second step came in 1979 when then Defense Minister Ezer Weizman personally sought to make Israel's entry into the U.S. defense market somewhat easier. In the course of bilateral negotiations stemming from the peace treaty with Egypt, Weizman presented the purchase of arms from Israel as one way of reducing America's direct aid commitments to Israel. The Memorandum of Agreement signed on 19 March 1979 finally authorized the Pentagon to make purchases from Israeli defense contractors by providing "competitive opportunities" for them to bid on certain Department of Defense (DOD) contracts without Buy American Act restrictions. Likewise, it was agreed also that Israel be entitled to sell its own defense products to a ceiling of 30 percent of annual U.S. military allocations to Israel ($1.7 billion for fiscal year 1983).[27]

But while the MOA remains in force, and despite repeated pledges of support for the idea in principle, from a practical standpoint Israeli companies have found it hard to overcome the various legal, technical, and political impediments. Consequently, efforts in this direction have been rather disappointing. It is estimated that from 1979 through 1982 Israeli industries sold DOD and DOD contractors approximately only $75 million worth of goods under the agreement.[28]

Again, in negotiating the 1981 Israeli-U.S. strategic Memorandum of Understanding, Secretary of State Alexander Haig committed the U.S. to buy some $200 million in military goods and services.[29] But this, too, encountered obstacles, as when the United States announced it would not be able to proceed with implementation of the understanding after Israel extended its law, jurisdiction, and administration to the Golan Heights.

Continued resistance to Israeli defense imports led Prime Minister Shamir, accompanied by Defense Minister Arens, to seek a reclarification of the supply relationship during high level talks in Washington in November, 1983. Among the requests granted by President Reagan were:

- opening formal negotiations on the possible establishment of a free-trade area between the United States and Israel, which, if put into effect, would extend to defense-related products manufactured by Israel;
- allowing Israel to spend 15 percent of U.S. foreign military sales (FMS) assistance, or as much as $200 million, in Israel rather than for purchases exclusively in the United States, a step designed to stimulate Israel's economy and to promote its industrial development;

- $300 million in FMS assistance to be spent on R & D on the Lavi plane, plus another $250 million in Israel itself;
- a reaffirmation of the 1979 MOA to enable Israel to sell $200 million in exports or services to the U.S. Defense Department;
- establishment of a joint committee to study additional options for strategic cooperation, including the purchase and use of Israeli storage facilities.[30]

Two requests not approved by the Administration relate as well to the arms export issue:

- that Israeli bids for U.S. defense contracts be on an equal footing with those submitted by America's NATO allies;
- that Third World recipients of U.S. military assistance be permitted to use some of their FMS funds for purchase of Israeli military products.

Rejection of these proposals, however, should not diminish the importance of the 1983 presidential decisions for Israel's defense sales to the United States.

Future prospects and potential transfers stand in sharp contrast at present to the modest U.S. procurement until now of Israeli goods. The following is a partial yet representative list of transactions as of mid-1982.

- DOD contract for overhaul of F-4 components ($1.7 million).
- United States purchased three mine plows for evaluations (for $190,000).
- United States leased six 105mm guns and purchased ammunition for evaluation. Further service evaluation is expected with possible buy thereafter (value unknown).
- Israeli firm won competition (joint effort) with McDonnell Douglas to sell B-300 assault weapon to U.S. Marine Corps ($11 million for fiscal year 1982, total contract value $300 million).
- Israeli firm won competition to produce AN/VRC-12 radios ($39 million).
- Israeli firm sold 9mm ammunition ($970,000).
- Israel sold tank parts for U.S. Army and FMS use ($5 million).
- Israeli firm sold pharmaceuticals to Defense Logistics Agency (value unknown).
- Israel provided ground support equipment for U.S. Air Force test. United States buy possible thereafter ($79,000).
- Israeli firm sold conformal fuel tanks for F-15 to McDonnell Douglas ($3.1 million).
- Israeli firm sold U.S. Air Force F-4 fuel tanks ($2.4 million).
- Israeli firm sold U.S. Navy A-4 fuel tanks ($2.0 million).[31]

Until 1983 Israeli companies, led by IAI and IMI, had not been able to sell more than about $10 million to $15 million a year to the Department of Defense.[32]

Since then, under the improved atmosphere of U.S.-Israeli relations since the war in Lebanon, the Israeli defense industries have redoubled efforts aimed at the American market. Tadiran won a U.S. Army contract worth $39 million. A first shipment of Galil rifles reached the U.S. at the end of 1982 but were earmarked for individual and private use only.[33] And in January, 1983, IAI spokesmen announced that the firm had outbid other European countries and would be refurbishing 100 U.S. Army helicopters, thereby netting $5 million.[34]

Far more important and large-scale were the procurement plans announced by Pentagon officials in 1984, including joint development of a new generation missile patrol boat, the Saar 5 class attack vessel, to be equipped with U.S. and Israeli weaponry;[35] and $27 million in funding a Katyusha rocket radar detection system.[36] Secretary Weinberger himself disclosed in May, 1984, that the U.S. Navy had bought "some" remote-controlled, small pilotless aircraft from Israel after concluding the IAI-Tadiran version was a superior product for the money.[37] In September it was announced that the Navy would lease twelve Kfir fighters to simulate Soviet-made MIGs in training exercises with U.S. aircraft, paying IAI $68 million during 3½ years to maintain the aircraft in the United States.[38] Yet in the aggregate such transactions represent a miniscule fraction of the total American defense market, and Israel still has not been given a status equal to NATO defense exporters.

If the Israeli defense industry has not been entirely successful until now it is not for lack of effort or inattention to the opportunities and potential found in the United States.[39] Tadiran, for example, accepted an invitation by the U.S. Army in June, 1984, to demonstrate its Mastiff reconnaissance aircraft, as did many of the leading defense industries, including IAI, IMI, Elbit, Urdan, and others, with encouragement from the Ministry of Defense.[40] The preferred course, "direct" sales to the American government, has been almost minimal until now, however, about $50 million.[41] (Table 9.1). In lieu of direct access to the U.S. military forces, Israel pursues two indirect approaches: One approach is to service American equipment in Israel, such as contracting to overhaul and maintain engines and components for U.S. Air Force planes.[42] In addition to port calls at Haifa the U.S. Sixth Fleet has spent millions of dollars on repair work at the Israel Shipyards, alleviating severe underemployment there.[43]

A second and more important indirect approach is through "offset" agreements with those U.S. companies from which Israel fills its own military orders. In June, 1983, the General Accounting Office (GAO) released an unclassified version of a report by the comptroller general of the United States, *U.S. Assistance to the State of Israel.* One chapter is devoted to Israel's defense industry development and global arms trade; it pays particular attention to the call for government authorities to encourage major military equipment exporters to conclude buy-back arrangements with Israeli manufacturers, also known as offsets, which are commitments by U.S. firms supplying Israel mil-

Table 9.1. Department of Defense Direct Purchases
from Israel.

Fiscal Year 1982 ($ Thousand)

Aircraft and spares	2,688
Combat vehicles	1,630
Weapons	504
Ammunition	971
Electronics and communications equipment	39,352*
Medical and dental equipment	118
Maintenance and repair	87
Chain and wire rope	16
	45,366

*This unusually large sum reflects the single contract won that year
by Tadiran.

From Jacques S. Gansler, vice-president, The Analytic Sciences
Corporation (TASC), a seminar on marketing arms sales, Tel-Aviv,
17–19 June 1984.

itarily to purchase a specified amount of goods or services equal to 25 percent of Israeli purchases of $1 million or more.[44] For example, in August, 1983, in the most expensive arms deal contracted for by Israel, it purchased 75 F-16 jets costing some $2.7 billion. Under the terms of the agreement, General Dynamics, manufacturer of the plane, agreed to Israeli firms producing components for the F-16 in Israel; such purchases would be worth more than $300 million.[45] At least ten Israeli companies have offset agreements with General Dynamics, including the Israel Aircraft Industries, Elbit, Elta, IMI, and Tadiran.

The advantages of offset arrangements with American manufacturers are at least two. They, indeed, "offset" the cost of arms purchases in the United States, in the case of F-16s, some 10 percent of the transaction. In addition, they enable Israeli defense firms to maintain close to full operation; thus, by supplying components for the F-16, IAI should be able to keep its production line busy in the interim between halting manufacture of the Kfir and starting to build the Lavi. Offsets can be expected, therefore, to constitute a focus of future marketing efforts aimed at the large and lucrative American market. As though to give expression to this promising direction, many of the larger arms manufacturers have recently opened offices in the United States or have hired the services of American lawyers as consultants and as their representatives in making useful contacts and negotiating transactions.[46]

Were economic utility to be the sole determinant then Israeli-American joint military development and manufacturing ventures would make a great deal of sense. Coproduction and increased military purchases from Israel would ease the burden of American economic aid to Israel. They surely are far more desirable than Israel either deferring or, worse, defaulting on even some of its $9 billion debt to the United States. Not only face-saving, the purchase by the American military of Israeli military products would be mutually advantageous.

On their own merits certain items manufactured by Israel are cost competitive and might fill certain gaps in American military preparedness, such as the sore issue of spare parts from prime contractors charging inflated prices. Other testimony reveals structural faults in American industry, in addition to a lack of cost consciousness, which challenge its ability to meet the specifications and production schedules set by the Pentagon.[47] One of the maladies has been shoddy military production by domestic firms shielded from foreign competition and holding to low standards of quality control;[48] another is the tendency of U.S. manufacturers and their military sponsors to favor newer systems and high-tech projects, like the DIVAD antiaircraft gun, the Americanized Roland missile or the Aquila RPV, at the expense of upgrading those of proven effectiveness,[49] or adopting cheaper and effective weapons already in use by Western allies.

The opportunity for an Israeli breakthrough into the American defense market therefore exists. One proof is that when given a fair chance to compete, Israeli firms have done well. However, the obstacles are less economic than political. Intense opposition from several American quarters is illustrated in the controversy sparked by Tadiran, which successfully underbid a Texas company, E-Systems, by 20 percent and won a U.S. Army tender to supply radio equipment valued at $39 million.[50] E-Systems, also an electronics manufacturer, objected to the Pentagon decision and then launched a campaign popular in American business circles to stop foreign industries from selling weapons to U.S. forces. Joined by a number of congressmen sensitive to possible military dependence on outside sources and to the issue of unemployment at home, opponents seized on the Tadiran contract as a test case and sought to push through an amendment to the defense authorization bill that would prohibit buying military equipment from a foreign manufacturer, no matter what the saving, if that company became the sole supplier.[51] Opponents of Israel, or of a closer U.S.-Israeli defense and security assistance relationship could be expected to add their voices in opposition to providing Israeli competitors in particular with any such opening or advantage.

In sum, high barriers remain to Israel's entry into the U.S. market: legislative and bureaucratic as well as competition from U.S. firms backed by congress in pressing for "buy American" policies. There have even been a few recent cases where an Israeli firm was the low bidder and still was not awarded the contract. Notwithstanding, Defense Minister Arens gave expression in 1984 to the confidence of many in Israel who regard America as the most important market in coming years when he voiced the hope of possible sales of Lavi aircraft to the United States in the late 1990s.[52]

Two possible grounds for this optimism are apparent. The first is that Israel is not alone in insisting that the United States open itself up to competition and turn defense collaboration with its Western allies into a "two-way street." The American market for military goods has been one of the most protected in world trade and increasingly is the target of NATO criticism as being inimical to solidarity. The Europeans are calling for greater standardization in weapons systems, production-sharing, and for the U.S. military to buy more defense equipment from NATO countries also involved in international arms sales and upset at their trade imbalance strongly in favor of the United States. Should the NATO allies of the United States succeed in establishing a more cooperative effort, logically it could facilitate Israel's call for a comparable relationship with the United States. Here Israel might actually be rendering a service to an industry sorely needing the discipline of more competition, and to an allied military establishment that ought to be interested in yielding a more cost-effective solution to its military requirements in conventional arms and innovative technologies.

The second opening could be provided by the 1985 bilateral framework of the approved free trade area between the two countries. If realized, Israeli exports in general might reach as high as $5 to $7 billion by 1990 — trade with the United States was $1.3 billion in 1983; preferential treatment would have the additional effect, one assumes, of facilitating military-related exports as well. But for the meantime, sensitivities aroused in a climate of American protectionism, together with an Israeli-U.S. political relationship always subject to strain, suggests that the prospects for an easy flow of arms *from* Israel *to* the United States are limited at best. Grounds for such caution stem from the fifth and final point at which the United States enters the calculus of Israeli weapons transfer policy: when American business interests perceive of themselves as direct competitors with Israel for overseas markets and clients.

THE UNITED STATES AS RIVAL

American officials in general are concerned that the dissemination of military technology may undercut existing markets. Accordingly, the United States, along with other major suppliers, has begun to examine more critically requests for various types of aid (data transfers, coproduction, licensing) and as a rule is less supportive of Third World countries with ambitions to develop weapons capabilities and an independent export program. In the late 1970s U.S. opposition was principled, as part of the Carter emphasis upon multilateral arms restraint; in the 1980s the opposition is even more intense, but now it arises from largely commercial considerations, such as the scramble for contracts and the elimination of competitors.

In this prevailing climate of protectionism, and at a time when the national trade deficit totaled $123.3 billion in 1984, American arms trade specialists tend to take a dim view of Israel's position. Criticism has already been heard that U.S. aid only serves to increase Israeli independence; that Israel has incorporated sophisticated American military technologies in weapons systems which it then proceeds to export in competition with U.S. products and possibly in contravention of the United States policy; that in parlaying smallness into an asset Israel meets production schedules ahead of American companies and offers Third World customers an excellent cost-competitive alternative to buying American. Arguments like these dovetail with the view of some American Middle East policymakers who prefer to ensure Israel's dependent status militarily as as effective means of exercising political control.

The clearest expression of aroused American concern at the longer-range implications of U.S. military assistance is, again, the previously mentioned 1983 GAO Report. It notes, for example, that Israel, more than any other FMS recipient, has been provided with a high percentage of military technologies having export potential. What results is a dilemma of importance for future Israeli-U.S. relations. On the one hand, liberalized FMS support helps Israel to maintain its qualitative military and technological edge. Support for the Lavi program will not only keep 20,000 workers employed in Israel's aircraft industry and lower unit cost of the plane, but as a result Israel will also have an advanced aircraft that could provide possible export monies.[53] On the other hand, however, American officials are cognizant of the domestic, political, and economic repercussions for the United States of aiding a foreign country's aircraft program. As the report observes, Israel's accelerated defense sales, together with the trend toward increasing assistance requirements, greater relaxation of restrictions on the use of FMS funds, competition with U.S. production, and setting of precedents that other countries may seek to emulate, could "cause an adverse impact on the U.S. economy," especially on its industrial base and employment, and "can affect U.S. ability to control proliferation of these technologies."[54]

The Reagan administration has put the United States back on its previous course of easing arms sales curbs and engaging in security assistance programs all around the globe. The more aggressive the United States becomes in promoting weapons transfers to the Third World the greater the inevitability of preempting Israeli representatives, whether in selling M-48 tanks to Thailand,[55] in sending military equipment to strengthen Costa Rica's tiny defense force,[56] or in encouraging the interest of ASEAN countries in U.S.-made jet planes. With a foreign trade deficit of its own, the idea of selling abroad probably has never been more important to America's economy or politics.[57] The aim, therefore, is to sharpen American competitiveness, extending to defense sales, against all other countries. Israel would be no exception.

THE AMERICAN VETO, EXPLICIT AND IMPLICIT

Greater independence has been Israel's traditional argument for making and exporting arms. Yet the problematic relationship with Washington suggests a serious impediment to Israel's future arms export diplomacy. Dependence upon the United States for arms procurement and military financial assistance is public knowledge.[58] Even so, this is but one part of the problem. Less known or discussed is the virtual stranglehold retained by the United States over key areas of the Israeli military sales program.

This capacity for upsetting Israeli plans expresses itself in a number of different ways and at several pressure points. The form of leverage used or threatened by the United States is likely to depend upon which of the five roles prompts it to intercede — as enthusiast or critic, as supplier of data, purchaser, or competitor.

The excessive use of Israel as a surrogate in extending U.S. and Western military assistance, in Latin America for example, could prove embarrassing in two ways. Pressure from Washington on Israel to act as supplier to dubious regimes nevertheless deemed worthy of being propped up against local subversion would be difficult for Jerusalem to resist repeatedly, especially if presented in terms of the least the United States might have the right to expect of its Israeli ally or if presented as a quid pro quo. Repeated acquiescence, on the other hand, would identify Israel too directly and too closely with the United States, branding it as the sword-bearer for American or Western interests.

What happens, however, when an American government falls out with Israel over arms transfer practices? One means available to the United States is preventing Third World clients from using American military or economic aid to purchase Israeli arms. Equally effective and far more embarrassing would be a scenario in which American officials willfully determine to discredit Israel or to damage its image with the American public. As seen previously, early traces of such a ploy were evident in 1982, when information apparently was leaked to the press about Israel's arms activities in the case of Iran, and again in supplying Argentina during the Falklands fighting. Compromising Israel by specifically mentioning it as a merchant of arms to countries with a poor human rights record, or simply as a major arms exporter, offers another way of exerting leverage.

Inadvertent or not, newspaper articles citing unnamed Washington sources and headlining Israel as the seventh ranking world arms exporter, aside from being somewhat exaggerated, fall under the category of damning with faint praise.[59] What they accomplish is to call undue attention to Israel and cast it in a less than favorable light. So, too, does editorial opinion arguing that the American interest lies in using what political and moral leverage it has to encourage unregenerate regimes like those in Argentina and Chile to return to the democratic fold, and not to permit them to diversify their arms suppliers; this alongside reports of Israeli arms and advisers to Latin American juntas.[60]

While available to the White House when it seeks to act as a critic of Israeli arms policy, publicity can also be wielded in expressing dissatisfaction at non-arms policies as well, such as Lebanon or negotiations on autonomy.

In December, 1981, the State Department announced:

> The President has decided that the U.S. will not for the moment proceed with further discussions on some Israeli proposals for purchases of defense-related goods and services in Israel; on authorizing Israel to use some Foreign Military Sales funds to purchase Israel-produced goods and services; or on the possible use of Foreign Military Sales funds by third countries to purchase Israeli defense items and services.[61]

The announcement was one of a series of sanctions expressing American opposition following the extension of Israeli law to the Golan Heights. Taken together, these three steps, worth several hundred million dollars to the Israeli economy, specifically affected different dimensions of Israeli arms sales diplomacy.

It is equally apparent that Israel could easily be undercut by a concerted U.S. effort to sell arms to states which have turned to Israel as their supplier. The economic motive, reinforcing political differences, is best seen in two recent areas of friction: the Kfir and the Lavi.

That American controls exist and have been applied is best documented in the Israeli campaign to sell its Kfir aircraft. Because production of the fighter in the 1970s required American technological assistance, the Kfir has a General Electric J79-17 engine. And because the original contract contains a clause requiring U.S. approval for sales of systems with American parts to a third party, each transaction is subject to veto by the American government. Consequently, the original high expectations for a brisk trade in the Kfir have suffered from the vagaries of U.S.-Israeli relations. According to one foreign source the IAI as of 1983 had sold 256 Kfirs. Of these 200 have gone to the Israeli air force; only fifty-six to foreign customers, including Colombia (12) and Venezuela (24).[62]

Despite periodic reports of arms deals which include the Kfir, its export record is not impressive. Thus, for example, in February, 1977, the first foreign order for the Kfir—twenty-four fighters by Ecuador—was vetoed by President Carter.[63] Shortly before the 1980 elections the administration announced that Israel would be allowed to offer the Kfir to Mexico, Colombia, and Venezuela, but by then they had contacted alternative suppliers. In June, 1978, when the United States allowed the sale of up to sixty Kfirs to Taiwan, public disclosure forced embarrassed Chinese officials to reject the offer;[64] Austria, sensitive to Arab reactions, terminated negotiations on twenty-four Kfirs in 1978.[65] As late as December, 1982, a State Department spokesman confirmed that the United States had denied Israel authorization to sell Skyhawk planes to Argentina.[66]

This power of the United States to determine whether Israeli weapons sales are to become limited almost exclusively to conventional small arms manufactured entirely in and by Israel or to be competitive in the rush to manufacture complex weapon systems can be seen in the Lavi project. The program, aiming at manufacturing a more advanced multipurpose jet fighter for the 1990s, was approved in 1980. One might argue that even by then the disappointing experience with the Kfir ought to have cautioned against any dependence upon the U.S. if foreign sales were to be a factor. Still, much of the research funds for the Lavi come from the American aid package. Despite pledges of technical and scientific assistance, delays have been experienced, and feasibility studies withheld, especially in the wake of the Lebanese fighting.[67] The State Department, for example, denied permission at the end of 1982 for the release of independent studies on design proposals for the plane ordered by Israel from three U.S. manufacturers.[68] Not until 1984 was executive approval given for the Phase 3 production technology on wing and tail assemblies to be given Israel.

Technical data packages are one American pressure point; another is direct U.S. financing, since in the first stage of developing the Lavi a large share of the funding is meant to come from American military assistance.[69] The third potential pressure point lies in the more distant future, when the plane becomes operational. Once again, some components are on order from American companies (Pratt and Whitney, Hughes, ITT, Bendix, Goodyear), making exports of the Lavi ultimately subject to U.S. government approval.[70]

In testimony before the U.S. House Foreign Affairs Committee, Defense Secretary Weinberger justified withholding assistance for the plane's manufacture on both political and commercial grounds. He argued that there was no need for Israel to develop a new-generation fighter since the F-15 and F-16 in use by the Israeli airforce were superior to the projected Lavi; and that the real reason why Israel was so anxious to build the Lavi, in his opinion, was in order to promote its own exports and compete for foreign markets with U.S. planes.[71]

The latter factor should not be deprecated as a source of friction. At first glance American fears of Israel as an arms competitor seem unwarranted, if not absurd, given the U.S. share of the market—some 32.4 percent of the world total during the period 1971–1980.[72] Yet both the U.S. and Israel are among the few Western exporters of the most advanced weapons technology. Thus, among the reasons for a delay in technology transfers for the Lavi project are concerns expressed by at least one major U.S. aircraft company, Northrup, that the Israeli plane eventually might compete with American fighters in the export market.[73] American uneasiness was raised by changes introduced gradually into the plane's design, performance characteristics, and envisioned level of technology, making it more than merely a replacement for Israel's own aging A-4 and Kfir aircraft.

Weinberger returned to this theme in talks with Defense Minister Arens in July, 1983. Challenging Israeli figures of a production run of 300 Lavi planes, he insisted that only with 700 planes coming off the production line would the plane cover development costs and show a profit. The only possible conclusion, therefore, was that Israel would be compelled to turn to overseas markets to sell the necessary critical mass of 400 additional aircraft in competition with the American aircraft industry.[74] Even though the unit "fly-away" price of the Lavi has increased from the initial estimate, according to American sources, of $7 million in 1979 to about $15.5 million per aircraft, should that price be kept it would compare favorably with the cost of at least $12 million for its U.S. counterparts, the F-16A by General Dynamics and Grumman's F-5G.[75]

Israeli experts were quick to take issue with Weinberger's analysis. They insist that Israel really needs the Lavi in place of the Skyhawk and the Kfir for ground support and in order to give the air force control over the rate of production (independence rather than reliance on U.S. supplies); also, that exports of the Lavi could be expected only after it was fully operational and in large enough quantities in the Israeli Air Force (IAF).[76] Moshe Arens, however, seems to have revealed this longer-term objective in suggesting that the Lavi's superior quality and lower price might even make the United States as well as other countries a potential customer.[77] Yet the immediate implication of this U.S.-Israeli debate was to delay the entire project.

Indirect U.S. sanctions have resulted already in delays which threaten to set back the program considerably, inflate costs, and put Israeli salesmen at a definite disadvantage vis-à-vis French, German, British, Spanish, Italian, and American competitors also racing to produce a marketable new jet fighter. Timing is critical for the Lavi project's success. The original timetable, as carefully worked out and approved, stresses two salient elements. One is the production schedule: initial test flight in 1983, manufacture to begin in 1990, satisfying IAF orders for 300 planes by 1995, and only then making exports possible. The other, related statistic is the expected cost per plane, which has already been revised upward several times. Only a relatively low cost would make the Lavi attractive to potential customers at the end of this century.

Behind the shifts in the pendulum it was apparent that American support for sophisticated defense exports by Israel, whether to the U.S. armed forces, or to those of other countries, would be less than enthusiastic in the future. The Lavi experience so far thus points to more sophisticated means than an outright veto available to the United States should it wish, for whatever motives, to hamper Israeli military production and weapons export plans. Unless Jerusalem can reach agreement with United States on a range of bilateral issues, only some of which stem directly from respective military transfer policies in the 1980s, and unless it receives a freer hand in weapons sales, the American multiple veto will loom increasingly large as a restraint upon Israeli arms diplomacy. This capacity of the United States at present and in the future to embarrass, short circuit, obstruct, and, if necessary, directly veto Israel's moves in the international arms arena serves, in turn, as a prelude to assessing the prospects lying ahead for Israel.

NOTES

1. The reader interested in the larger Israeli-American relationship will find the following useful as an introduction: Nadav Safran, *Israel. The Embattled Ally* (Cambridge: The Belknap Press of Harvard University, 1978); William B. Quandt, *Decade of Decisions* (Berkeley: University of California Press, 1977). The latest book on the subject is Bernard Reich, *The United States and Israel. Influence in the Special Relationship*. (New York: Praeger, 1984).
2. As as example, President Reagan in April, 1983, stated he would not permit the transfer of 75 F-16 planes held back since the previous summer until Israel withdrew from Lebanon. *IHT*, 2–3 April 1983.
3. *IHT*, 18–19 December 1982.
4. Informed sources, in demonstrating the atmosphere of reciprocity between Israeli and U.S. intelligence services, were quoted as using the example of Israel's having provided some well-concealed financial assistance to U.S.-backed *Contra* guerrillas through a South American intermediary, *Washington Post*, 21 May 1984. *Time*, 7 May 1984, cited other reports of Israel's funneling arms and providing trainers.
5. *NYT*, 26 February 1983.
6. *IHT*, 20 July 1983.
7. In April, Reagan said he ordered $32 million in arms shipments to El Salvador, because "we cannot turn our backs on this crisis at our doorstep," after Congress adjourned for a ten-day recess without voting on whether to approve the emergency aid request, *IHT*, 26 April 1984. Two months later the Senate voted to delete funds for construction of two advance military bases in Honduras sought by the President, *IHT*, 11 June 1984.
8. *NYT*, 15 March 1983.
9. *IHT*, 8–9 January 1983.
10. *IHT*, 22 July 1983.
11. *IHT*, 22 March 1983.
12. Two excellent expositions on Israel's value to the U.S. are Eugene V. Rostow, "The American Stake in Israel," *Commentary,* **63** (April 1977):32–46; and Steven L. Spiegel, "Israel as a Strategic Asset," *Commentary,* **75** (June 1983):51–55.
13. Cited in *IHT*, 18–19 December 1983.
14. Brecher, p. 63.
15. Brecher, p. 68.
16. See, for example, Mark Helprin, "American Jews and Israel," *New York Times* Sunday Magazine, 7 November 1982.
17. "Conventional Arms Transfer Policy," *Department of State Bulletin*, September, 1981, p. 61.
18. See, for example, *Haaretz*, 25 December 1983.
19. *Haaretz*, 22 November 1983.
20. *Haaretz*, 27 February 1984. In April the State Department's head of Middle Eastern

affairs formally asked Iran's suppliers, including Israel, to comply with an American request to halt the further supply of arms and spare parts; *Haaretz*, 30 April 1984.

21. General Accounting Office, Report by the Comptroller General of the United States, *U.S. Assistance to the State of Israel*, Washington (24 June 1983).

22. In the case of the Merkava $181 million in foreign aid earmarked for the purchase of U.S. M-60 tanks was made available instead for development of the Israeli tank, *Wall Street Journal*, 22 June 1984.

23. *NYT*, 11 November 1983.

24. Details of the controversy in *WSJ*, 22 June 1984; *J P*, 12 October 1983, *Haaretz*, 27 January 1984; *IHT*, 12–13 November, 1983.

25. Victor Basiuk, "Security Recedes," *Foreign Policy* 53 (Winter 1983–1984):49–73. He presents the anti-liberalization argument in order to minimize the damage from foreign competition. Analysts of the American scene by 1984 were beginning to speak of economic nationalism, citing as proof the staggering trade deficit of nearly $150 billion, urging "America Must Look Out for Number One." Kevin Phillips, *WP*, 16 December 1984.

26. Text in John Norton Moore, ed., *The Arab-Israeli Conflict. Readings and Documents* (Princeton: Princeton University Press, 1977), pp. 1219–1223.

27. *Maariv*, 26 February 1982. The Department of Defense can waive the Buy American Act with respect to Israeli products in awarding contracts for such items as parts for the M-60 and M-1 tanks; missile components; ammunition, bombs, grenades, and fuses.

28. GAO Report, p. 46.

29. *Maariv*, 11 March 1982.

30. *J P*, 30 November 1983; White House background briefing, 29 November 1983; courtesy of USIA office, Tel-Aviv.

31. GAO Report, p. 46; *Haaretz*, 27 June 1982.

32. *NYT*, 26 June 1983. The $39 million communications equipment deal is exceptional. Estimates of the potential for military trade vary from $100–$300 million a year in Israeli sales. This and other aspects of U.S.-Israel military cooperation are discussed in the 1984 staff report for the Senate Committee on Foreign Relations, pp. 32–35.

33. *Maariv*, 15 October 1982.

34. *Haaretz*, 31 January 1983.

35. *J P*, 25 May 1984.

36. *Maariv*, 22 June 1984.

37. *J P*, 18 June 1984; Navy spokesmen acknowledged making the RPV purchase but said that the exact number of drones, the cost, and whether they were for experimental or operational use was classified information; *IHT*, 25 May 1984.

38. *J P* 10 February and 18 May 1984, *Maariv*, 5 June 1984, *WP*, 10 September 1984.

39. *J P*, 30 December 1982.

40. *Maariv*, 4 March 1983.

41. Figure offered by Jacques S. Gansler at a Tel-Aviv seminar, 17–19 June 1984, sponsored by the Jerusalem Institute of Management.

42. Martin Indyk, Charles Kupchan, and Steven J. Rosen, *Israel and the U.S. Air Force* (Washington: American Israel Public Affairs Committee, 1983), p. v.

43. *J P*, 13 January 1984; such sales of goods and services to U.S. troops abroad are known as "offshore," in contrast to "offsets."

44. GAO Report, pp. 48–52.

45. Terms of the transaction reported in *J P*, 21 August 1983; the $300 million figure also cited in *Haaretz*, 25 August 1983, quoting Israeli sources.

46. An episode involving Assistant Secretary of Defense Richard Perle has also shed

some light on the use of American consultants by Israeli contractors in an effort to gain a foothold in the U.S. arms market. It was revealed that Perle, an authority on strategic affairs, served in 1980–1981 as consultant to Israeli arms dealers representing Soltam. Perle later acknowledged that in his official capacity in 1982, although no longer on a retainer, he had written an internal memorandum urging Pentagon evaluation of the Israeli company's weapons and recommending that the Army consider buying mortars manufactured by Soltam strictly on their merits, *IHT*, 18 April 1983 and *Maariv*, 29 April 1983.

47. Comments by Rear Adm. Frank C. Collins, Jr., Executive Director for Quality Assurance at the Defense Logistics Agency, *NYT*, 26 June 1983.

48. U.S. Army Chief of Staff John A. Wickham, Jr. criticized faulty procurement practices, *IHT*, 10 August 1983. Test flight failures and manufacturing deficiencies, such as with the F-18 plane, led *The New York Times* to editorialize: "What kind of procurement process is it that designs weapons inferior to those they replace, and buys them even when they flunk their tests, investing $40 billion in its mistake?" "When Weapons Flunk," *NYT*, 14 July 1983.

49. Pursuing this line the *NYT* returned to the subject in a later editorial, "Getting High on High-Tech Weapons," 28 August 1983. "The Army chose to build the hot-rod M-1 tank instead of doing what the Israelis did: improve the reliable old M-60 so well that it smashed the Syrians' Soviet-supplied T-72's." See also references to Israel as a model of industrial success in the sharp *NYT* editorial, "Beating Swords Into Lemons," 27 November 1984.

50. *Yediot Achronot*, 20 October 1983.

51. On the obstacles before Israel in reaching the U.S. market, see *Yediot Achronot*, 12 July 1982; *IHT*, 13 July 1982; *Haaretz*, 14 July 1982. The Tadiran system is described in *Maariv*, 4 July 1982. The problem of coproduction is dealt with in Efraim Inbar, "The American Arms Transfer to Israel," *Middle East Review* **15** 1–2:(Fall and Winter 1982/3):47–48.

52. *J P*, 24 June 1984.

53. GAO Report, p. 56.

54. GAO Report, pp. iii–iv, 49, 52.

55. *IHT*, 16 April 1984.

56. *IHT*, 5–6 May 1984.

57. *NYT*, 29 June 1983.

58. On U.S. arms flows to Israel, see David Pollock, *The Politics of Pressure* (Westport, Conn.: Greenwood Press, 1982).

59. *The Christian Science Monitor*, 4 January 1983.

60. Cf., a *Washington Post* editorial, "Of Arms and Rights," 24 January 1983 and the article by Leslie Gelb, *NYT*, 20 December 1982.

61. U.S. Department of State Bulletin, 18 December 1981, announcing formal suspension of the strategic understanding; see also *J P*, 26 March 1983.

62. *Haaretz*, 11 May 1983, relying on *Flight International*'s report.

63. Explanations vary from U.S. principled opposition to a global race in conventional arms sales, the desire to curb arms to a volatile region like Latin America, and policy differences with Israel all the way to eliminating competition for the United States; see Neuman and Harkavy, p. 307; *Fortune*, 13 March 1978, p. 73.

64. Goren, p. 53.

65. Ibid., p. 54.

66. *Haaretz*, 9 December 1982.

67. *Haaretz*, 28 October 1982, *Maariv*, 29 October 1982, *J P*, 25 November 1982.

68. *J P*, 30 December 1982.

69. *Maariv*, 4 March 1983.
70. *Haaretz*, 19 January 1983.
71. *J P*, 23, 24 February 1983.
72. ACDA, 1983, p. 31.
73. *J P*, 16 February 1983.
74. *Haaretz*, 28 July 1983.
75. GAO Report, p. 56; senior defense industry sources in May 1983, offered a projected basic unit cost for the Lavi of approximately $11 million, compared to the anticipated $18 million cost of the F-16, *J P*, 29 May 1983.
76. Remarks by Israeli Air Force Commander Amos Lapidot, *J P*, 24 February 1983.
77. "It could conceivably happen," said Arens, "if the airplane turns out to be as good as we hope it's going to be." Interview in the *Wall Street Journal*, 22 June 1984.

10

LIMITS TO GROWTH

In its fourth decade of independence Israel has earned prominence for itself as a supplier of arms and military assistance. We began this study of Israeli arms sales diplomacy by looking at the interplay of political, strategic, and commercial objectives. Subsequent chapters focused on two domestic factors, manufacturing skills and consensus-building, which have made Israel perhaps more effective a seller than others.

We then examined Israel's weapons inventory and trading partners in chapters 7 and 8 in order to underline the hypothesis of flexibility and of diversity revealed in the implementation of its arms sales policies. The previous chapter dealt with the United States as a potentially critical factor in the arms equation, interpositioned strategically at several sensitive points, and with the potential to act at any given moment as a further impetus or, alternatively, a major impediment for Israeli arms export diplomacy. In this chapter our intent is to suggest at least three prospective challenges or limitations to Israel's further ascendance in the area of conventional weapons transfers.

SMALL STATE LIMITATIONS

Small states such as Israel always walk a fine line in matters of national security and foreign policy. Where the margins for error are so narrow and the risks even higher, prudence becomes essential rather than merely laudable. And when the issue is as sensitive as current international weapons transfer practices, due consideration must be given to costs as well as gains, to failures no less than to accomplishments. Also, for the sake of prudence, reservations ought to qualify optimistic market forecasts which predict an even greater potential for Israeli arms sales.

Reassessments, however, are limited by two existing realities. The first reality is that the role of arms supplier is no longer simple and unambiguous and is too far advanced to merit a simplistic either/or response or, for that matter, a sharp policy reversal. Arms sales are now firmly ingrained in Israeli national security policies as they are in international politics. Israel, through its own labors in consciously overcoming a number of formidable obstacles, has earned a place in the world arms trade. As a result, its foreign and economic policies are so geared to this fundamental proposition that the military assistance program in general and arms transfers in particular are no less critical today for the survival of the state than is its parallel weapons procurement. Indeed, one of the purposes of this study has been to underline the high degree of Israeli commitment to arms diplomacy.

A second reality is that selling arms is ultimately a political decision and must be judged on those terms. The question of morality, while a definite factor, is not the sole determinant. Our criteria for judgment, again, are essentially political: What is the political fallout from weapons transfers? Their military impact? The economic consequences? Just how durable a foreign policy tool are such transfers likely to be in longer-term service of Israel's security and international status?

If Israel is to persist as an arms supplier, its leaders must be prepared to incur substantial costs and risks. Their caution is heightened by either of two possible situations: first, when global demand gives no sign of abating and market opportunities abound—if not in one region or country then in another—and when each successful transaction breeds greater confidence, further reinforcing the domestic consensus on behalf of an even more aggressive arms policy; or, second, when global recession shrinks the arms market, making competition for remaining outlets that much more intense.

Reservations about Israel's ability in the coming years to sustain the momentum of its arms sales drive are warranted by clearly evident challenges from at least three different directions: bilateral, systemic, and internal. These challenges are: the mutability of supplier-client relationships; the very nature of the conventional arms race, which is becoming increasingly competitive; Israel's own shortcomings. Of the three the first two owe to the external forces of supply and demand. Only the latter is within the power of Israel to control. This dependence upon outside market forces in itself says much about the limits to growth.

REDUCED DEMAND AND CLIENT UNDEPENDABILITY

Advocates of an expanded arms exports policy for the 1980s and 1990s should be forced to address the potential setbacks traceable to the unreliability of customers. It has happened more than once that interested foreign governments, armies, or firms entered negotiations only to renege at the last minute, because better terms were obtainable elsewhere, because the threat of Arab countermeasures was taken seriously, or because of U.S. opposition.[1] This problem of sensitivity is further aggravated whenever reports of a pending transaction find their way into the press prematurely, or if the purchaser gets cold feet because of a particular item's high visibility, such as the Kfir or Merkava.

Unreliability finds expression, secondly, in the danger of defaults or delays in payments for arms purchases. A purchasing country's foreign reserves, after all, should be a primary restraint on its capacity to acquire arms. The recent wave of arms-selling happens to coincide with a world recession and at a time when the total debt burden of the developing nations was estimated at $737 billion at the end of 1984, compared with $450 billion in 1979.[2] Given the arms client relationships emphasized and encouraged by Israel with Third World nations, their economic slowdown and present monetary crisis pose an acute problem.

Evidence indicates that some of Israel's best customers are on the edge of penury. Countries like Argentina, Kenya, Mexico, Nigeria, and Zaire are experiencing serious economic difficulties, reflected in balance of payment deficits, high annual inflation rates, mismanagement and corruption, lower government revenues, a slowdown in economic growth, less receipts from commodity exports, and poor terms of trade and scarcity of foreign exchange.[3] In South America alone three reported customers — Ecuador, Peru, and Venezuela — are wrestling with the effects of the economic crisis: renegotiation and restructuring of foreign debts parallel drastic cuts in public spending called for by international bankers and monetary agencies.[4] During the Falklands crisis, for example, the Argentinian junta was hard-pressed to finance urgently needed arms replacements through European banks. Cost considerations and credit ratings thus are likely to figure more prominently in international weapons transfers negotiations hereafter.

Exactly how much the burden of financing arms imports contributes to the Third World crisis, or what impact this period of domestic economic adjustment and international debt crisis will have on the international arms trade is as yet unclear.[5] There are those who maintain that rearmament is a constant and that arms imports tend to be comparatively inelastic, ensuring a steady flow of orders and weapons transfers to countries with domestic or regional security problems. Others argue that the fiscal problems of the heavily indebted countries will force them to reduce arms imports, perhaps only temporarily, within the austerity programs and reforms insisted upon by international lending institutions. Industrialized arms suppliers, for their part, can be expected to promote weapons transfers as part of the need for income, markets, and continued production lines, but in doing so they are likely to come up against emergency measures by potential or even previous LDC arms customers compelled to reorder import priorities in striving to regain their own economic growth and stability.[6]

The risks for Israel are two-fold and more real than hypothetical. Arms shipments will add to the negative image, and Israel may be charged with draining scarce monetary resources from impoverished countries. This risk is perhaps more easily dealt with since a determined buyer will have no difficulty in finding any number of other suppliers, although on less liberal terms (arms for bases, hard currency versus barter). The second risk, harder to cope with, is that a buyer might choose to defy its suppliers, Israel included, by not paying for military arms and services rendered. Debt repudiation might be entertained by a desperate country in the belief that it can do so with impunity, especially because Israel has neither vital leverage nor much political recourse.

In 1984 Israeli companies were already reported as standing to lose as much as $60 million in Latin America and Africa. Prior to that time the Israel Foreign Risks Insurance Corporation, a government-sponsored company, had had to pay out about $25 million for losses incurred in Iran ($5 million) and Uganda ($20 million), both arms purchasers at one time.[7]

Lower oil earnings combine with reduced government spending and a recent decision to slash imports by 50 percent, for example, to make Nigeria less attractive, at least on economic grounds, to Israeli exporters of military as well as nonmilitary goods or services. Therefore, at some point in the decision-making process, a client's credit-worthiness had best be weighed carefully. This is especially so if, as the statistics cited earlier suggest, the short-term economic motive is a primary consideration in approving many Israeli sales. It was perhaps for this reason that former Defense Minister Sharon, in boasting of the military aid agreement with Zaire, hastened to add of Kinshasa, that "it has made its payments meticulously."[8]

If the goal is to establish an ongoing arms relationship rather than merely to cash in on a one-time transaction, then a third client limitation arises. Most black African and South American armed forces have a limited absorptive capacity when it comes to military hardware. Their ability to continue effectively to assimilate advanced weapons systems or large quantities of Israeli arms as part of their national force postures is circumscribed not only by financial problems but by such things as lack of adequate infrastructure or manpower. What with the massive inflow of equipment in recent years some of these countries may be getting close to the saturation point. A variant of this limitation occurs in the opposite direction, as happened in the case of Idi Amin, who escalated arms demands beyond the point which Israeli leaders were either willing or able to meet; he then responded by severing ties. Already there are signs of strain with Zaire over Mobutu's unfulfilled expectations.[9]

Coproduction arrangements on a bilateral basis pose a fourth risk. Israel's success, as we have seen, owes in no small measure to its selling military technology as well as arms themselves. The licensing of military assistance, no matter how carefully screened and policed, demands the exchange of at least some military secrets and technological know-how. Adams and others attribute the South African relationship to such sharing; in January 1983, however, the arrest of the director of the naval shipyards at Simonstown on charges of spying for the Soviet Union led to rumors that operational details and construction designs may have fallen into enemy hands.[10]

Fifth is the risk of embarrassment to Israel resulting from the repressive domestic policies of some of its clients. Israeli military cooperation with Zaire coincides with efforts by other countries, including Belgium, to distance themselves from the corruption-ridden regime of Mobutu Sese Seko. That Israel is unable to influence corruption in Zaire, human rights violations in Chile or Argentina, or racial separatism in South Africa, yet suffers from guilt by association, serves to capture something of the risk factor involved. It leads to condemnation from many quarters; for example, the denunciation of Israeli official visits and arms sales to unnamed Latin American countries and the increase of U.S.-Israeli intervention in the region at a conference of non-aligned nations in January, 1983.[11]

Unreliability also becomes an issue when the recipient lacks political stability. Israel, having pinned its prospects for an enduring relationship in Iran on Shah Reza Pahlavi and in Nicaragua on the Somoza regime, saw its preferential position disintegrate when they fell from power. Indeed, in the Nicaraguan domestic struggle Israeli arms were used by both sides, which underlines a basic hazard of arms trafficking: it has little long-lasting positive impact and has no political guarantees whatsoever.

The problem of unreliability is compounded when two recipients clash, further putting Israel on the spot politically. These conditions exist at present in Central and South America where Israeli clients are embroiled in territorial and frontier disputes. In the 1976 border conflict between El Salvador and Honduras, Israeli arms were used by both antagonists. The list of potential conflict is extensive: Peru-Ecuador, Argentina-Chile, Honduras-El Salvador, Honduras-Nicaragua, Nicaragua-Colombia, Venezuela-Colombia, and Guatemala-Belize. The danger is by no means limited to the southern hemisphere. Reports of Israeli aid to Mobutu led Angola to fear an Israeli presence which might portend a U.S.-inspired challenge to the Marxist regime of Roberto Holden. This, in turn, led Defense Minister Sharon at the time to declare publicly that Israel would not become involved in any fighting within Zaire, nor "in any war between states."[12] Nevertheless, conflict contingencies involving Third World clients of Israel abound. In the absence of strict controls by Jerusalem the chances of being implicated in local wars, unsympathetic coups, or revolutions could multiply. Too liberal and loose an arms policy is bound to result, sooner or later, in diplomatic complications for Israel.

Such forecasts were confirmed in the Falklands war. It added a slightly different dimension when the fighting involved two states with diplomatic ties to Israel but from different regions. The crisis arose when the British government, officially protesting rumors of Israeli arms reaching Buenos Aires, insisted upon a clarification of Jerusalem's arms relationship with Argentina and an immediate halt to all arms shipments.[13] In reply Foreign Minister

Shamir initially denied supplying arms, and then stated Israel's revised position: It wished to stay out of the Falklands dispute, and had concluded no additional arms deals since the dispute erupted. However, Israel would honor any contractual obligations already incurred.[14] On the one hand, by delivering as promised Israel demonstrated its reliability. But on the other hand, Anglo-Israeli relations, although strained even before the crisis, became acrimonious for a while when Israeli leaders and the media recalled British conduct in selling to Argentina and in supplying arms to Arab states located in the Middle East war zone. To further compound the perplexity, supplying arms to Argentina discomfited the Anglo-Jewish community too. In the labyrinth which is the international arms trade, such diplomatic sensitivities may sometimes call for transferring weapons through a third party — country or private agent — so as to avoid complications and to enable spokesmen to insist that arms are not being supplied to a belligerent directly.

Left for last in this discussion of the problems arising for Israel by the very nature of supplier-client arms transfers is the prospect of the recipient itself becoming an arms producer and exporter. It is apparent from the arms trade flow patterns that some of Israel's favorite customers in the past, especially those classed as pariahs, have reached their own takeoff stage of military production thanks to Israel's aid during the preliminary stages. While acknowledging this assistance by Jerusalem, such countries gradually enter the international arms trade themselves in order to help sustain their own local armaments industry. Marketing war materiel fairly similar in composition to that of Israel's arms inventory, they in fact stand to become serious competitors. Such is already the case with South Africa, manufacturing medium-level technology items independently, successfully reducing the proportion of its defense budget spent on imported arms from 70 percent in 1966 to a mere 15 percent in 1982, and now boasting of the tenth largest arms industry.[15] Singapore, modeling itself on the Israeli model, illustrates the emergence of yet another independent, internationally competitive arms industry. Membership in the Association of Southeast Asian Nations (ASEAN) gives Singapore a tremendous advantage in seeking prospective customers closest to home, and those previously cultivated by Israel. South Korea and Taiwan, traditional Israeli clients, are other Third World countries making impressive strides in producing low technology armaments. Their entering the market both raises questions as to the credibility of these ties with Israel in the future and points to the second challenge for Israeli export momentum: the competitiveness of the present arms market.

EXCESS SUPPLY AND THE COMPETITION

Not only consumer-supplier relations are uncertain and evolving at present. Particularly ominous for Israel as it seeks to sustain defense exports is the intensifying competition for markets among the growing list of arms suppliers.

In order for Israel to realize its expectations for defense sales growth, both in terms of national trade and its share of the international market, it will have to contend with the presence of too strong and too many competitors.

Weapons transfers, to repeat, are an area of international commerce long known for high competition and low ethics. Yet so intense has the fight for arms contracts now become that it threatens to ignite an arms trade war of unprecedented rivalry with no holds barred. In such a situation the advantages lie with the present leading and major supplier nations. Israel, to be sure, emulates the major world arms suppliers in scrambling for new markets and opportunities. Yet it does not, and cannot, compare to countries like the United States, the Soviet Union, France, Britain, or West Germany either in terms of national resources committed to the arms sales contest or in the ability to absorb setbacks. Like Brazil, its major Third World competitor, Israel is simply unable to continue pumping money into the arms export program.

The chief competitors have tended until now to be rather tolerant of Israel as a marginal supplier. Hereafter, however, they can be expected to stiffen the competition since for them, as well, local arms industries and war preparedness increasingly have become linked with, and dependent upon, weapons exports. Their commitment to defense sales, in short, is no less real or total than is Israel's. As the competition becomes more desperate and cut-throat, Israel cannot expect to equal others in the scale of arms, in largess, and in special terms, in offering goods at dumping prices, or in value as a military or diplomatic ally. In a word, therefore, Israel must fully expect in some instances to lose whatever comparative advantages it may have enjoyed previously. It stands to be squeezed out of arms deals by rival suppliers perhaps less objectionable or controversial politically and more endowed economically, who establish the norms Israel must strive to meet.[16]

Second, the trend toward a demand for quality weapons shows no sign of abating. SIPRI arms trade registers, for instance, identified approximately 1,100 separate transfer agreements covering major weapons on order or being delivered in 1981. Ninety-four percent of these contracts were for new weapons systems, 4 percent for refurbished weapons, and only 2 percent for second-hand weapons.[17] Furthermore, there are strong incentives for more rapid weapons modernization programs, and weapons planners foresee a new generation of arms deriving from advances in physics and computers which will boost weapons research and development budgets even higher.[18] In the case of Israel both trends are ominous. Some of the more attractive items in its arsenal are not for sale to foreign governments for reasons of security.[19] Others are subject to American approval before they can be exported. Still other projects have already been frozen at the planning or blueprint stages due to prohibitive R & D costs made all the more so because their export value cannot be guaranteed. One source of compensation, though, is the advantage, enjoyed almost exclusively by Israel, of systems with proven performance and credibility.

The two superpowers show no hesitancy in setting an almost impossible pace for Israel and the others. Prior to his death Leonid Brezhnev warned that as regards military technology, lagging behind is "inadmissible" for the Soviet Union; he pledged that Russia would spare nothing in countering the American arms buildup by a new wave of weapons modernization.[20] Recent history suggests that each new generation of arms releases older but still sophisticated ones for overseas export. Under President Reagan the United States, for its part, has signaled its determination to compete even more vigorously for these overseas markets. Security assistance is viewed by the administration as the very key to its global and regional strategies of increasing its influence, gaining or holding access to bases, assisting nations threatened with internal or external aggression, and of countering a nearby Soviet presence.[21] The U.S. government's efforts now extend to legislation which would streamline the commercial arms sales process and help other American companies to sell abroad.[22] One result is that in the scramble to meet some of China's arms needs Israel could find itself competing directly with the United States.

In the face of this intensified competition and demand, other sellers are confronted by the choice between dropping out of the race, redoubling their efforts, or pooling their resources in undertaking joint projects.[23] Western European governments, troubled by the world economic slump, have become cautious about supporting aerospace ventures such as new tactical fighters. Israel, by contrast, has decided to go ahead with plans for producing its own Lavi fighter despite these limitations.

Nevertheless, the Western Europeans are very much intent upon pushing more conventional arms sales. The socialist government of Francois Mitterand has not curtailed French arms export policy. If anything, it has intensified support for the national defense industry, as reflected in the flow of Mirage fighters and Exocet missiles to many nations, including Argentina and those, like Iraq and Chad, caught in a conflict situation, as well as to the Persian Gulf sheikhdoms. Great Britain is another active supplier to the Middle East; and partly due to pressure from its labor unions and as part of plans for the recovery of the British economy the Thatcher government saw fit, in 1981, to lift the embargo on arms transfers to Chile. Still pending is West Germany's proposed large sale of Leopard tanks to Saudi Arabia which, if approved, would constitute a major revision of its policy against selling to areas of tension. For these and other established suppliers the prime motivation becomes that of hedging against depressed sales or the loss of previous contracts.[24]

But the threat does not come solely from the major suppliers. In the midst of the economic cycle and recession which even extends into the arms market, additional suppliers have emerged from among the non-Western industrializing nations. Retaining their hold over the world market for conventional arms is what joins the U.S., the Soviet Union, and the large European dealers together. By contrast, it is the prospect of entering this marketplace and of making any sales whatsoever which forms the developing countries into a third subgroup of suppliers following the two superpowers and the Western Europeans.

This rise of Third World sellers is one of the more remarkable and least analyzed trends in conventional arms proliferation. SIPRI cites at least thirty-one states in Africa, Asia, Latin America, and the Middle East that produce arms. Years of investing heavily in R & D activity enables Third World arms industries to emulate Israel in the sense of beginning to compete with their own partners on the world market. During the 1970s almost three-quarters of the global arms trade consisted of Third World imports from the industrialized countries. The present decade has seen a growing number of Third World countries developing their own productive capacity. Even the poorest of them now has access to advanced forms of military technology. In consequence, the volume of trade in weapons between Third World countries is claimed to have grown ten-fold,[25] or even beyond in cultivating military trade ties with the West, sometimes through joint production ventures and licensing.[26] The end result is that for the first time the smaller arms producing nations have begun to make serious inroads into the export trade—a development already treated as a routine aspect of the global conventional arms transfer process.

For Israel the trouble is that alleged licensees and users of its military and technological assistance may become competitors in the conventional arms trade, if they are not already so. Perhaps the two best examples are Singapore and South Africa. Because the former now can produce modified Skyhawk planes cheaply, for example, it has the prospect of outbidding for buyers in Asia, Africa, and South America;[27] certainly in terms of Asia it has to be seen as a preferential supplier by virtue of its geographic location. In the case of South Africa, the experience of arms deprivation that led it to turn to outsiders for help in the field of military technologies has enabled it not only to catch up but to engage in selling arms to others as well, to the point where it is now the tenth, perhaps the seventh largest supplier.[28] Argentina also appears to be making a major arms export drive.[29]

From the perspective of Israeli arms producers, then, the appearance of these Third World exporters signals still newer entrants in an already crowded market. They raise the question of exactly what types of weapons Israel wishes to push in the world market. All types? Major weapons systems—tanks, planes, etc.? High-tech component systems? Or the traditional kind, like the Uzi, which proved so successful at an earlier stage of Israel's conversion into a weapons supplier?

In the field of emerging technology (ET) weapons Israel is at a disadvantage against the big suppliers. It is estimated, for instance, that the U.S. Department of Defense has spent about $2 billion just on researching and devising nonnuclear laser weapons.[30] As the experience with the Lavi reconfirms,

Israel cannot anticipate these kinds of sums to invest in independent R & D. To contract with foreign companies is only to complicate further the existing problem of securing later approval for selling systems with foreign components. In the narrower field of sophisticated tanks, missiles, naval craft, and planes, aside from the U.S. veto and Israeli reluctance to give these items wide distribution for security reasons, it seems clear that the competition from countries like Britain, France, West Germany, and Italy—or for that matter Brazil, South Africa, and Singapore—will be heavy and competitive in the extreme; which leaves the third category of standard conventional small arms, parts, and ordnance. However excellent the quality of Israeli merchandise, these are the types of weapons which every small and aspiring supplier is likely to promote in its immediate regional sybsystem, so that here, too, the competition will only get worse from Israel's standpoint.

Israeli exporters are thus beginning to find themselves caught in a squeeze between the really big arms merchants, with whom they cannot easily compete, and these new suppliers who, pursuing export promotion strategies of their own, are making inroads into Israel's traditional markets. Within the group of Third World sellers, and especially those with whom it is loosely associated as part of the newly industrialized yet pariah countries, a great deal depends on Israel's success in continuing to set an example. The challenge for all of them is to avoid extreme competition by vying for the same limited market and instead somehow to retain the same spirit of tacit cooperation that enabled them to become arms producers.

There are thus ample question marks as to Israel's ability to remain: (a) independent, (b) competitive, and (c) immune to unstable client relationships. Yet few would deny that Israel has proven itself capable of conducting an impressive if at times unorthodox defense sales program. Rather the doubts tend to center about Israel's capacity to build further upon its past record. The last of the three basic causes for concern focuses not upon recent trends in the international arms trade but upon Israel's own limitations.

CAPABILITY VERSUS CAPACITY

Not to be ignored in the list of problems originating in the arms trade competition are Israel's objective limits, such as in the pool of prospective customers. "Market access" is as much a term of politics as it is of economics, being a function of a country's power, prestige, influence, and centrality. Some of the largest and most lucrative markets, including virtually the entire Middle East, are closed to Israel for political reasons. If reports of arms assistance to the People's Republic of China are true, it suggests that diplomatic obstacles are not insurmountable. Nevertheless, Israeli foreign policy may not always be able, given greater diplomatic and economic adversity, to keep open as many doors as necessary to sustain the export drive and to replace markets as they dry up.

It is not at all certain these dangers are fully appreciated by policy planners in Jerusalem, least of all by enthusiasts within the military-industrial complex. SIBAT takes due note of the fact that weapons sales are the most hazardous branch of export, given the transient nature of supplier-client relationships and rapidly changing political circumstances. But what conclusion do Defense Ministry planners derive from this sober analysis? They advocate neither withdrawal nor closer scrutiny of arms recipients but, rather, attempts to "deepen" political and strategic ties with "many states" while striving to "widen the circle" of contacts.[31]

There is also the issue of whether, in the delicate conduct of arms trading, Israel, as an undisciplined democracy and open society, can succeed in monitoring itself. One major source of embarrassment are premature reports which originate in Israel from time to time of arms transactions pending and under negotiation. Solely from the standpoint of policy effectiveness this phenomenon of repeated leaks is inexcusable and borders on gross irresponsibility.

Rarely do events converge to dramatize Israel's vulnerability in the role of arms supplier as occurred in May, 1982, when front-page headlines in the world press reported two items about arms flows implicating Israel. The first referred to U.S. customs agents in New York detaining an Ecuadorean cargo plane carrying a shipment of Israeli-manufactured arms destined for Ecuador yet believed to be actually meant for Argentina.[32] The second item reported remarks made by Defense Minister Ariel Sharon who chose a visit to the United States to confirm publicly for the first time that Israel had continued to supply $27 million worth of arms to Iran during the hostage crisis and even afterwards.[33] The adverse publicity was damaging in itself, presenting Israel as a country willing to supply arms to active combatants.

Sharon's insistence that the supply of spare parts to the Khomeini regime was done with U.S. approval had little effect on the American public and media. But in addition the episodes exposed a basic difference of political assessment between Jerusalem and Washington over the Falkland issue and the Iran-Iraq war as well as Iran's ultimate stability.[34] Sharon went so far as to charge the U.S. administration with conducting a press campaign to undermine Israel's standing and to push through Congress the pending arms sale to Jordan.[35] Revelations about supplies to Iran reportedly came as a surprise to the Prime Minister and dismayed other Cabinet members.[36]

Yet the Iranian affair was not the first nor the last time that Israeli officials have displayed a penchant for serving as the sources for press leaks. One earlier instance came in 1977 when then Foreign Minister Moshe Dayan openly discussed military ties with the Marxist government of Ethiopia. A second instance also occurred in May, 1982, when the Prime Minister cited Switzerland as an example of courage in withstanding Arab pressure by agreeing to purchase military equipment from Israel worth $220 million.[37] This met with a prompt denial from Bern. Later in the year the Swiss Army decided against the Merkava tank.[38] Again, at the close of 1982, the visits of Foreign Minister Shamir to Zaire and of the Foreign Minister and Defense Minister Sharon to Central and South America fueled press speculation, usually based on comments from members of the official delegations, about new deals, leading one Israeli newspaper to editorialize: "publicity now precedes delivery."[39]

In the covert and clandestine world of conventional arms salesmanship, discretion is usually prized as essential. And even in the event of press speculation the ground rules call for either denial or no comment. Too much prominence in the media and excessive attention upon Israel's moves in the role of arms supplier are a separate source of embarrassment for Jerusalem, prompting one to assume greater reticence on the part of Israeli arms diplomats. Solely in terms of effectiveness and policy success, the quiet style of a David Kimche in pursuing, renewing, or strengthening arms contacts and military aid relationships are to be preferred to the too candid and undisguised—one might say, undiplomatic—approach of an Ariel Sharon.

At the domestic political level there are some early signs of discomfort if not of open dissent, at the magnitude and direction of Israel's military assistance relationships, as well as specific ties. Reservations were expressed in 1984 as to the wisdom for Israel in becoming implicated in Sri Lanka's civil struggle, especially with its potential for spilling over into tensions with India. Reports of Israeli aid to Nicaraguan rebels likewise evoked voices of concern that Israel might slip into the role of proxy for the United States in contravention of the Contadora Act by Central American nations calling for mutual reductions in arms, troops and foreign military advisers or assistance. Some voices expressed discomfort at Israel's identification with Zaire's regime. Still others saw potential trouble in ties with South Africa while Jewish liberals abroad were joining in the chorus of calls for punitive measures against Johannesburg and its apartheid policy.

To the extent that these signs reflect anything deeper, the implication may be a lessening of the traditional solid consensus behind the forward arms export campaign. One explanation is sensitivity to Israel's negative world image. A second, sociological explanation may lie in the initial traces of an Israeli brand of antimilitarism stemming from the nation's one long and unending war with its neighbors, from independence in 1948 to the heavy military presence in Lebanon. This self-doubt as to the marginal utility of military force and fear of the militarization of Israeli life and politics could extend to the military-industrial complex's influence and to pushing arms.[40] While not necessarily representative, it is interesting to note an editorial comment not too long ago in the English-daily *Jerusalem Post*, entitled "Unsavory Trade." Citing foreign press reports of Israeli arms to Nicaraguan rebel forces and denials by the Foreign Ministry, the paper referred to weapons transfers in general as a "morally unsavoury, politically delicate and commercially risky business." Cautioning that Israel has become cynical in this trade, it sought to make a distinction:

> To sell arms out of necessity—more justifiable in Israel's case than in that of any other country in this awful trade—is one thing. To act as an agent of a CIA . . . is another thing altogether.[41]

The editorial ended by suggesting that this trade, "on which Israel has become dependent," should be the subject of a "thorough political and economic review." Were public sentiment against trafficking freely in arms to gain momentum, which seems unlikely at the time of writing, it could serve as a second check on Israeli effectiveness.

Transfer policy is vulnerable, too, to government changes. Earlier Labor cabinets proudly deepened relations with Iran. Likud leaders followed by marshalling arguments in favor of assistance to revolutionary Iran. But in February, 1985, Prime Minister Shimon Peres, on behalf of the National Unity Government, revealed a sharp alteration of policy. He firmly denied that Israel was selling arms to Iran and added, "We are not going to sell any arms to Iran."[42] Peres said, "We consider the Khomeini revolution a very sad experience in the 20th century. It is a very extreme and hostile movement and we do not have any reasons to support Khomeini."

There is also the economic factor involved in the relationship of foreign arms sales to the country's industrial capacity and growth. One finds a slight awareness, but nevertheless an awareness, of the fact that, as Pierre points out, self-sufficiency in arms is illusionary.[43] Merely to cite defense sales of $1 billion and more is to offer an incomplete economic picture, ignoring, for example, the high costs initially incurred in manufacturing the arms (import of raw materials, labor costs, R & D, etc.). One billion dollars does not represent net gain or profit margin. On similar utilitarian grounds, the growth in Israeli exports has been more than matched by a growth in its imports of sophisticated arms and technology from the United States.

There are other signs that Israel, its economy worsening, is approaching the limits of military industrial growth. Indeed, Israel has outdone itself, going beyond what might have been predicted by economic indicators alone. Still, in terms of the future, Israel's unique arms export diplomacy will be imposed upon a shrinking economic base. One telling example is the Lavi whose production costs already exceed estimates by Israeli experts.[44]

As a result the economic structure of Israel is in danger of becoming over extended and too dependent upon the manufacture and export of military equipment. In 1981 more than half of local arms production went for exports; these military exports, in turn, represented more than 20 percent of industrial exports.[45] Professional opinion is that arms should not rise above 25 percent of total industrial exports;[46] yet if present trends continue Israel may rather quickly be approaching that point, if it hasn't already done so.

One such warning came in the wake of the Iranian revolution when foreign orders dropped markedly. One company, Soltam, saw its arms sales plummet from over $100 million a year to zero and had to fire 800 workers.[47] These limitations were as much as admitted by government officials who insist that given the country's economic condition, it is all but unthinkable to proceed simultaneously with such major projects as a Dead Sea-Mediterranean canal, nuclear reactors, and, most notably, the Lavi fighter project.[48] Sudden fluctuations in the world arms market could threaten the collapse of any economy whose industry becomes so geared to arms exports.

Furthermore, Israel stands to lose more and more of its earlier overall comparative advantage, even to LDC exporters like Brazil, as the world arms market becomes increasingly predatory. While some resources, such as skilled and experienced labor, engineering and technical know-how, are readily available, others, like raw materials and large capital investment, are in short supply. Cuts imposed on the defense budget, dictated by high annual rates of inflation, have had the immediate effect of reducing local procurement by the Ministry of Defense. As a logical consequence state-directed defense industries were encouraged to intensify their export marketing in the hope that the real cost to the economy of R & D and production might still be absorbed abroad as overseas purchasers took up much of the slack.[49] Not even the 1982 Lebanese campaign and the unanticipated extended stay and redeployment of forces prompted IDF and Defense Ministry leaders to reclaim for the military industry its previous role of primary local supplier. Some reserves which otherwise might have been freed for export, however, had to be drawn upon.

Depending on the IDF's needs in the coming year or two, exports could be less prominent; or else local purchasing, concurrent with further government budget cuts, could be reduced following a restoration of military force levels, thereby releasing military production once again for a renewed export drive. In any event, the export pattern becomes erratic.

1982–1983: CYCLE OR DECLINE?

Others' competitiveness, cutbacks in orders by some of Israel's best customers, and its own limited capacity are three factors to be watched in the future. Their influence appears to have been evident in 1982–1983, when statistical evidence suggested only a slight rise in defense sales. Certainly there was no high rate of increase in exports as in preceding years, which suggests the drive ran into trouble, unless significant transactions went undetected.

Beginning with the last quarter of 1982, industrial exports began to decline rather appreciably. From October to June, 1983, they fell by some 25 percent. Hardest hit were the metals and electronics sectors, down by 35.7 percent in March alone compared with the previous year.[50] Economic analysts pointed to a variety of factors in addressing the sustained decline in export figures: the persistent economic recession in the West; the lower profitability of exports to Europe caused by the strengthening of the U.S. dollar and the slower rate of shekel devaluation; the financial crises suffered during 1982 by several LDCs, forcing them to reduce all imports from Israel.

Few commentators drew attention, however, to sectoral problems, more specifically to the impact reduced arms sales might be having upon export figures as a whole. Yet bits of the evidence were there to be pieced together. March, 1983 export figures led Industry and Trade Ministry sources to note, for example, that in March, 1982, there had been an exceptionally large sale of aircraft not repeated the following year.[51] One or two economic reporters analyzed that as much as 85 to 90 percent of the export decline in the first quarter of 1983 could be traced to a fall in the overseas sales of metals and electronics (25 percent in January–May), meaning primarily military-related equipment.[52] By August government economists claimed that the drop in arms sales abroad was responsible for the 25 percent decrease in exports compared with August, 1982.[53] Figures for the first nine months of 1983 revealed that exports of metals and electronics had fallen by seventeen percent.[54] Yearly figures for 1983 published by the Central Bureau of Statistics pointed to a 3 percent decrease in exported goods, the loss of $200 million in industrial sales resulting from a 6 percent decline in industrial and farm products, and a drop of 5 percent in overseas military sales; metals and electronics exports fell from $1.5 billion to $1.3 billion in 1983.[55] The Industrialists' Association attributed this generally disappointing trade performance to a single cause — the sharp reduction in foreign military sales.[56]

The accuracy of their analysis was as much as admitted by the Minister for Industry and Trade, Gideon Patt. He revealed that military exports fell by $170 million in the first four months of 1983 and accounted for 90 percent of the poor record registered by the industrial sector, excluding diamonds.[57] Patt went further in offering a two-fold explanation: (a) the sale of planes to Argentina had not gone through because of political complications connected with the Falklands war; (b) in the wake of the Lebanese conflict the military industry was forced to divert some of its energies from the foreign market in order to fulfill its primary role, that of supplier of first instance to the Israeli army. What remained to be added, though, were the adverse effects of greater arms trade activity by other countries, and the credit problems in arms procurement by those who would buy from Israel under better circumstances.

It remains to be seen whether the downward trend in defense-related exports around 1983 represented a temporary lull in the sales campaign of recent years or if it is indicative of a deeper, structural crisis suggesting Israeli weapons transfers might have been stretched to their limits. Worth noting is that the decrease in defense sales, whatever its causes, is not voluntary or because Israeli planners have seen fit to impose self-restraints. Both the impressive export figures for 1979–1981 and the 1982–1983 decline serve to underline for us the contribution of arms exports to the national export effort, and the precarious nature of this policy. Recognizing uncertainties about future prospects for arms sales apparent in 1984–1985, now is the appropriate moment to draw some conclusions about Israel and the international arms trade at mid-decade.

ISRAEL'S STANDING AS A SUPPLIER

After analyzing Israel's foreign military relationships and domestic military industries, we find the role described for it in previous accounts to be exaggerated in some ways and underestimated in others. At the international level, and in terms of global patterns of conventional weapons transfers, Israel does not rank as a major arms supplier; yet neither is it inconsequential.

Respected to the point of being described as the world's fourth strongest military power, Israel was also graded as high as seventh in the sales of conventional weapons in 1981.[58] This prominence, while possibly flattering to arms enthusiasts and lobbyists in Israel, is unwarranted on the basis of comparative data and in light of more recent developments.

Certainly Israel qualifies for inclusion among the twenty largest suppliers, especially when allowing for "invisible" sales which remain undetected and unreported. Nevertheless, its true position is probably closer to fifteenth than it is to seventh (Table 10.1). These findings further show Israel to be marginal in terms of each country's volume of weapons transfers and also in its share of the total market.

Four countries—the United States, the Soviet Union, France, and Britain—dominate the market and do business worth billions of dollars each year. They accounted for 87.5 percent of the value of arms supplied to the developing world during the decade of the 1970s.[59] Despite mounting competition, in 1980 these four major suppliers still managed to divide something like 77 percent of the market between them.[60] The United States alone reportedly earned $18.3 billion from the sale of arms during 1982–1983.[61] As for the next largest West European suppliers, France, illustrating the magnitude of sales as compared with the $1 to $1.5 billion earned by Israel from all its transfers, is said to have sold approximately $5 billion worth of military equipment to Iraq alone since the outbreak of fighting in the Persian Gulf in 1980.[62]

Furthermore, this initial gap between the top arms export leaders and Israel is constantly widening. Even other developing countries like Brazil are coming to surpass Israel in the volume of their sales. The Third World share of the global trade in major conventional weapons is, in any case, relatively small—2.4 percent for the period 1979–1981 according to SIPRI; under 8 percent in 1980 on the basis of ACDA data.[63] Of the six largest Third World

Table 10.1. Leading Arms Exporters, 1982.

1980(a)	1981(b)	1982(c)
1. Soviet Union	Soviet Union	Soviet Union
2. United States	United States	United States
3. France	France	France
4. United Kingdom	Italy	United Kingdom
5. West Germany	United Kingdom	Romania
6. Czechoslovakia	West Germany	China
7. Italy	Netherlands	Italy
8. Yugoslavia	Sweden	Czechoslovakia
9. Poland	China	West Germany
10. Switzerland	Czechoslovakia	Brazil
11. South Korea	Switzerland	Poland
12. China	Canada	Spain
13. North Korea	Japan	North Korea
14. Netherlands	Brazil	South Korea
15. Saudi Arabia	Israel	Israel
16. Turkey	Libya	Libya
17. Austria	South Korea	Egypt
18. Israeli ⎫	Egypt	Switzerland
19. Belgium ⎬ *	Saudi Arabia	Canada
20. Brazil ⎭		Netherlands

*Arms exports for all three countries given as $140 million each.
Derived from (a) ACDA, 1971–1980, pp. 75–116; (b) SIPRI Yearbook, 1982, pp. 188, 192–193; (c) ACDA, 1972–1982, pp. 58–94.

exporting countries, Israel was listed by SIPRI as second (21.1 percent of total Third World sales), with Brazil in first place for the years 1979–1981 at over double the figure (45.6 percent).[64] Israeli transfers, in sum, represent but a tiny fraction—somewhere between 0.6 percent and 4 percent—of total major world arms exports.[65]

It further helps to maintain a sense of proportion by recalling that no country in the world derives all—or most—of its armaments from Israel alone. Each state receiving weapons from Israel also gets arms from other countries. In addition, Israel is more likely to pursue small, unobtrusive sales unlike the pacesetters in quest of large contracts and political gains. Finally, because of their marginality, Israeli arms alone cannot really be viewed as the primary cause for regional instability. Argentina could, and did, get military aid elsewhere than from Jerusalem alone.

A clearer, more balanced perspective, therefore, is needed. While marginal, nevertheless, Israel has to be recognized as the fifth or sixth largest pro-Western supplier after the United States, and among the top three Third World suppliers, making it significant as a supporter of Western global interests and as representative of the arms export trend characterizing the newly industrialized countries like Singapore, South Korea, Taiwan, Brazil, and Argentina.

Israel's real importance for students of the conventional arms trade lies in this latter category. Perhaps the most interesting trend at present is the growing number of non-Western, developing countries active in promoting weapons transactions of their own. Arms exporters can be classified in three broad categories: principal, secondary, or developing suppliers of weapons.[66] In 1965 monetary terms $80 million per year in arms sales or equivalent aid value qualified a nation as a principal supplier, while the difference between secondary and developing supplier countries was $10–$80 million and $1–$10 million respectively. Retaining this range of sales activity while allowing for inflation and the boom in the arms market since then, Israel fits the middle category of second-tier suppliers. One of the first developing nations to supply its own needs and to achieve exporter status, Israel had gained recognition as a secondary supplier by the early 1980s yet stands only on the fringe of the circle of principal supplier nations. By understanding the Israeli experience in responding both to adversity and opportunity, one may be better able to follow the conversion process from arms import through indigenous military production to arms export now underway in other Third World nations intent on catching up.

In sum, the question whether the Israeli arms sales program is major or marginal does not lend itself to a single, definitive answer. The answer depends really upon a second question: major or marginal from what standpoint? In international terms Israel's military assistance, while significant in a few specific areas, is nonetheless marginal, whereas from a domestic perspective the impact and present importance of the military industry and its arms sales are in fact of major consequence.

Among the weightier domestic considerations are: full employment and sustained production in the defense-related industries primarily charged with meeting Israel's own requirements in military equipment; the fact that a science-based, military-oriented technology of high standards is one of the country's few marketable assets; surplus stocks of weapons of proven performance under actual battlefield conditions. Other pressures include: the need for hard currency in view of an alarming national balance of payments problem; a no less serious trade imbalance; and the search for diplomatic leverage with foreign governments some of which are unprepared at the moment to maintain formal ties, yet are quite willing to accept military aid and to purchase arms from Israel. Or as it was put by one Israeli official in referring to how the United States and the others see Israel's trade: "For them it's a drop in the bucket. For us it's vitally important."[67] Thus the real question becomes whether Israel, poised at the mid-1980s, will see defense sales stabilize at present levels—and possibly even decline both in dollar terms and market share—or whether it will have the forward momentum, the industrial and techno-logical capacity, and the opportunities to meet the challenge, retaining the stake it has fought so hard to achieve.

Nor are international conditions especially propitious. Israel's diplomatic exclusion, uncertain client relationships, and the shadow of the United States over Israeli weapons development are serious constraints. Two other world trends are relevant for the immediate future. Arms markets may not expand appreciably in the future. Due to payments problems as well as to problems involved in the ability to absorb weapons, the cycle of "big buys" which prompted the spectacular arms export growth rate recorded in the late 1970s may well yield to a period of more modest purchases. Similarly, even as the market begins to decline, Israel finds itself competing against other Third World suppliers like Brazil, South Korea, and Singapore enjoying certain ad-vantages—of resources, of contacts, of location—of their own.

If the outside environment is changing, so, too, is Israeli policy. In fact several trends are underway. First, the convergence of diplomatic, strategic, and economic interests, always strong, has become that much more power-ful. Together they make the need to sell, as well as the wisdom of military transfers by Israel, axiomatic. Israeli foreign military assistance is accepted, and appreciated, as a vital component of external relations, as an essential element of the national defense posture and, now, as a pillar of the economy. By reinforcing each other the triad of arguments and incentives provide an overarching rationale on behalf of a continuing arms supplier role for Israel. This will remain so even if and when the costs, or possibly the risks, in any single given area should increase.

At the same time, however, the position of the three basic Israeli national interests within this larger pro-arms export argument—the relative emphases of each—appears to be undergoing revision.

At the diplomatic end of the scales, arms themselves, as opposed to less visible military assistance (training, advisers, etc.), have moved from a minor and inconsequential position to that of an indispensable instrument of Israeli foreign relations. While the diplomatic argument itself has been weakened by an inability to reverse Israel's decline internationally through statecraft or arms alone, some useful lessons have been learned from previous disappoint-ments with military aid. Expectations have been adjusted downward and changes of approach introduced so that no longer is it anticipated that arms supplies will be rewarded by open support for and identification with Israel. Arms relationships are pursued discreetly, on a quid pro quo basis and in-directly, sometimes through third party arms brokers. The revised policy re-flects greater realism in acknowledging the tenuous nature of political influ-ence and the limits to diplomatic leverage by a small state.

Second, as diplomatic considerations hold fast, the military or strategic factor has increased in the 1980s. In part this reflects greater Israeli attention in the present decade to military relationships with other countries: on the one hand, with the developing nations, and, on the other hand, with the United States. As a result, Israel has adopted more of a global view in perceiving where its vital security interests lie and how they might best be secured. Defense sales, in short, provide Israel with a global reach. The effects can be seen most recently from reports of Palestinian pilots active in Central America countered by Israeli activity such as defense equipment and assistance in what amounts to the internationalization of the core Arab-Israeli conflict. The other explanation for this wider security perspective stems from the pivotal role of the Israeli defense establishment in making arms sales policy—indeed, in making foreign policy—as well as in its execution.

Third, and particularly noteworthy for the future course of Israeli arms diplomacy, the economic motivation of late has become foremost. It merits repeating that were the military assistance and sales program to be terminated entirely, or even in part, whether voluntarily by Israel as a conscious government decision, perhaps on moral grounds, or because arms diplomacy was no longer effective in opening arms relationships, this would have the most adverse consequences for both the economy and society of Israel. Israel's Defense Minister Arens represented this dominant school of thought when he argued in 1983:

> It is widely agreed, and incontrovertibly substantiated by the facts, that the defense industry is today one of the most advanced and efficient sectors in the Israeli economy. Our military exports are a very large component of overall industrial export. . . . Revitalizing the economy and making it more progressive requires that the defense industry be encouraged . . . [68]

Israeli commercial interests, such as maintaining both the standard of living and international trade relationships, are increasingly difficult to resist.

It follows that if weapons transfers are an economic necessity even more than a military and diplomatic priority today, it is unreasonable to assume that Israel would reject arms deals worth millions of dollars or suddenly reverse course by curtailing or terminating the weapons export program. After all, as a small state with an unenviable challenge to its security and with little else going for it in the equation of international power and influence, it should not be expected to forego so valuable an asset, least of all unilaterally, in the absence of multilateral agreement among the major arms traders and without a genuine Middle East peace. On the contrary, and until such regional and global conditions prevail, both the Israeli public and its leadership remain convinced that it makes good military, political, and business sense to sell arms.

Israeli arms sales activity, emulating that of the pacesetters in the world arms trade, suggests that economic criteria are no longer easily subordinated to political or diplomatic considerations. The conventional wisdom about weapons transfers used to view them primarily as an adjunct of a state's foreign relations. This thinking is challenged once exporting arms and military technologies comes to be seen as economically indispensable. In Israel's experience until now, these economic and commercial considerations, together with the diplomatic and military ones, by and large have tended to be positive and mutually reinforcing. What remains to be seen is whether good business can be prevented from making for bad international politics on the part of Israel.

NOTES

1. Donor-recipient patterns are analyzed by William H. Lewis, "Political Influence: The Diminished Capacity," in Neuman and Harkavy, pp. 184–199. Egypt's unilateral termination of its military relationship with the U.S.S.R. in 1972 is, of course, a classic example of client undependability.
2. A. W. Clausen, "To Help Developing Countries Sustain Growth," *NYT*, 22 February 1983. Subsequent developments in *IHT*, 22 September 1983, citing the U.N. Conference of Trade and Development (UNCTAD).
3. *Haaretz*, 21 October 1982; on 8 December 1982 *Haaretz* published reports that Nigeria's unpaid account with the Israeli construction firm, Solel Boneh, amounted to millions of dollars. This recent phenomenon is ably dealt with in Harry J. Shaw, "Debts & Dependency," *Foreign Policy* 50 (Spring 1983): 105–123; see, as well, the three-part series by Charles William Maynes, "The Third World Crisis," in *IHT*, 20–22, September 1983.
4. On Venezuela, *IHT*, 14 December 1983; on Peru, *IHT*, 22 September 1983; on Ecuador, *IHT*, 6 June 1984.
5. On the arms imports factor, Alan B. Mountjoy, "Third World Military Spending," *Third World Quarterly* 5 (January 1983): 139–140; Michael Brzoska, "Research Communication: The Military Related External Debt of Third World Countries," *Journal of Peace Research* 20 (1983): 271–277.
6. This "flattening out" is the impression of SIPRI analysts, SIPRI Yearbook 1983, pp. 270–272. They note that from 1963–1967 to 1968–72 the volume of arms flows doubled; doubled again in the next five-year period, 1973–1977, but from then to the most recent five-year period, 1978–1982, the increase was down to fifty percent. The reasons given are: the world recession and the budget constraints it has brought with it, and the possibility of market saturation.
7. *J P*, 11 April 1984; at that time Israeli exporters were owed about $40 million by Nigeria, Argentina, Mexico, Venezuela, Peru, and Brazil, each $10 million, with Ecuador owing about $5 million.
8. *J P*, 23 January 1983.
9. Related in Abba Eban, *An Autobiography* (Tel-Aviv: Steimatsky's, 1977), p. 602. Mobutu's disgruntlement and efforts by Israel businessmen to mollify him were reported in *Maariv*, 7 December 1984.
10. *Haaretz*, 28 January 1983 and 15 September 1983; *IHT*, 12 June 1984; also in Adams, pp. 108 and 208, based upon his conversations with Israeli officials.
11. Excerpts from the "Communique of Managua," critical of Israel in *J P*, 16 January 1983.
12. Israel Radio, 22 January 1983; see also *J P*, 23 January 1983.
13. *NYT*, 9 May 1982; *Haaretz*, 31 May 1982; *J P*, 29 April 1982.

14. *Haaretz*, 30 May 1982.
15. Joseph Lelyveld "South Africa Actively Courting Arms Clients," *IHT*, 15 December 1982; Richard Leonard, *South Africa at War* (Westport, Conn.: Lawrence Hill and Company, 1984).
16. Much of the demand for arms has been stimulated by the supplier countries themselves through price cutting and the use of generous export credits and financing techniques.
17. SIPRI, 1982, pp. 176–177.
18. *IHT*, 30–31 October 1982.
19. The government refuses, for instance to allow major Kfir subsystems to be exported on grounds of security, Goren, p. 47.
20. *IHT*, 28 October 1982; the Soviets, hard-pressed for foreign currency to buy grain and technology, earn about $16 billion a year from arms they reportedly sell below market price, *Wall Street Journal*, 29 June 1982.
21. *NYT*, 8 August 1982.
22. *IHT*, 31 July–1 August 1982; it is estimated that in 1981 U.S. arms transfers were valued at $25 billion, as compared with $15 billion in 1980, *Wall Street Journal*, 29 June 1982.
23. Britain, for example, undertook a major arms selling drive in 1983. The plan included sending a floating exhibition of British arms manufactures to the Middle East due to interest created by the Falklands campaign.
24. On the French arms industry and its renewed drive, see *IHT*, 10 January 1984 and 31 March–1 April 1984. Pressure upon the West German government to ease limits on arms exports is described in *IHT*, 6 September 1983 and in *Haaretz*, 24 and 27 February 1984. On how individual firms are being affected, see the story on Belgium's Fabrique Nationale, the world's largest private maker of small arms, whose revenues have shrunk appreciably, *IHT*, 18 October 1983.
25. Mountjoy, p. 139 and Moodie, p. 62.
26. Brazil, for example, coproduces a NATO warplane with Italy, *IHT*, 15 February 1984. Developing countries as exporters of industrial technology are closely analyzed in Sanjaya Lall, *Developing Countries in the International Economy* (London: The Macmillan Press, 1981). Military applications of these capital and technological skills are reviewed in Rodney W. Jones and Steven A. Hildreth, *Modern Weapons and Third World Powers* (Boulder and London: Westview Press, 1984). For whatever reason the authors have not included Israel among the countries investigated in a project sponsored by the Center for Strategic and International Studies of Georgetown University on "Modern Weapons: Third World Motivations, Capabilities, and Performance."
27. *IHT*, 30 June 1983; it is making the plane in a joint production arrangement with six U.S. or Western European aircraft manufacturers. On Singapore's arms industry see *The Economist*, 30 July 1983.
28. *Yediot Achronot*, 2 July 1984, citing a report by London's Royal Armed Services Institute.
29. *The Economist's* "Foreign Report," 24 November 1983, pp. 6–7, on the Argentinian military industries led by the powerful conglomerate, Fabricaciones Militares.
30. *IHT*, 29 April 1983.
31. *Israel Government Yearbook*, 5742, p. 124.
32. *J P*, 27 May 1982.
33. *J P*, 27 May 1982; *Haaretz*, 31 May 1982.
34. U.S.-Israeli policy differences were reported by the *IHT*, 29–30 May 1982. In October, Ambassador Arens repeated that Israeli arms to Iran in its war with Iraq were conducted in coordination with the United States "at almost the highest lev-

els," *J P*, 22 October 1982.

35. Sharon, upon his return to Israel, claimed that the United States had released the information intentionally, *J P*, 30 May, 31 May 1982.
36. *Maariv*, 27 May 1982.
37. Maariv, 26 May 1982; *J P*, 27 May 1982.
38. *Haaretz*, 5 October 1982.
39. *Haaretz*, 12 December 1982.
40. Alex Mintz addressed this theme in a recent article, "The Military-Industrial Complex: The Israeli Case," which appears in a special issue of *The Journal of Strategies Studies,* **6** (September 1983): 103–127, devoted to Israeli society and the defense establishment.
41. *J P*, 26 April 1984.
42. Remarks by Premier Peres in *NYT*, 5 February 1985.
43. Pierre, p. 126.
44. *Haaretz*, 7 December 1982.
45. *Yediot Acharonot*, 27 August 1982.
46. Evron, p. 297.
47. Interview with Koor's Director-General designate Yeshayahu Gavish, *J P*, 21 July 1982.
48. *Haaretz*, 28 April 1983.
49. Ze'ev Schiff, "Honduras and all the Others," *Haaretz*, 17 December 1982. Commerce Minister Patt attributes the drop in the percentage of production for foreign customers to increased demand by the IDF to fill its own depleted stocks, *J P*, 19 June 1983.
50. *Newsview*, 21 June 1983; *J P*, 11 April 1983.
51. *J P*, 11 April 1983.
52. See Shlomo Maoz, *Haaretz*, 10 May, 8 June 1983. The pattern of falling exports continued through the end of the year. Exports in November dropped by about $70 million and included, in particular, diminished military sales, *J P*, 8 December 1983.
53. *Haaretz*, 12 September 1983.
54. *Haaretz*, 9 October 1983.
55. 1983 figures reported in *J P*, 11 January and 2 February 1984, as well as *Haaretz*, 2 February 1984.
56. *Haaretz*, 12 March 1984.
57. *Maariv*, 17 May 1983.
58. *Christian Science Monitor*, 5 January 1983; Israel ranked eleventh in the period 1977–1980, accounting for 28.9 percent of all Third World arms exports. In 1981 it was placed seventh among the world's exporters of weapons and defense-related equipment, with sales for the year ending 1 April 1981 of about $1.3 billion—a 40 percent increase over 1979–1980, SIPRI Yearbook, 1981. pp. 116, 188; *NYT*, 16 March, 1982, quoting British sources.
59. Pierre, *Global Sales*, pp. 10, 13.
60. ACDA, 1983, p. 31.
61. *Haaretz*, 20 November 1983, citing American sources.
62. *IHT*, 29 June 1983.
63. SIPRI, 1982, pp. 176, 187; ACDA, 1983, p. 30.
64. SIPRI, 1982, pp. 176, 187–188.
65. SIPRI, 1981, p. 188; *Monitin* (July, 1983), gives the figure of 4 percent.
66. Frank, pp. 50–51.
67. Quoted in *J P*, 24 November 1983.
68. Arens, *Maariv*, 19 August 1983.

11

CAN ISRAEL KEEP PACE?

In comparison with other Third World and secondary suppliers of conventional weapons, Israel had the benefit of a headstart. As an enterprising small state with clearly-defined vital national interests, it has pursued low-cost opportunities for increasing security and influence through modest weapons transfers. This has continued for some three decades during which time domestic, regional, and global conditions have for the most part been favorable. But now Israel may be at a critical turning point in its remarkable arms sales diplomacy.

In anticipating current market trends and future prospects, our study finds Israel probing the outer limits of its growth, not so much as an arms manufacturer and producer, where its capacity still appears to be great, as in the role of arms exporter and international weapons trade competitor. Among the more serious constraints on further defense export achievements which we found are: reliance in certain critical areas on the United States, which, in turn, reveals America's own ambivalence toward Israel as both ally and competitor; increasing competition for markets among the major suppliers, and unreliability for a small state like Israel of contemporary supplier-client relations in a fluid global market and at a time of national and worldwide economic recession.

Nevertheless, there is no reason why Israel should not be able to cope with these limitations without having to forego what has been, and remains, a legitimate as well as effective instrument of foreign relations. To do so requires greater thought to what we see as the determinants of success.

ISRAELI POLICY ALTERNATIVES

How might Israel best respond to contemporary pressures and challenges in preserving its status and competitiveness within the conventional arms trade? The question as phrased intentionally rules out one theoretical option: that of self-abrogation, or withdrawing itself from the competition. The entire thrust of our analysis has been to show just how deep and serious the Israeli commitment is. Rather, the following guidelines might be incorporated as part of an Israeli effort to combine maximum effectiveness with minimum risk in its weapons transfers practices during the remainder of this decade.

Some of the pitfalls in the conventional arms trade are implicit in the international setting and therefore beyond Israel's control. Others, such as undue adverse publicity, however, can be avoided or minimized through greater care for how the arms policy is designed, debated, and executed at home.

A Clarified Arms Sales Strategy

Foreign military sales are means to identifiable ends. These ends deserve to be clarified, first, in the minds of those responsible for making Israeli policy; and second, to a greater extent than at present, in the minds of the broader Israeli public. Success in the use of arms transfers will depend directly on the perceptiveness and validity of the strategy guiding them and on the popular consensus—as opposed to parochial support by any particular sector or group—lining up behind the policy. In each instance sales consciously must be subordinated to strategic and foreign policy objectives which oftentimes seem to be lost upon government officials as much as they are upon the wider public.

Failure to establish and maintain general policy guidelines, publicly enunciated and carefully enforced, could be detrimental. The entire effort might remain clouded in obscurity. Individual sales will be treated ad hoc without being integrated into the larger framework of policy. A feeling that arms sales practices were irrational, irresponsible, and inconsistently applied could take hold at home, and even abroad by friends of Israel. The end result could be a series of setbacks and embarrassments because thorough prior consideration had not been given to the unintended consequences arising from random, uncoordinated, case-by-case and country-by-country sales.

Admittedly, judgments about arms transfers are not easy to make, and they often invoke conflicting aims and values. Yet governments inevitably must wrestle with these questions. For Israel, sending equipment to countries accused of violating human rights may be unfortunate. Yet if the reasons for doing so are sound, then the case ought to be presented as forcefully as political prudence allows. In thinking about this and related military aid questions, Israeli leaders can only stand to benefit from clarifying the soundness of national goals and then measuring their achievements against these objectives. In sum, principles of foreign military assistance and arms transfers ought to be discussed more openly; not, however, the particulars of various transactions.

Tight-Lipped Diplomacy

Logically one would expect the validity of concepts underlying arms actions to be tested in the public domain, with the actual handling of policy being done professionally within authorized government agencies and removed from the public eye. Of late, however, the reverse situation seems to have prevailed, with an audible silence as to principles contrasted to inordinate official utterances and government leaks concerning the details and modalities of specific military partnerships. Statements about arms sales should be issued only after they have been approved in an authorized forum. It seems elementary that like everything else connected with arms diplomacy, announcements should come from government circles rather than from individual officials. This is one area at least which is under Israel's control and where greater self-restraint should be shown.

Trading in arms is, along with intelligence-gathering, military planning, secret overtures, guaranteeing energy sources, and antiterrorism, one of those six most sensitive areas of Israeli foreign relations where discretion is absolutely essential. For this reason, the *details* of the scope, mechanics, tactics, and implementation of country-to-country transfers ought to be shielded from public scrutiny, unless, of course, there are compelling reasons for doing otherwise. Discretion in the reporting of defense matters, including specific defense sales, is a traditional Israeli practice which has been seriously breached in recent years, causing damage to sensitive political relations with clients as well as with the United States and to Israel's image, resulting from undue publicity or premature disclosure. Premature disclosure of the extraordinary effort at arranging the exodus of Falashan Jews from Ethiopia and Sudan to Israel in January, 1985, serves here as an object lesson in quiet diplomacy and what happens when its special rules are disregarded.

Improved Policymaking Procedures

The third area for improvement concerns process. Insisting upon greater discretion is merely the first requisite for procedural change. There remains room for tightening other controls over the military assistance program. In order to better explain Israel's position and motives the diplomatic, military, and economic considerations need to be more closely integrated with the information services. Bureaucratically, all too often in the past, personal or interdepartmental rivalries and the absence of close coordination, especially between the defense and foreign ministries, have been permitted to handicap arms trade diplomacy. At the same time unanimity within policymaking structures runs the risk of overvaluing the policy.

The very existence of such a multifaceted national effort legitimately reemphasizes the need for a national security council framework. Periodic review, debate, and controls become a vital safety net against miscalculation and against excessive dependence on this one area of activity. Convening the Ministerial Committee on Weapons Transfers was a step in the right direction by the Begin government. Nevertheless, it may be that the scale of effort has simply outpaced and outgrown the structures needed for managing the production and flow of Israeli arms. For example, at no level is there provision for a process of comprehensive arms policy evaluation, nor is there at present a permanent unit charged with considering the political implications and economic consequences of defense sales.

That the sum is larger than its parts may be a political truism, yet one which must find institutional expression. A policy planning staff is needed, for example, to bring together civilian and military perspectives, immediate circumstances with larger global patterns and trends. Export controls should be meshed more closely with foreign policy, and any organizational change should come through either a security council or strengthening the Foreign Ministry, especially considering the Defense Ministry's extremely close working relation with the special interest groups which make up the armaments industry. Alternatively, or in conjunction with the government, the twin tasks of monitoring policy and international developments would benefit from closer involvement by the Knesset's Foreign Affairs and Security Committee.

In addition, the aid of independent think tanks and strategic studies centers in Israel might profitably be encouraged in defending the country's arms trade position against either of two undesirable eventualities—a traumatic loss of markets and sudden decline in military exports, or no less ominous, exaggerated expectations and a headlong rush to fill orders occasioned by a steady flow of sales opportunities. If Israel's desire is for deeper and ongoing arms partnerships, then it is clear that government agencies and private firms alike will require more highly trained personnel. International relations experts, international economists, and regional specialists sensitive to both systemic factors and local conditions are no less important as risk consultants for a balanced national policy than are retired army officers knowledgeable about Israeli weapons systems or their operational use.

The Exercise of Greater Circumspection

The logic for selling arms will always appear strongest in the case of smaller suppliers like Israel; so, too, the impulse to grab at the opportunity for promoting military products. It is all the more important for Israel's self-image as well as its world reputation, therefore, that principles be maintained concerning categories of weapons made available and their prospective recipients, including, for example, prohibitions against the sale of weapons for use in civil wars or the suppression of domestic opposition. A certain deterioration or lowering of standards seems to have taken place over the past several years which ought to be arrested.

Market diversification can be combined with greater selectivity in conferring upon Israel this necessary latitude should it prefer not to sell particular items to a particular country or regime at any given time. Such circumspection seems politic on two counts: externally, in not appearing overeager or indiscriminate; domestically, in preserving support for the existing policy, since it appears that the overwhelming majority of Israelis do not object to the general thrust of arms-selling, merely to the impression sometimes given, as with Zaire, of impulsiveness, mismanagement, or simply too much noise.

Cautionary measures, however, go beyond individual client countries, weapons, or transactions. Given Israel's economy and industry approaching the mid-80s, military sales come close to dominating the country's foreign trade and certainly its industrial exports. Estimates of the latter ratio range between one-fifth and one-third. Even if effectively restricted to no more than one-quarter of industrial exports, the sale of arms, acknowledged generally to be one of the more unstable and unpredictable areas of international commerce, would in Israeli terms be excessive. A sudden drop in sales, due perhaps to being edged out by other sellers or possibly because a good customer can no longer afford additional purchases, has no use for them, or is itself manufacturing comparable items, would introduce profound shocks in an already shaky economy. Hence the need is for establishing aggregate limits — and for adhering to them even in the face of additional seductive opportunities which, in toto, would overcommit and further distort the economy.

In effect, an institutionalized program of sales restraint, with built-in controls and inhibitions is called for. The burden of proof should no longer rest with the opponents of arms shipments. It should be the duty of officials, arms producers, and arms dealers to prove that an arms sale is absolutely necessary and justified in terms of the national interest. This will necessitate closer scrutiny as well as better coordination of arms sales proposals in the future. Arresting the process of nearly automatic sales authorization clearly depends on the imposition of deliberate checks and balances.

Restraining the Special Interests

Unquestionably, the most politically sensitive issue will be whether, and in what way, to monitor the influence on policymaking of the military and industrial interests. One acknowledges the profound and positive contribution made in the course of modern Israel's history by the defense industries. If not for them it would be hard, if not impossible, to picture the position of Israel in the three critical areas of defense, economic growth, and international respect.

Yet the existence of a powerful military-industrial complex which subscribes to the series of politico-strategic and commercial propositions current in Israeli thinking toward arms export diplomacy, nevertheless, poses a problem. These interlocking groupings form the domestic framework for defense production and export, and they share in the assessment that the weapons trade serves the national interest and is as promising as it is profitable. They present a weighty argument and exert a strong influence on the decision-making process. Moreover, their preoccupation with promoting foreign military transactions inadvertently only further strengthens what has become a form of dependence on external factors under unstable circumstances. Once these defense industries, government agencies, private corporations, and their overseas sales representatives become so export-oriented, the sale of military hardware in effect becomes an end in itself. As the industry has grown, so have its sales abroad and so, too, its impact on the government and the national defense exports policy.

The director-general of Rafael has explained that due to the classified nature of its weapons development work his company's export sales remain limited to about $10 million per annum. But he then proceeds to argue that in order to attract new sources of outside funding and as a means of lowering the costs of newer systems for the IDF, the contribution made by exports must increase, and in fact is "vital" for the future of Rafael.[1] One consequence of the influence of the military-industrial complex and its lobbying could well be a relaxation of standards which at present exclude many military products from the arms export inventory. As of now these standards represent possibly the greatest single limitation on the further development of Israel's arms export potential. The influence exercised in favor of weapons transfers by Israel's nationalized, seminational, and private business interests, as well as by a government agency like SIBAT within the defense establishment and charged with promoting arms sales, argues for the progressive liberalization of these standards.

Arms diplomacy, if it is to achieve its combination of strategic, economic *and* political objectives, must not be allowed to become the captive of special economic interests. A political arms supply policy must involve restraint; yet an arms supply policy dominated primarily by economic considerations cannot afford restraint. Industrial and commercial objectives may well run counter to political objectives, and a policy which concentrates on the former could prove, from the long-term standpoint of Israel's international position, to be myopic.

In Israel the defense industrial base remains a national resource. Therefore, insofar as exports contribute to the survival of defense industrial capacity, and in the absence of alternatives, the government is committed to promote them. Except that with a relatively small home market, policymakers now find themselves under growing pressure to permit companies to export well over half of their annual production in order to maintain the economic viability of the defense industries. Intense pressures from the military-industrial sector, for example, prompt skepticism at the government's declared intention not to permit military exports to exceed 20 percent of total industrial exports.

First, because the logic of opportunism and necessity, backed by enthusiastic administrators and salesmen, encourages everyone actively involved in the arms export drive to aim for constantly higher annual performance records; to hold steady is to recede. Secondly, even were arms sales to remain

at their present level of more than one billion dollars, as long as other export sales, such as of textiles, continue to decline, the effect automatically
will be to elevate the status of military transfers within the totality of Israeli
exports. Thus, while the arms boom continues, and unless a major overhauling of the national economy takes place, economic dependence upon this
single — and singularly vulnerable — sector seems likely to continue.

Thus in 1982 Israel had one of the highest ratings in the world in terms of
arms exports in relation to total exports. Statistical computations by the U.S.
Arms Control and Disarmament Agency placed Israel fifth, with a ratio of
6.9 percent based only upon known or verified transfers. This figure was exceeded only by Egypt (9.3 percent), Romania (9.5 percent), the Soviet Union
(12.5 percent) and in all probability North Korea (13.2 percent in 1976).[2] Israel
presently leads the Western and the democratic states. The United States, for
all its major arms export efforts, still manages to preserve a low ratio of 4.5
percent of military sales to total export sales. It is that much more disturbing, therefore, to read of official government reports, like that of the Yiftah
Commission in 1984, which confidently note that the defense industries are
far from realizing their full export potential and which enthusiastically encourage an export campaign aimed at marketing the Merkava tank and, later,
the Lavi fighter plane.[3]

That such defense-related shipments might be unavoidable and even vital
from a national standpoint would be a legitimate even if uncomfortable argument. Less acceptable, however, would be such prominence owing to particularistic or private concerns which took for granted that their interests were
somehow synonymous with the national interest. "What's good for General
Motors is good for the nation" has yet to make its way into Israeli political
culture or parlance; still, it may not be so removed from reality. The distinction between the defense complex and the state is an important one; it needs
to be made and, no less important, to be retained.

Giving Thought to Reconversion

An alternative approach to imposing immediate export limits takes the
longer view. It acknowledges that defense sales have a definite role to play
in the future economic independence of Israel. It calls for a two-fold program: (a) encouraging dual-use manufacture of military systems which also
have a civilian application; (b) redirecting the arms industry, or, more precisely, certain selected sectors within it, to civilian purposes. However, the prospects of success for, and the initial effect of, such a program are not immediately apparent; moreover, even this gradual conversion from defense to
social expenditures would be resisted by some of the most powerful industrial
and military sectors.

Yet it would not, in principle, be harmful to the economy as a whole in the long run. Neither would this conversion entail any major switch of resources from the defense sector. Initially, all that is required is a joint effort by the government and the defense industries to explore models for converting military production facilities to civilian-related production. This in itself would signal greater restraint. Indeed, the spin-off benefits for nonmilitary research and development always have been presented as a principal selling point for Israel's undertaking such major and ambitious projects as the Merkava, the Kfir, and the Lavi.

Continued Resourcefulness

If Israel's arm diplomacy is to survive, it must continue the tradition of industriousness at home and resourcefulness abroad. Today, in order to compete, a supplier state must have several requisites. These include: a well-developed internal production capability, financial resources, scientific and educational potential, organizational and political abilities, an extensive reservoir of industrial know-how and human skills, large and continuous requirements for its armed forces, and the willingness to export defense products to other states. With the exception of financial resources, Israel possesses every one of these requisites. It has both the industrial base and the manpower base; unlike other LDC defense industries which tend to level off at the intermediate stages of production capability as the skills required for more advanced weapons design elude them, Israeli manufacturers continue to master today's most innovative technologies, like microelectronics, computers, and a new generation of precision-guided, so-called "smart weapons."

For this reason alone the Lavi project is of vital importance. Production of the Lavi goes beyond mere national pride or symbolism and is meant to preserve if not widen Israel's technological lead over other rival suppliers. Its fulfillment means reduced dependence on arms supplies from outside sources. Full production means employment, scientific research, and economic spin-offs. The Lavi project will build up the domestic arms industry and preserve Israel's status as a world leader in aerospace; there is also at least a prospect of the Lavi joining the inventory of Israeli military exports. If American ambivalence, private and government, toward the project cannot be resolved in favor of the project, and if Israeli leaders are determined to see it through to completion, then efforts must be redoubled to find alternative sources of financing and technological cooperation. Reports along these lines referred to interested private American investors; to discussions between Defense Minister Arens and French defense officials on the possibility of Franco-Israeli arms cooperation; and, by August, 1983, to unspecified orders for Lavi parts placed by the Israel Aircraft Industries with European firms.[4]

Whatever the economics involved, the political implication seems rather clear. Squeezed between dependence on the United States and the mounting payments deficit, Israeli arms enthusiasts are strengthened in arguing that the country is forced to make greater efforts to expand its own weapons export campaign.

This situation makes resourcefulness that much more imperative. Achievements notwithstanding, Israel's deficiencies cannot be swept aside. Like the heavy costs of military research and development, or factors of scale, they are real, and a daily fact of life. Among the important weapons producers in the Third World, only Israel is not included in the group of states with a relatively large GNP.[5] Certain countries have apparently already overburdened their economies by ambitious arms-production programs. Israel is a particular case in point, since it ranks only approximately twelfth on the list of arms production potential.[6] At least sixteen other countries have a domestic arms-manufacturing capacity extensive enough to enable them to become significant exporters within this decade.[7]

In this emerging competitive system, functional specialization and comparative advantage will largely determine the fate of Israel's diplomacy of military transfers.[8] Two groups of arms suppliers are likely to emerge: the largest and most industrialized countries, which will concentrate on developing sophisticated technologies, and the smaller arms-manufacturing countries will be left with less advanced systems and standard items. Presently Israel is positioned in the middle, yet leaning heavily toward the former group. Exactly where it will fit in the coming decade is unclear as yet, to be decided by the gravity of the possible challenges and the nature of the Israeli response. A good deal will depend upon the ability and ingenuity demonstrated so often in the past in adapting to change.

Flexibility in Terms of Trade

One possible demonstration of resourcefulness can be shown in the fight to retain arms clients. Like any other supplier, Israel's obvious preference is for deals on a cash-and-carry basis, with prompt payment and in hard currency. In striving to maintain their competitive position Israeli negotiators and contractors already show a good deal of realism in offering liberal repayment conditions. Still, there is certain to be a problem as the list of cash-short debtor countries grows. It is suggested, therefore, that Israel give greater consideration to the idea of countertrade. This entails a willingness by Israel as supplier of military arms and aid to accept, in lieu of cash, an equivalent amount of goods or raw materials. This practice, in effect, represents a type of barter which could be beneficial to Israel.

Economists purport to identify the emergence of a new international economic order, one of whose central features is a return to the former practice of barter due to the shortage of convertible currency. Thus many developing countries subject to financial constraints arising from their foreign debt position are reverting to countertrade to fill part of their import requirements. Third World countries insisting upon countertrade are making it an important consideration for their international defense purchases;[9] and if Israeli government arms salesmen want to compete successfully abroad they will do well to emphasize such arrangements.

Fortunately, while some suppliers anxious for hard currency have not overcome their distaste for countertrade, Israel has never precluded such arrangements. Quite the opposite. Barter has worked well in the past. A notable example was the military partnership with the Shah of Iran based upon arms-for-oil. Similarly, Israel is reported to have a barter arrangement with Argentina, by which it receives approximately $100 billion worth of beef for arms.[10] A barter arrangement could facilitate further transfer relationships as well with countries like Mexico, Venezuela, and Zaire. In fact, receptivity to barter transactions is the declared policy of the Ministry for Industry and Trade.[11]

Balance in the Mix of Arms

It is clear that in keeping with the principle of diversification, Israel wishes to preserve all options in marketing the widest possible range of defense goods and services: from standard arms to state-of-the-art complete weapons systems, from actual hardware to technical advice and scientific data. Yet it may be that some options are more effective and promising than others.

The entire impetus originally for a modest arms diplomacy came from the shipment of simpler items and small arms like the Uzi, and, more recently, the versatile Galil light-assault rifle. Even now they account for a substantial percentage of Israeli sales. On the one hand, these sales do add up; another advantage is that they are less likely to be detected or traced. On the other hand, they are the least profitable and are unsuitable to serve as the core component of a sophisticated sales program, especially when one considers the manufacture of similar items by so many other countries, including new Third World arms exporters.

Historically, it is worth remembering that Israel has carved out a niche for itself in the arms trade by successfully countering the cost increasing tendency of new weapons technology for itself, and then passing these savings on to others. It has designed processes for increasing the lifetime of existing weapons systems and platforms by improvements and retrofits in an older system, thereby extending its use and effectiveness by many years. One Israeli researcher estimates that by using these proven technologies, Israel averages 5 to 6 years to design and deploy a weapon system, while the United States typically requires 10 to 12 years.[12]

Of late, however, Israel has shown signs of going to the opposite extreme in attempting to carve out a wider niche for itself, namely, by aiming at the market for top-of-the-line technologically sophisticated and very expensive systems. Yet in doing so Israel may be aiming too high. The fact is that it has done less well in securing orders for complete systems such as the Kfir plane or the Merkava tank, where competition from the larger Western or Soviet blocs is so much greater, where the demand is limited, where the Israeli product is so glaringly obvious, where Israel has little if any comparative advantage, and where the value added may be less than anticipated.

Of equal concern, national planners may be repeating this cavalier abandonment of cost restraint mechanisms in the Lavi program. The mistake lies not so much in undertaking the project but in permitting it to evolve as it has. For a variety of reasons, including bureaucratic pressures and defense thinking, the original design was expanded to even higher degrees of utility and sophistication, accompanied, of course, by cost increases. In the end some of its more striking virtues, such as light weight, small engine, and low cost, have been sacrificed. As a result, barring other obstacles or delays, particularly a U.S. veto of sales, even when the plane is placed on the open arms market it is certain to encounter stiff competition from other producers of jet fighters.

Instead, it would seem that Israel would do better to shift more of its production and marketing skills from explicit sales of large, complex, and expensive weapons systems to the potentially more rewarding area of data and technology transfers. There is going to be a growing worldwide demand, which will include the American and Western European markets, for military high technologies: electronic, optical, acoustic and other sensors; computers and warning systems; precision-guided weapons, featuring more accurate missiles and homing devices. Israel and its military-based industries have earned a deserved reputation in these fields and retain a significant comparative advantage. The Lebanese fighting stimulated this international interest by disclosing a number of new indigenous products: electronic warfare devices, command and control systems, and Scout mini-RPV reconnaissance equipment.

The supply of defense software, of specialized component systems for ships, tanks, and aircraft, and of military-related scientific data packages, therefore, represents a major opportunity for Israel. It is less direct, less conspicuous, and highly profitable in today's market for weapons. Such items have the additional virtue of flexibility, since they can be contracted for either through actual sales or through any of the various forms of joint ventures, primarily offsets, licensing or coproduction.

Supplier Coordination

From its present position of strength and respectability within the conventional arms trade, Israel might wish to consider a political initiative aimed at preventing unbridled competition among weapons suppliers and assuring a place for itself. Here three possibilities present themselves: bilaterally, with the U.S.; with the Western Europeans; and with certain Third World countries which have also emerged as sellers of some importance.

The United States is one key to Israeli defense sales prospects in at least two ways: as a market for high-quality systems and components; and as a competitor in Third World LDC's leaning politically toward the West. For both reasons it is advisable to initiate a bilateral U.S.-Israeli dialogue on aspects of the conventional arms trade in an attempt to reach some kind of understanding about weapons sales.

At a time of unprecedented American sensitivity to the financial burden of supporting Israel — witness the 1983 GAO *Report* — it is hard to anticipate an enthusiastic reception for Israeli defense sales contracts in the U.S. market. Such prospects will be poor unless a skillful political and public relations campaign is waged to present Israeli defense sales in general, and to the United States and its allies in particular, in a positive light.

Anything that gives Israel better access to the American market will help exports, the Israeli economy and the balance of payments. Worth emphasizing is that Israel's success in independently marketing its military products and the income derived therefrom become a substitute for U.S. loans and grants. It should be noted that unlike other grantees of military credits, including Egypt, Israel has never failed to make its interest payments and is determined to fulfill its debt obligations. Also, that the Israeli defense industry's own innovations, the refinement of American weapons systems tested in battle, and Israel's acting in the role of arms surrogate, represent substantial cost savings to the U.S. government — part of Israel's value as a strategic ally. It should be noted that in instances where the United States cannot overtly or directly help certain countries, such as Iran or Argentina, it might be very convenient to provide this assistance through Israel or by encouraging Israel to increase its arms exports to these countries. Finally, a diplomatic approach to Washington must press for full implementation of the clause in the 1981 strategic memorandum pertaining to U.S. purchases of up to $200 million a year in Israeli military supplies.

Alternatively, should local resistance to Israeli sales to the U.S. armed forces be so great, then Israel ought to press at least for an American recognition of its role in the Third World market. Save most notably for Iran, Argentina, and prevention of early sales of the Kfir, the United States has not interfered with Israel's arms sales program. Israeli proposals might help to ensure that in the future as well such activity outside of North America will be appreciated as complementary to the United States efforts.

China, Ethiopia and Honduras serve as illustration. In the case of the former, the Chinese leaders recently have forsaken — at least temporarily — heavy investment in weapons production and eagerly seek outside assistance in modernizing their largely outdated forces. While particularly interested in

U.S. assistance, China has not wanted to make too public an issue of coopera-tion with Washington, hence the potential role for Israel as a subsidiary sup-plier specializing in some of China's needs. In Israeli terms, even a small por-tion of the large Chinese military market would be significant. In the case of Ethiopia, the resumed supply of arms by Israel would satisfy the goals of all three parties concerned: for Israel, restored influence and access to the remnants of the Falashan community; for Ethiopia, help in contending with Eritrean rebel groups; for the United States, the prospect of weaning the pres-ent Marxist government away from its Soviet suppliers. Honduras points to American concern at the reported steady buildup and influx of armaments into the Central American region contrasted with refusals by Washington of requests from Honduras for such arms aid as F-5 fighter planes in reaction to perceived threats from Nicaragua. Planes upgraded and modernized by Israel, as well as light tanks, would continue to provide countries like Hon-duras or El Salvador with ungraded defensive equipment yet without direct-ly involving the United States. Subsuming arms sales within the larger strategic dialogue would seem to have been one of the topics under discussion when high Israeli officials visited Washington in the first half of 1984.[13]

A bolder initiative might apply to a broader strategy of coordinating not only United States and Israeli defense sales activities but also those of the NATO allies as well as smaller, pro-Western Third World arms exporters. At the present time a renewal of the Conventional Arms Transfer (CAT) talks with the Soviet Union depends on the vagaries of *détente*; but that need not deter the leading Western weapons suppliers from convening a somewhat more restricted forum to explore possible steps to regulate the trade deriving from shared strategic interests in a strong anti-Communist, global-wide col-lective containment and security system. Currently the competition is un-regulated and obviously works to Israel's disadvantage, outmatched as it is against the larger suppliers like Britain, France, Italy, and West Germany, while also resulting in senseless duplication.

In calling for such a conference Israel might propose a more equitable redivision of the market while acknowledging the economic importance of the conventional arms trade for all of the industrialized states. Coordination could be facilitated along regional and geographic lines, or, alternatively, by categories and types of weapons. In the same vein, the industrialized Euro-pean countries themselves are a target for Israeli products, especially those proposed above in the general category of emerging military technologies.

In Israel's favor are heightened European sensitivities about the long-term consequences of either acute dependence on the United States for advanced weapons and military technologies or falling behind the U.S. and Japan in the next generation of civil and military technological products. At the same time all the NATO countries face the need to upgrade their conventional forces and are determined to produce high-technology conventional weapons themselves, even if it costs more and takes longer than buying from the Americans. In December, 1984, NATO defense ministers agreed on a six-year, $7.85 billion package of basic improvements in conventional defense to upgrade ground equipment and boost ammunition stocks. Possibly here is a "window of opportunity" for Israeli manufacturers provided by an assertion of European independence from America, in a strategic and economic sense, and a rediscovery by Europeans of the value of Israel as "the Japan of the Middle East."

Due to this desire for "Europeanization," and given Israel's affiliate status with the EEC, the foundation exists, as Defense Minister Arens said in June, 1984, in London, for exploring technology-sharing and cutting defense and manufacturing costs through coproduction as well as other forms of cooperation on both sides of the Mediterranean. In any case, in the rush to enter the U.S. market, Israelis are advised not to write off or otherwise neglect Western Europe.

These countries, along with the United States, could fulfill a multiple service for Israel: aiding in its economic recovery; achieving greater strategic coordination—and through Israel, with some of the pariah countries further removed; and giving Israel the latitude which might enable it to reject certain borderline or dubious types of arms deals. Nor would this purchase of Israeli military products and services qualify as altruism. The Europeans would be helping themselves: improving their own force capabilities, achieving standardization and harnessing Israel's military technologies and experience to the common defense of the Free World.

Similarly, as discussed earlier, there is a role for Israeli diplomacy in seeking some minimal understanding among the Third World suppliers for whom outright, unrestrained competition—both in products and customers—could be ruinous. It is not enough for Israel to make quick sales in helping pariah states in their hour of procurement need, thereby aiding in the construction of their own industrial infrastructure. Beyond that lies the task of preventing such industrializing countries from subsequently becoming tough competitors insensitive to Israel's particular arms diplomacy motivation.

Despite the difficulties, this coordination requires greater diplomatic effort, both because of the dangers and possible gains for Israel. An example of the former is the case of Brazil, which is pushing vigorously into the Arab arms market. In return for technical aid by the Brazilians, Saudi Arabia is expected to help finance the development of a new Brazilian ship-to-ship missile system which could eventually emerge as a competitor to the Gabriel. Such cooperation would undoubtedly put an end to Israel's hopes of selling Brazil its Gabriel missile under an agreement that would have curbed Brazil's future sales to Arab clients. There is no evidence to suggest the issue received highest priority in Jerusalem. Conversely, greater coordination and agreement among some of the Third World arms exporters, particularly the pariah states, could be used to advantage in showing the United States and others that Israel is not quite so isolated as is often assumed but rather a key connecting link in a bloc of states of strategic value in a global context.

ARMS TRANSFERS AND ISRAELI FOREIGN POLICY

In the course of its history Israel, for a complex of reasons, has violated the first rule of weapons transfer politics: avoid becoming dependent upon a single arms supplier. Largely in order to ameliorate this disturbing condition and pronounced trend, the country's leaders adopted a program aiming at an independent arms production capability. However, in the process of converting this capability into arms exports Israel at times gives the impression of approaching the brink of a second and no less dangerous pitfall, that of mistaking arms sales diplomacy for foreign policy.

There is a thin line between arms transfers as an auxiliary to foreign policy or as a substitute for it. An ominous shift in the latter direction came about toward the end of the 1970s as Israel's economic strength, political image, and diplomacy waned, leaving arms sales as one of the few ways to stem the decline. At a moment when Israel's missions abroad were being reduced, the attractiveness of military assistance and weapons transfers in, first, preserving existing links and, second, renewing ties should be obvious. Certainly this branch of external relations would appear to receive far greater emphasis than diplomatic initiatives, for example, or than information campaigns aimed at improving Israel's international image. Indeed, so salient is the weapons transfers program in the mid-1980s that it has come to constitute one of the principal factors determining Israel's reach abroad.

Until now this diplomatic exploitation of military sales has, for the most part, been beneficial for Israeli national interests. Returning to our initial set of three criteria, this diplomacy continues to be *necessary* since it stems from imposed circumstances. On the whole it is a *balanced* policy and also rather *effective* in serving and promoting Israeli national interests. Indeed, the real danger lies in possible excesses. Recent success represents a potential long-range liability unless a balance can be struck by cautioning against undue reliance on arms diplomacy as the panacea for the country's diplomatic, military and balance-of-payments problems.

Because a philosophical and operational basis still has to be found for integrating the benefits of arms sales and the standards of restraint that may preserve diplomatic objectives, one wonders whether perhaps the pendulum has swung too far. Can the pro-arms sales coalition any longer differentiate between profits and politics? Of late the weight of the argument reflects a perceptible shift toward sanctioning sales on economic rather than diplomatic grounds. This merely reinforces a feature long identified with Israeli international behavior: the preference for a short-range military/security approach to what are fundamentally political and diplomatic issues. If dollars must be valued above image, principles, and sometimes even elementary prudence, then at a minimum the Foreign Ministry and considerations of statecraft must be encouraged to play a more central role—which leads to a final cautionary statement.

DON'T CONFUSE ENDS AND MEANS

As successful as they have proven, arms transfers alone are nevertheless merely a tool. They also tend to be effective only as short-term influence. In world politics what is valid in the short-run may become conspicuously invalid in the longer-term. By the same token, short-range benefits often are offset by long-term costs. The answer lies neither in abstinence or restraint for its own sake, nor in an unrestricted cash-and-carry attitude, but in producing an integrated, coherent strategy resting on defined national interests, recognized limitations, and possible pitfalls.

Isolated transactions—now Honduras, now Zaire—however successful and lucrative, still are no substitute for a comprehensive policy which links arms sales to clearly adumbrated political objectives. Somewhere in the institutional process of policymaking there ought to be an agency or individual sensitive to the web of possible linkages between any single bilateral arms relationship and its regional or even international context; the instance of Argentina, Britain, and the Falklands comes readily to mind. Anthony Sampson has characterized arms sales at present as the "blind spot of a generation." They must not become the "blind spot" of Israeli foreign policy.

In the real arena of world politics and *raison d'état* highmindedness is misplaced. All countries find security assistance essential. Israel, with its advantages, has every justification for presenting itself as a small yet important supplier of such assistance. Arms are one of its fields of expertise; and Israel stands ready to assist many of those countries concerned with buying reliable weapons at a reasonable price—and with few if any political strings attached.

Still, for Israelis and their supporters ethical considerations ought to serve as a partial check against indiscriminate or hasty transactions. Policy should not be driven by relentless pressures both internal and external to sell arms at all costs, including moral and diplomatic. Thus, for example, if Israel is perceived as unprincipled, the diplomatic campaign waged on moral grounds against European arms sales to Arab countries is weakened. Paradoxes and dilemmas extend as well to the Jewish factor. Israeli arms may keep the window open to communities in the Diaspora; but they may expose Jews overseas to intimidation and reprisal as a hostage to the arms relationship, while evoking criticism from world Jewish organizations which take issue with, and criticize arms practices by the government of Israel.

The proper relationship between principles and politics is but one of the policy dilemmas with which weapons transfers are fraught. Such transfers could be perceived of as inherently wasteful or even evil, and politically tending to draw the supplier into domestic or interstate conflict. But by the same token Israeli arms may serve to restore a local imbalance, perhaps deter aggression, and generally enhance stability. While the answers often reside in the specifics of each case, they depend, too, upon perceptions in Israel of the very nature and utility of military transfers in general. Clarifying these basic perceptions and achieving a broader perspective of the many issues involved in a diplomacy of arms sales would be two of the purposes of a policy review of ends and means eleven years after the Yom Kippur War and the acceleration of arms exports which followed in its wake.

Can Israel keep up its active and extensive arms diplomacy? Should it even want to? Does the policy justify itself on all three grounds of diplomacy, strategy, and sound economics? If the answer to each is positive, then Israel, in continuing to walk the thin line, must do so with its eyes open, fully alert to the risks as well as the incentives. Friends may be won and people influenced by selling arms. Yet the history of Israeli military assistance is instructive for its failures and shortcomings as much as for its diplomatic breakthroughs. To repeat, arms diplomacy ought not to be encouraged to serve as a substitute for an active foreign policy.

To study Israel's defense sales diplomacy is really to probe the nature and limits of contemporary Israeli foreign relations. Since the struggle for acceptance within the world community and for security within the Middle East continues, final judgment on the country's military assistance and weapons transfer policies must be suspended, at least for the present. In the interim, answers must be conditional at best and tentative. But in closing this initial inquiry into the arms balance sheet one last comment is in order. Criticism of Israel's foreign policy as conservative and unimaginative is commonplace. This may be valid only if we confine the analysis to diplomacy in the formal sense, such as in the area of Middle East peace initiatives. Yet we insist that in the case of Israel this represents merely the tip of the iceberg.

Were the full record of Israeli arms diplomacy to be known, it would present Israel and Israeli external affairs in quite a different light. Defense sales and foreign military assistance are a vital element in the spectrum of relations. They have been marked by industriousness and ingenuity in the face of adversity, by dedication, discretion, and flexibility in responding to fresh opportunity. It is doubly regrettable, therefore, that because of various sensitivities serious study of the entire subject has been discouraged; there is too little recognition of the major effort involved in an effective day-to-day management of the security assistance program and of its contribution in keeping the State of Israel respected, developed, and secure. Conventional arms, in short, have been converted by Israel into unconventional diplomacy.

NOTES

1. *Haaretz*, 15 and 25 February 1983; in a meeting with local electronics manufacturers, the Director-General of the Defense Ministry, Menachem Meron, encouraged them to compensate for reduced IDF orders by redoubling export efforts, *Maariv*, 29 July 1983.
2. ACDA figures for 1982, *World Military Expenditures and Arms Transfers, 1972-1982* (April, 1984), pp. 53-94.
3. *Haaretz*, 17 July 1984.
4. *Maariv*, 3 June 1983 and, again, 5 August 1983; see also *Haaretz*, 2 August 1983.
5. Peleg, p. 215.
6. Herbert Wulf, "Developing Countries," in Ball and Leitenberg, p. 325.
7. John Stanley and Maurice Pearton, *The International Trade in Arms* (New York: Praeger, 1972), p. 229.
8. Neuman, p. 188.
9. On barter, see Hunter Lewis, "Coming Up, A New International Economic Order," *IHT*, 18 January 1984; David Goldfield, "Countertrade," *International Perspectives* (March/April, 1984): 19-22; David B. Yoffie, "Profiting from Countertrade," working paper (HBS 84-17), Harvard University Graduate School of Business Administration (October, 1983).
10. *The Israel Economist*, July, 1984, p. 22.
11. *Haaretz*, 9 March 1984.
12. Gerald Steinberg, "Recycled Weapons," *Technology Review* (April 1985): 28-38.
13. The Foreign Ministry's David Kimche held talks in Washington in April, 1984.

INDEX

ABOUT THE AUTHOR

Aaron Klieman is professor of international relations and former chairman, Department of Political Science, Tel-Aviv University, and visiting professor at Georgetown University, 1984–85. His publications include *Foundations of British Policy in the Arab World*; *Soviet Russia and the Middle East*; *Emergency Politics and The Growth of Crisis Government*; and *Israel–Jordan–Palestine: The Search for a Durable Peace*.

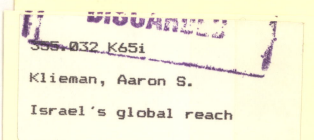